OX AGAINST THE STORM

A biography of Tanaka Shozo (1841*–1913)

Beaten, buffeted
By the rain and the wind,
An ox drags his load
Past, and is gone —
Leaving only
Wheeltracks in mud
And the sadness of things.
TANAKA SHOZO

*According to the oriental zodiac, 1841 was a Year of the Ox.

OX
AGAINST
THE STORM

A BIOGRAPHY OF TANAKA SHOZO
- JAPAN'S CONSERVATIONIST PIONEER

KENNETH STRONG

JAPAN
LIBRARY

OX AGAINST THE STORM
A Biography of Tanaka Shozo

First published 1977 Paul Norbury Publications

First paperback edition published 1995 by
JAPAN LIBRARY

Japan Library is an imprint of Curzon Press Ltd
2 Park Square, Milton Park, Abingdon, Oxon, OX14 4RN

Transferred to Digital Printing 2004

© Kenneth Strong 1977

All rights reserved. No part of this publication
may be reproduced or transmitted in any form, or by any
means without prior permission in writing
from the publishers.

British Library Cataloguing in Publication Data

A CIP catalogue record for this book is available
from the British Library

ISBN 1-873410-14-X

Contents

	Acknowledgements	*viii*
	Introduction	*ix*
	List of illustrations	*xiv*
1	Village headman's son	*1*
2	Feud in a fief	*8*
3	Murder on a frontier	*17*
4	*'Totchin'*	*30*
5	Democrat versus developer	*45*
6	'Gift of a priceless jewel'	*58*
7	Pollution: the prelude	*65*
8	Pollution: growth of a crisis	*81*
9	*'To kill the people is to kill the nation'*	*99*
10	Appeal to the highest	*128*
11	New directions	*141*
12	Murder of a village	*150*
13	*'The care of rivers is the Way of Heaven'*	*181*
14	*'Over withered fields'*	*199*
15	Jottings	*215*
	Epilogue	*225*
	Selected Bibliography	*230*

Errata

p. viii Read Oguchi for Oguichi Ichiro
p. 13 Footnote (See above, p.16 should read p.7)
p. 176 Footnote 2. See above, p.164 n.2 should read p.172 n.2
p. 178 Footnote 2. See below, p.215 n.1 should read p.225 n.1
p. 154 Footnote 1. p.166 should read p.175
      Footnote 2. p.175 should read p.157

For Mari, Adrian, & Naomi

Acknowledgements

This book could not have been written without the help and guidance of many Japanese students of Tanaka Shozo. I am indebted in particular to: Professor Hayashi Takeji, Principal of Miyagi College of Education (and formerly Professor of Philosophy at Tohoku University), and Mr Hinata Yasushi, both of Sendai; Professor Shiota Shobei, of Tokyo Metropolitan University; Mr Amamiya Gijin, lately Principal of Moka High School in Tochigi Prefecture (who most generously provided me with copies of many of his unique collection of photographs); Professor Mitsue Iwao, of Obirin College, Tokyo; and Professor Amano Shigeru, of Hijiyama Woman's Junior College, Hiroshima. To all of these scholars, who gave unstintingly of their time and learning, I express my warmest thanks. I share with them a great debt to Mr Shimada Sozo, Tanaka's 'disciple' and amanuensis in the last decade of his life, for his careful recording of a vast amount of detailed information relating to those years.

My thanks are also due to the Meiji Bunken Publishing Co. for permission to reproduce the woodblock prints from Mr Oguichi Ichiro's striking volume *No ni sakebu hitobito* (Men crying in the wilderness); to Mr Satish Kumar, editor of *Resurgence* (Felindre Farchog, Crymych, Dyfed, Wales), for permission to use the material quoted from that journal in Chapter 15; to the staff of the National Diet Library in Tokyo, for their assistance in tracking down valuable bibliographical material; to the Japan Information Centre, London; to Mr. Richard Storry, of St. Antony's College, Oxford; and to Mr Paul Norbury, of Paul Norbury Publications, whose encouragement and enthusiasm were as welcome to me as they have been to many others concerned to interpret modern Japan to the West. Finally, my thanks and that of the publisher are due to the Inter-university Committee of the Japan Foundation Endowment for their generous grant towards publication of this book.

Japanese names

The names of all Japanese mentioned in this book are given in the Japanese order, i.e. with the surname first.

Pronunciation

Vowels are pronounced much as in Italian, and a final 'e' is always sounded. Thus 'Otome' is pronounced *Oh-toh-meh* (spoken rather rapidly). Each syllable is accented.

Bibliographical Note

All the material upon which this biography is based is in Japanese. To avoid an inordinate number of footnotes, detailed references to the Japanese books and articles consulted have not been included. A bibliography at the end of the book does, however, list the main sources upon which I have relied.

K.S.

Introduction

A number of biographies of prominent Japanese now exist in Western languages. The earlier examples dealt with figures of historical or political importance in the conventional sense of those terms, such as the great sixteenth-century general Hideyoshi, or Marquis Okuma, one of the founders of the modern Japanese state. More recently the biographers have begun to cast their net wider. Ralph Hewins' *Japan's Miracle Men* provides sketches of some of those responsible for the country's leap from austerity to affluence; studies have also appeared of the present Emperor, of religious leaders of different periods, such as the eighteenth-century Zen priest Hakuin and our near-contemporary Nishida Tenko, founder of the syncretic religious community known as the Garden of the Single Light, and of two revolutionaries, even — Kita Ikki and Kotoku Shushui. Most of these men, however, fit comfortably into the Japanese tradition, as pillars of a very old Establishment, and the fame of even the two revolutionaries derives (one suspects) not so much from their radicalism itself as from the single-minded intensity of their commitment to it, a quality traditionally much admired in Japan.

Tanaka Shozo, though he certainly shared this single-minded intensity, is not to be so easily categorized. Rooted in traditional society and its ethics, yet a lifelong rebel against some of its most characteristic practices; an uncompromising individualist in a conforming, collectivist nation, yet with a profound, old-fashioned reverence for the Emperor, symbol of the authoritarian family-state; lonely champion of people and nature against industrial pollution, but lacking any definable 'ideology' — characterized during his lifetime alternately as a saint, a charlatan and a madman, and forgotten almost totally on his death in 1913: even now, when the new explosion of concern for pollution has led to the rescue of this nineteenth-century 'outsider' from sixty years of oblivion, his countrymen find it hard to decide whether Tanaka is to be seen as an antiquated, if heroic, figure, belonging essentially to a past that seems to many of them almost as distant as our own Middle Ages, or as a prophet of a future whose outlines are just now beginning to be glimpsed in both East and West. For us in the West, Tanaka's life offers the compelling spectacle of a tough-minded individual waging a one-man war against injustice in a country where it is often assumed that such refusal to conform is all but unknown. Nor was he primarily influenced in his stand, like most modern Japanese progressives, by Western liberal or socialist thought: his dynamism was the product of oriental attitudes, functioning in a character of extraordinary energy and stamina. Christianity he did discover, it is true, but only towards the end of a lifetime of action according to his own principles, which makes his reaction to it the more interesting.

His struggle against pollution, too, owed nothing to foreign example. As a result of direct experience of large-scale contamination of agricultural land by industrial effluent, Tanaka became in effect an ecologist and environmental conservationist long before these words came into use. Almost no one paid any attention to him when as a penniless old eccentric, all his other causes shattered, he preached his gospel of 'caring for mountains, forests and rivers'. Then, he seemed to sensible men merely a freak — a picturesque freak, no doubt, the Lear-like, massive figure with the black topknotch tied with a piece of string or straw (because he never had time to get it cut) blowing in the wind, tramping the fields of his native Tochigi in a threadbare cotton kimono and a peasant's straw cape to keep off the rain — but still a freak, with no observable relevance to the 'real' problems of the day. Today, however, he is not dismissed so lightly. Most Japanese have in the last few years become only too well aware of the baleful effects of pollution on health and well-being, in that they live in one of the most heavily polluted countries (if not *the* most heavily polluted country) in the world. One result of this awareness has been a rediscovery of Tanaka Shozo and his significance. In the autumn of 1969 and the spring of 1970, when I was in Japan working on the material for this book, few Japanese apart from a handful of specialists even knew his name. Since then, several books on his life and work have appeared, together with a flood of articles in newspapers and journals. The dramatic finding in 1975 of a mass of Tanaka's papers that were thought to have been lost caused a minor sensation.[1]

Tanaka's isolation during so much of his anti-pollution work was compounded by the historical tendency of Japanese governments to side with industry against all forms of popular protest; a tendency stronger in Japan than in Western industrialized countries, since the modernization of Japan was largely made possible by active state

---

1. These papers — 582 letters, 92 diary extracts, and 20 photographs, all concerned with the last nine years of Tanaka's life — were originally deposited with his friend and supporter, Henmi Onokichi, who ran a canning factory in Tokyo. Henmi died in 1940. When the factory was evacuated during the Pacific War to Kamaishi in Iwate Prefecture, the two bundles of documents went with it; the factory was subsequently destroyed in an American naval bombardment, and the two or three people who suspected the existence of some such material assumed that it, too, had perished in the flames. In 1973 Henmi's adopted daughter, who was still living in the old family home in Tokyo, decided to knock the house down and rebuild it on the same site. As the work was about to begin, the two bundles were discovered in a box 'under the verandah', carefully preserved in waterproof paper. She, however, had no idea that these old papers were of any importance, and did not trouble to open the bundles. Only in 1975, when she was asked by Professor Hayashi Shigeru of Tokyo University (who was then working on a new edition of all Tanaka's writings) if the family had any Tanaka material in its possession, did the documents finally come to be recognized for what they were.(*Yomiuri Shinbun*, September 15, 1975; *Asahi Shinbun* (evening edition), October 20, 1975.)

Introduction

support of industrialists and by innumerable close links between business and the bureaucracy. Further, the obvious and overriding need to build a strong industrial base that would enable Japan to compete on equal terms with the Western powers meant that in the 1890s, when the pollution Tanaka fought against was at its worst, the government could count on overwhelming public support for its policy of favouring industry rather than agriculture, at least until Tanaka and his supporters could *prove* the true scale of the disaster pollution was causing to thousands of families in the affected farming areas. However objectively convincing the proofs he collected, it was difficult to put them across in Tokyo, where the dynamism of the new industrial Japan was centred and where talk of the sufferings of small rural communities of peasants and fishermen, even though they were no more than 50 or 60 miles away from the capital, seemed remote and irrelevant to the great themes of the age.

Now, in the late seventies, the situation is very different. The so-called 'Pollution Diet' of 1970 enacted no fewer than 14 anti-pollution measures. There remained the possibility that the continuing close ties between government and industry would blunt the sharp edge of such legislation; and judging from the dismal lack of success registered by sporadic protests against pollution during the sixties, the omens were not very good. But in the last five or six years the rapidly growing strength of the citizens' protest movement has ensured that the legislation has at least a chance of reversing the drift towards even greater pollution that until very recently was threatening Japan's crowded islands. A number of important test cases, involving the courts and a new government-sponsored Pollution Disputes Mediation Committee (attached to the Prime Minister's Office), seem to be setting a hopeful trend[1]. Difficult though the task of present-day Japanese environmentalists may be, it stands a much better chance of success than Tanaka did in his all-but solitary campaign of eighty years ago. Tanaka was certainly far from successful in achieving *his* aims, which were radical indeed; but his failure is full of lessons for his successors[2]. Above all, the courage he displayed in his lonely fight remains as a permanent inspiration. In the 1970s his career is worth recording outside the purely Japanese context, as an early outrider's gallant skirmish in what is now increasingly recognized as a worldwide campaign for ecological survival. It also raises interesting questions for the student of the nature of the consensus upon which Japanese government rests, and of the effectiveness or otherwise of Japanese protest movements in

1. See the Epilogue to this book.

2. Contemporary Japanese conservationists have been making a comprehensive study of what are now the most effective methods of bringing pressure to bear on polluting enterprises, public authorities which give them tacit support, and scholarly 'experts' who are often called in to justify a no-change policy by juggling with statistics. See, for example, an article by Ui Jun, The singularities of Japanese pollution, in the *Japan Quarterly*, vol. XIX, no. 3.

general[1]. In this book, however, my concern has been simply to tell the life-story of one outstanding protester, rather than to discuss the larger issues involved.

To young Japanese of the present time, the atmosphere and attitudes of the Japan of the Meiji period seem remote indeed. So much in Japanese life, they feel, has changed so radically since then. There is much, too, that has not changed but the Japanese themselves *feel* very clearly this sense of remoteness, and if that is how *they* feel, it is evidently much more difficult for a foreigner, writing for foreigners, to bring to life a figure from that seemingly distant period. One special difficulty is that of language. The peculiar style in which the men of Meiji wrote conveys to perfection the medley of the naive, the heroic and the sentimental that gives the period its peculiar fascination. That style has vanished now; nor, unhappily, can its unique flavour survive translation into English. The Japanese of that time were not always strong on logic as we understand it, and much of their writing — Tanaka's diaries, for example, and many of his numerous 'unpoetic' poems — are so disconnected and impressionistic that they would appear in translation as either unintelligible or oddly childish, though neither of these judgements would be deserved[2].

There are severe limitations, therefore, on the amount of original materials that can be quoted in a biography of this kind but Tanaka's story is sufficiently dramatic to be of interest to us in the West in spite of this drawback. Few men even in that exciting age can have lived more eventful lives or have been more abrasively involved with such a wide range of their fellow-countrymen, from peasants to Prime Ministers. Equally compelling is his personality, the outlines of which are clear, though the full colouring must be difficult to convey to anyone without some knowledge of Japanese society and psychology. Like many of his Meiji contemporaries who responded with such energy to the challenges of the age, he gives the impression of an epic, larger-than-life quality. What makes him unique is the unvarying courage with which he was ready all his life to fight battles of public principle on his own, abandoning the security of party or faction in a country where till recently (and change in this respect is slow even now) an individual could hardly be said to exist apart from the group or groups to which he belonged by birth or attachment. His integrity was not acquired overnight. Ambition, of a certain kind, and a pugnacious nature, helped to propel him through his early trials. But experience of conflict, instead of teaching him the great Japanese goal of harmony based on mutual yielding, only deepened his

---

1. For a discussion of these issues, see Symposium: The Ashio copper mine pollution incident, in *Journal of Japanese Studies (University of Washington)*, vol. 1, no. 2 (Spring 1975).

2. For these reasons, and in an attempt to convey something at least of the spirit of the original, I have allowed myself considerable freedom in translating extracts from the diaries, particularly in Ch. XV.

Introduction

convictions; and it is this process of spiritual growth in one who was at the same time the perfect type of the man of action, that lends a further dimension to his biography. Retirement from the world into a meditative life as one grows older is a commonplace of oriental tradition. But Tanaka refused to follow the pattern. The deeper his insights grew into the problems of men and society, the more earnestly he strove to act in the public world in accordance with those insights, though on an ever smaller stage as the years went by and men cared less and less to listen to his message, even those few who had admired and thought they understood him choosing, in the choice Japanese phrase, to 'honour him at a distance', while they told each other that he was now no more than a harmless crank.

In a series of eulogies published shortly after his death some of his friends, recalling his one-man campaign against the central government of nearly twenty years before, likened him to Cromwell, to Luther, to Hugo, to Oshio Heihachiro, the Japanese reformer of the early nineteenth century whose tenacity drove him in the end to suicide, to John Ball, the mad priest of Kent, to General Nogi, one of Japan's most celebrated military men of the modern period, and last but not least, to Ch'ü Yüan, the Chinese poet and patriot of the third century B.C. Such a haphazard series of comparisons only shows how little insight those who made them had into the meaning of his life as it moved through its last strange decade. Yet it is true that while remaining in many ways quintessentially Japanese, Tanaka had finally outgrown Japanese frames of reference. If at first sight he resembles his fellow-countryman Sakura Sogoro, who petitioned the Shogun on behalf of his oppressed fellow-peasants in 1651, there are aspects of his life and character that remind one — allowing for the many differences — of Mahatma Gandhi, of Danilo Dolci. If such men as these continue despite the buffetings of time to be seen as forerunners, perhaps the same honour may one day be accorded to Tanaka Shozo.

But it is out of delight in the man himself, as much as from admiration for the steadfastness of his lifelong fight, that I have chosen to attempt this biography. An irascible man, with not a few other foibles besides his over-quick temper; heavily built and formidable in appearance, yet surprisingly gentle with children and ever ready with laughter; a peasant and a fervid parliamentarian; careless of his person and possessions and not at all averse to interrupting a conversation in order to de-lice his kimono; with little formal education but much reading, not a little of it achieved in prison; given to jotting down poems to record his moods or amuse his friends; a collector of small shapely stones picked up by the roadside. ... At this level, that he was a Japanese, and a Meiji Japanese at that, ceases to matter. If his political and ecological message is universal, so is the appeal of his humanity. KENNETH STRONG
London, 1977

Illustrations

	Page
[1] Shozo and Satori Hikojiro examining poisoned plants	20
[1] Shozo showing a poisoned plant to the Diet	40
[1] The River Watarase, before pollution	60
[1] Mounds of poisoned topsoil	80
[2] Poisoned fields in Yanaka	100
[2] Unryuji Temple as it was at the time of the demonstrations. (It now has a tiled roof.)	120
[1] The River Watarase in flood	142
[1] The destruction of Yanaka	158
[1] Gathering for Shozo's funeral	180
[2] A shack built by a Yanaka family after their house had been destroyed	198

[1] OGUCHI ICHIRO'S DRAWINGS

[2] PHOTOGRAPHS

Japanese characters for Tanaka Shozo

1

Village headman's son

The fertile Kanto plain, stretching northwards from Tokyo for 60 miles till the ground climbs suddenly into the southern spurs of the Nasu volcanic mountains, seems an unlikely background for a rebel. Least of all its remoter northern reaches, for whose inhabitants life had for centuries been easier than in most other parts of Japan.

The River Watarase contributed in several ways to this prosperity. Rising in the mountains near Nikko, each summer after the alpine snows had melted it spread over countless low-lying fields, in floods that had long been regarded not as a calamity but as a boon, a layer of rich damp manure from the mountain forests, which helped to give the region one of the highest cereal yields in the whole of Japan.

Thanks to the purity of the mountain water and its suitability for dyeing processes, a silk weaving and dyeing industry had flourished on the banks of the Watarase for over a thousand years. And that was not all. The river abounded in fish; a catch of a hundred pounds' weight in one man's net in a single night was nothing uncommon, so that a good living could be made in this way if a man had no land to grow his rice, and in the mid-nineteenth century nearly 4,000 fishermen worked the Watarase and its tributaries. The bulk of their catches went for sale in Tokyo, or Edo as it was till 1868.

Transport presented no problem, for the river was also an arterial highway, easier to negotiate than most roads of the time. Boats sailed downstream to the capital daily, with cargoes of rice, textiles, fish, and another speciality of these fortunate plains — enormous bamboo poles, a foot in circumference, that were highly prized by Edo builders.

This comparative affluence, in a country where natural disasters were common and austerity had been invested by the ruling classes with an almost religious approval, had made for a more relaxed life along the banks of the Watarase than was possible for most Japanese country-dwellers. Though in other parts of Japan holidays in the modern sense were unheard of till after the Pacific War, the people of Shimotsuke (as this part of the Kanto plain is called) long ago adopted the custom of 'spring and autumn visits', when peasants would lay aside their work and travel in groups to neighbouring villages, staying overnight to eat and drink at leisure and enjoy the pleasures — according to their age and sex — of wrestling, dancing and the singing of old ballads.

Like so much else in pre-modern Japan, these 'visits' were strictly controlled. Boys and young men could take a week or ten days off, girls only three or four days, and men over thirty-five a mere two or three. But of the gaiety of these occasions and of the unusually carefree life they reflected, there is no doubt. The shock was all the more severe, therefore, when the region began to experience in the eighteen-nineties what was probably the most dramatic and large-scale example of industrial pollution anywhere in the world during the last century, if not since the first Industrial Revolution. Ease had also bred in the people of Shimotsuke a trait that made it all the harder for them to face the calamity when it came: a smug narrowness of mind that made them indifferent to the troubles of any beyond their immediate neighbourhood and reluctant to band together even in resisting adversity.

Into this placid region, nearly fifty years before industry poisoned the river that was the direct or indirect source of nearly all its riches, Tanaka Shozo was born in 1841. In the country at large the year was one of some disquiet. The pressure of the wider world outside Japan was beginning to make itself felt. The conservative Tokugawa government was clamping down on scholars and others who advocated the ending of the nation's two centuries of seclusion; a typical case was that of Watanabe Kazan, one of the best-known of such 'advanced' thinkers, who committed suicide when he was arrested and condemned to perpetual confinement to the territory of his own clan.

But these tensions did not disturb the peaceful prosperity of Shimotsuke. In spite of its nearness to the capital, it never became a centre of the anti-government feeling that was gradually fomenting in other, remoter provinces and led eventually to the downfall of the feudal system. Shozo's father Tomizo was *nanushi* or headman of Konaka, a straggling village of some 200 households five miles from the River Watarase. The family were primarily peasants cultivating their own land but kept a little shop as well in front of their house. A short walk away through the fields was the Buddhist temple of Jorenji, where Tomizo ran a *terakoya* or temple-school for the village children.

Tomizo evidently deserved his position as headman of Konaka. The post was not an easy one. Under the peculiar administrative system of the Tokugawa, the *nanushi* or headman, an elected official, was expected to fulfil two apparently inconsistent functions. The lord of his domain held him responsible for the payment of taxes due from his village, and the village looked to him for protection against oppression or rapacity on the part of the lord. The task sounds impossible, yet men who combined tact and strength of character in the necessary proportions were sometimes found to work the system with surprising effectiveness. Of these Tomizo was one.

Stubbornly honest, energetic but quiet and steady, he was popular with the peasants and trusted by the fief officials. In the thirty years that he held office, he had never once been heard to speak in anger, villagers recalled a generation later, instancing in quaint proof of his lifelong evenness of temperament his fine head of hair, which remained jet-black till his death at the age of 76.

The same could not be said of Shozo's mother Saki. When she died, in middle age, her hair was already white — the reflection, not of domestic or other cares, but of her own restless nature: talkative, open-hearted and excitable, Saki could hardly have been less like her solid headman husband. Their son Shozo was to take after them both in good measure. As if in sign of this dual inheritance of principle and passion, his own hair took on a freakish division of colour from his fifties right up to his death — a venerable white beard under a fine black samurai-like topknot.

Shozo's grandfather was the other obvious contributor to Shozo's make-up. Shozo Senior (the grandson was named Kenzaburo, but took his grandfather's name as a young man) was a cheerful extrovert, who drank himself to death at the age of 35, but not before he had served six years as headman, the first of the family to be elected by the villagers to the post. His addiction to saké did not prove to be hereditary; taking warning from his example, Tomizo and his son both gave up drinking in their early thirties[1]. The optimism and the streak of eccentricity and flamboyance reappeared in Shozo Junior, to diversify his inheritance still further.

As a child Shozo attracted attention chiefly for wilfulness, an atrocious memory, and unusual physical strength. When he was five he raged one evening at the family servant, who had given what Shozo thought was too lukewarm praise to a drawing Shozo had made, and refused to do a better one himself when the boy ordered him to. His mother, furious at her small son's treatment of an inferior, drove him howling out of doors into the night, to soak in the pouring rain till he could repent. Fifty years later, in an autobiographical sketch of the first part of his life related orally to a journalist and published in a national newspaper, he recorded his gratitude to his mother for teaching him thus so early — and so severely — to respect all men without regard to their station: a lesson of peculiar weight in Japan, where rank counts for so much. Its corollary — to respect no man for his station alone — he learnt much later, but just as thoroughly.

---

1. This, however, was one vow to which Shozo did not strictly adhere, as will be apparent from later Chapters.

His other childish fault, poor memory, was a deficiency less easy to correct. At the school classes held in the little shrine in front of the Tanakas' house by Akao Koshiro, a *ronin* or masterless samurai, Shozo regularly disgraced himself by his inability to memorize Chinese characters, without a good knowledge of which Japanese children could neither write their own language nor read the books that were the principal medium of education: the Confucian classics, and the commentaries on them by Japanese scholars. Fiercely determined to do better, he prayed fervently to the spirit of Mount Fuji for a better memory, and throughout the winter, unwilling to rely on prayer alone, would break the ice of a nearby stream day after day, to stimulate his mental powers by swimming in water so piercingly cold that it gave him (so he later averred) rheumatism for life. Neither Mount Fuji nor freezing water seem to have greatly helped him, however.

At Akao's school he remained a slow pupil but if he was a poor reader and writer, his aural memory was less defective, for he succeeded without much difficulty in learning by heart two of the most important texts, the Confucian Analects and Mencius.

These literary and philosophical classics, and the biographies of virtuous men of the past that were taught along with them, seem to have made more impression on Shozo than one might expect from the mechanical way in which they were set to be memorized in many schools of the time. In the diaries of his later life he would constantly quote sayings from these books, not as the few surviving tags of a half-forgotten book-learning, but in a way that showed he had made them a living part of his experience. Even in his childhood the villagers thought of Shozo as an unusually trustworthy boy, with strong notions of what was fair and just, and an exacting sense of responsibility in any activity he undertook, no matter how trivial.

Perhaps Akao, two of whose sons were to be executed in 1867 after a local 'freedom' uprising against the feudal regime, may have made more of the moral and humane precepts of the Classics than the common run of teachers — more, certainly, than the teacher of a small residential school where Shozo is said, according to one account, to have spent a few not very profitable weeks: no sooner were his charges asleep at night than the pedagogue in question would hurry away to the nearest brothel. Suspicious, Shozo feigned sleep one night, secretly followed his teacher to his destination, and left the school abruptly next morning after denouncing him in front of his fellow-pupils.

But for all his insistence that teachers should practise what they preached, or at least what the Classics enjoined, the boy Shozo was normal enough in other ways to keep his lofty moral notions from seeming to his fellows anything more than a likeable eccentricity. Dull at lessons and fond of wrestling, quick-tempered but forgetting a quarrel the moment it was over, he was naturally popular. Sometimes his forgetfulness and his sense of responsibility came into play simultaneously, with amusing results. Sent one afternoon on a family errand to a village some miles away, he was asked by a neighbour to take a verbal message to a weaver who lived near the village where his business lay. The errand performed, he came home — to realise he had forgotten after all to deliver the message to the weaver. By this time it was dark. He set out again and returned just before dawn, knocking up the neighbour to let him know he had spoken to the weaver as requested. The message was 'Please be quick with the weaving'!

When Shozo was fourteen his teacher, Akao Koshiro, died. Now that he seemed to have learnt enough Chinese characters to enable him to read the official documents that would come his way if, as was likely, he was chosen to succeed his father as headman of Konaka, his parents decided there was little point in his going elsewhere for another dose of academic education. They sent him instead to a small *juku*, or private residential school, to study *chikuga*, the art of painting the bamboo in Indian ink.

An odd choice, it might seem but not really so in Japan, where many such arts have for centuries been widely practised by all classes as 'Ways', or means to achieve mental and physical self-control. Since the discipline of *chikuga* is similar to that of calligraphy, Tomizo and Saki may have thought Shozo would benefit in his formative years from a 'Way' that was less encumbered with the learning of ideographic meanings that he found so difficult. Moreover, a special distinction clung to this particular teacher, by virtue of his friendship years before with the great painter and scholar of Western learning, Watanabe Kazan.

The plan did not work, however. In a boy of Shozo's obstinately independent temperament the rebellious years were rebellious indeed, the more strikingly so in a society where obedience to parents was universally held to be one of the supreme virtues. For a while his 'principles' went by the board. He made no progress in the Way of bamboo-painting, and spent most of his time wrestling or fighting with the other pupils of the school. After only a few months his parents brought him home again. They made no further attempt to school him into docility. A year later, by his own account, he caught syphilis, after being lured to a brothel by 'evil friends': shocked and humiliated, he tried to run away to Edo to get himself cured, but was caught by a messenger from his family when he was hardly out of the village and confined strictly to the house, for fear news of his sickness should spread round the district and damage his chances of a satisfactory marriage in four or five years' time.

Before long he ran away again, this time getting as far as an inn in a hot-springs resort in the mountains. Tracing him here a week later, his uncle ordered him to return home immediately, on the (false) ground that his grandmother had been taken ill. Shozo did not believe him but filial disobedience had its limits. Hiring a horse, he galloped the seventy miles home, arriving before his uncle — to find his grandmother as well as when he had left her. As soon as his uncle appeared, Shozo demanded a written apology.

The syphilis took three years to heal. Chastened, the boy settled down to work in his father's fields, and there were no more tantrums. His independent turn of mind now showed itself in other ways: his father had repeatedly to rebuke him for 'ideas above his station' when he argued fiercely that the taxes imposed by the lord of the domain on Konaka and the surrounding villages were unjustly high. His mother, too, warned him against the cardinal Japanese sin of outspokenness, which would bring him into bad repute with their neighbours.

Many things around him struck him as unfair. Shozo insisted, for instance, that the poorest peasant ought to have the right to wear the clothes he pleased — in itself a revolutionary opinion in Tokugawa Japan, where the behaviour and attire of every class, and particularly of the farmers, were regulated by degree according to each individual's place in the rigid social hierarchy. At the same time he abused to their faces the sons of well-to-do farmers who dressed too ostentatiously. Yet the fears of his parents proved groundless.

Hard work and a cheerful, straightforward disposition gradually earned respect for the headman's son. By painstaking effort he raised the yield of the rice-fields in his care to well above the average. To augment the family income he planted mulberry trees so that they could keep a substantial stock of silkworms. He also devised a plan to transplant pine-saplings from the mountains, with the idea of selling them for timber after twenty years (to much scoffing from some of the villagers, who were not in the habit of thinking so far ahead), and later started a little private industry of his own making indigo-balls to sell for dyeing (in this case against the wishes of his father, who held it beneath a headman's dignity to engage in 'trade').

Among his peers he quickly showed himself a leader. He it was, inevitably, who would carry the statue of Amida Buddha on its annual festive progress through the village. By all the signs, Shozo was on the way to becoming a solid and successful farmer, with a head for business as well as for the care of his fields; the type who might well seize one or other of the countless opportunities that were to present themselves to bold minds after the founding of the modern state in 1868.

At all events, when Tomizo was promoted in 1859 to the position of *warimoto*, or superintendent, of the eight villages that constituted the domain, the people of Konaka were happy to have his seventeen-year old son to succeed him as their headman. For Tomizo the new post brought considerable added dignity. For the first time he was officially allowed to wear a sword, and even to have a surname — until 1868 a privilege normally reserved for the ruling class of samurai.

Shozo, for his part, took his public responsibilities seriously. Apart from his tax-collecting duties, some of which he had to delegate because his arithmetic was not up to working out the necessary sums, he started his own temple-school, organized wrestling-contests among the young men (himself withdrawing before long, having inadvertently broken the arms of two of his friends) and persuaded the lord of the domain to award prizes every year to the most filial sons and daughters of the village. He set himself the following daily schedule:

Before breakfast: 1 hour's work in the fields
After breakfast: 2 hours' work in the indigo-hut
After supper: Teaching
Work in the indigo-hut
Reading Chinese books with other young men in the temple

The rest of the time was to be filled with the daily chores of a peasant and a headman. Now and then village affairs would call him away.

On one occasion at least, in a dispute between Konaka and another village over water-rights, he was not afraid to champion Konaka against his own father, who as *warimoto* decided the other village had a better case. But for the most part Shozo's life during these years of early manhood was that of a moderately prosperous peasant, working hard for long hours but still with leisure enough to enjoy a degree of communal recreation and culture above the average for a Japanese villager of his day.

Shozo himself looked back with pride on these years. 'I am a peasant of Shimotsuke', he begins the brief autobiography already referred to, compiled when he was well-known as a member of the National Diet. All his life he was fond of pointing to 'mattock-lumps' on his right hand, and 'sickle-scars' on his left; his only 'decorations', as he liked to call them. Nor was this the easy self-deception of a man who had accepted the ease and comfort of the capital: Shozo's later life was far harder and more austere than these youthful years at home.

Short but broadly built, immovably stubborn when his will was roused, he was in many ways the typical peasant, though with a special toughness of fibre, both physical and spiritual, as he was later to prove, that raised him to a different plane.

But a peasant the young headman of Konaka was not to remain, for in his twenty-third year there confronted him the first of the three severe trials that were to recast his life in a far less traditional pattern.

2

Feud in a fief

Konaka and seven other villages, with their outlying hamlets, comprised the domain of the Rokkaku family, feudal lords of modest territory and income but considerable dignity, for they were designated by the Tokugawa government as one of the *koke*, families charged with important ceremonial duties, such as receiving Imperial Messengers from the Court in Kyoto.

During the 1840's the peace of the little fief remained undisturbed. A competent *warimoto*, one Kobayashi Toshichi, kept both his lord's coffers full and the peasants contented. When Kobayashi retired to make way for his son, however, the delicate balance was threatened. The son proved well-intentioned but weak; the financial reserves of the House of Rokkaku melted rapidly away, till in 1859 Shozo's father Tomizo was appointed *warimoto* in place of the young Kobayashi.

Tomizo, working under the unusually able and honest Chief Steward who had chosen him for the job, managed before very long to wipe out the deficit and restore confidence. Unfortunately the Chief Steward died suddenly in 1862. His successor, Hayashi Saburobei, proved to be the worst kind of corrupt feudal bureaucrat, using his position and knowledge of the cumbersome domanial administration to enrich himself and a group of sycophantic supporters. Not long after his appointment began the seven years of misgovernment and unrest in the fief that impelled Shozo from his rice-fields and indigo-balls into public life, and subsequently to the politics of protest on the national stage.

The troubles that plagued the Rokkaku fief hold no special interest in themselves, similar as they were to the bouts of turbulence to which many fiefs were liable during this last period of weakening feudal authority. The details of plot and counterplot are in any case complex and obscure. Only the briefest sketch of the conflict need be given here, with some account of its impact on Shozo.

The origin of the canker was simple and commonplace enough. Hayashi, the new Chief Steward, at once began to publicise the desirability of building a new mansion in Edo against the day when the son and heir of the present head of the house, who was now thirteen, should be married. This solicitude for the young lord's future comfort was less innocent than it might seem, for it was the common practice in such cases for the Chief Steward of a daimyo to appropriate between thirty and fifty per cent of the money set aside for the building expenses, as compensation for his supposedly arduous labours in commissioning and supervising the builder; and to make matters worse, Hayashi clearly intended to finance the whole operation from the reserve of 3,000 *ryo* carefully accumulated by Tomizo and the previous Chief Steward. Tomizo was furious. As he only too easily foresaw, both the lord of the fief and his subjects would suffer. The treasury would be quickly depleted and heavy taxes levied on the villages to make up for the Steward's extravagance. Moreover, the time could hardly have been less suitable for the lord of a small fief to sink his modest capital in a project which would serve no purpose but to flatter his own vanity.

Since permission to reside in Japan had been granted to foreigners in the fifties, tension had risen throughout the country between those who demanded vociferously that they should be driven out and others who saw that their presence had to be accepted if Japan was to be 'modernized' and so avoid the danger of subjection to the still expanding Western Powers. When towards the end of 1862 the Emperor issued a decree ordering the Shogun to expel the barbarians, the Shogun could only state publicly that it was beyond his power to carry out the Imperial command. In a number of ugly incidents, the best-known of which is the murder near Yokohama in September 1862 of an Englishman who refused to give way to a leading samurai and his retinue, frustrated hotheads took the law into their own hands. Bombardments by British, French and American warships of ports in the territory of the more xenophobe clans followed. Slowly but inexorably the authority of the central government disintegrated; uncertainty and the fear of civil war seeped across the entire country.

In these circumstances it is not surprising that Tomizo managed to persuade the lord of the fief not to sanction plans for the new mansion. Hayashi was not to be put off so easily, however. In November 1864 the Shogun appointed the lord of Rokkaku to make an official visit on his behalf to Unebi, near the ancient capital of Nara, in west Japan, to view the newly-discovered tomb of the Emperor Jimmu, founder of the Imperial line. The elaborate nature of such ceremonial visits, not to mention the primitive state of even the 'trunk' roads in the feudal era, meant that the party would be away for several weeks. More important still, the incorruptible Tomizo was appointed to accompany his lord on the mission. The moment they left, Hayashi went into action. His emissaries toured the fief, attempting by various means to neutralise the opposition — most notably by bribing villagers to propose new headmen who would denounce Tomizo and support the Hayashi faction.

But there was one opponent whose calibre — misled, no doubt, by his youth — Hayashi had left out of account: Tomizo's son, Shozo. The young headman of Konaka cannot have seemed at first sight a likely source of trouble. Six months before his father departed on the mission to Unebi, Shozo had married Katsu, the daughter of a dyer from a neighbouring village.

A number of anecdotes about his relations with women at this period, some of them probably apocryphal, survive. According to one, his wedding scanted the formalities: meeting Katsu one evening on her way home from a lesson with a sewing-mistress, he proposed to her, and took her back home with him there and then, refusing to allow her to say goodbye to her parents, and considered her his wife from the following morning. Another story tells how he was visiting a girl in her home one day without the knowledge of her parents, who were away, when the father suddenly returned; the girl hid Shozo in the bath, keeping him there for nearly twenty-four hours until an opportunity presented itself for him to slip out of the house unnoticed.

A book entitled *Tales of the strange conduct of Tanaka Shozo* which appeared in 1902, when Shozo was sixty, has a choice drawing of him squeezed uncomfortably in the iron tub, with the girl furtively passing him a dish of food through the half-opened bathroom door. It seems improbable that the heroine of the incident — if indeed it ever took place — was the girl he married.

Katsu may conceivably have been a teenager of romantic inclination, but from her marriage onwards she proved to be a model of dutiful, self-effacing wifehood rare even by the Japanese standards of her time — so successfully self-effacing, indeed, that there is scarcely a mention of her in the records of Shozo's life. Poor Katsu, one cannot help feeling: not merely because so little is recorded of her, but because at the time of her marriage to an industrious and respected village headman nothing could have seemed less likely than that out of forty-eight years of married life they would never be together continuously for more than two, so momentous were the changes ahead.

For the moment, in the spring and summer of 1864, Shozo's existence must have seemed placid indeed, and likely to remain so. From that quarter at least, despite the opposition from Shozo's more experienced father, Hayashi anticipated no trouble.

In November, no sooner had Hayashi taken advantage of Tomizo's absence to launch his strategem to win over the villages than Shozo reacted vehemently. All his instincts were aroused: his pugnacious, uncompromising nature, the stubborn respect for principle that had made him stand out even as a boy, the inherited sense of responsibility for the just treatment of the villagers he represented.

His first act was to write to his father, who advised him, as he had often done before, to take no precipitate action and in any case to be sure not to act out of keeping with his youth and station. This counsel Shozo ignored. He too now took advantage of Tomizo's absence to send an angrily-worded petition to the Council of the House of Rokkaku in Edo, demanding that they take steps instantly to stop Hayashi's intrigues. Such a petition to the feudal authority, particularly one that took no pains to couch its accusations in the prescribed formulae of self-abasement, was in itself regarded as almost criminal. Shozo was at once dismissed from his office of headman.

A curious form of humiliation was then inflicted on him, which offers a glimpse of some of the bizarre practices in force during the declining years of the Tokugawa administration.

As news of the petition and its result came through, the priest of Jorenji Temple sent for Shozo. Jorenji was the temple to which Shozo and his family 'belonged', as parishioners; he had played in its grounds as a boy and may have borrowed its hall as a classroom for his village school. By virtue of extensive lands which it owned by direct grant from the Edo government, its incumbent was regarded as far above a mere headman in rank, which superiority he was no less inhibited in putting to use than some of the more worldly representatives of pre-modern European Christianity. Castigating Shozo for his insubordinate action — 'a disgrace to the parish' — the priest told him his dismissal was thoroughly deserved. The rest of the incident is better told in Shozo's own words, written years later:

As I had a larger purpose in mind, I did not want to argue with the old bald-pate; so I prostrated myself before him, agreeing that I was to blame for everything, and begging him to forgive me. That still wasn't enough for him, though. Getting more and more pompous, he said that asking forgiveness of a temple was no light matter, and that if I was serious in my desire to apologize, it was customary to make application to the main temple. I must go at once and take the necessary steps. . . . Again I made no objection, but went straight to the main temple. Here, when I explained the situation and asked how I should submit my apology, the priest's eyes gleamed, as if to say 'here's a catch indeed!' It was the bounden duty of a man of religion to assist his fellow-men, he assured me, and he warmly welcomed my application; but there were certain formalities. . . . These required that a supplicant should approach the temple in procession — in a chair, with a horse carrying a spear, a clothes-chest, and an awning-umbrella, and attended by two chair-bearers, a groom and a servant. A fee of 25 ryo was payable to the temple. . . . This time too I submitted. Finding I could just manage to pay the sum required from the money I had about me, I handed it over, fixed a date and time for the formal visit of apology, and took my leave.

When on the appointed day I donned a formal divided skirt and special straw sandals, as the rules demanded, and led my little procession through the temple gate, the sight must have been absurd beyond words, too ridiculous even for a music-hall story-teller. Who was it that made me perform this ludicrous little comedy? I had no particular wish to make a fool of myself, nor, I imagine, do men make fools of others unless there is some kind of reason why they should do so. Under the Tokugawa system, temples were a part of the bureaucracy. Quite apart from their religious function, they had charge of the register of households in their districts, issued passports to travellers, and had the privilege of direct access to the lord of their fief. The priest ranked above the headman, whose judgment in disputes he could overrule. In the case I have just related, the two priests must have planned the whole thing beforehand to get money out of me. How unspeakably degrading![1]

The villagers of Konaka, however, refused to accept this treatment of their elected headman. A deputation was sent to Edo to protest to the lord of the fief, who when he could be roused into action was evidently not without a sense of justice; he unhesitatingly revoked the dismissal. Unfortunately he died shortly afterwards.

Seizing his chance, Hayashi immediately ordered work to be started on the new mansion, at the same time taking further steps to undermine the opposition by bringing pressure on the councillors of the fief to replace some at least of the elected village headmen by nominees of his own and by forbidding Tomizo to continue some of the methods by which he had restored the domanial finances, such as borrowing from outside the fief at the lowest available rate of interest. In disgust, Tomizo and Shozo wrote formal letters resigning their respective offices.

These letters were taken to Edo on their behalf by two friends along with a document signed by 700 villagers denouncing Hayashi's malpractices. After an uproar at the fief headquarters the resignations were rejected, apparently out of fear of strengthening still further the support that had been gathering behind the two men. Tomizo and Shozo were merely reprimanded for insolence and trouble-making.

Hayashi now began to operate with greater subtlety, making use of old jealousies and prejudice to set village against village, faction against faction, and thus keep himself safely in power. His task was not very difficult.

---

1. The final twist to the story provides an instance of the violent upsets experienced by so many during the confused years after the beginning of the modern period. Shozo goes on:

Seventeen years later, in 1881, as a member of the elected Prefectural Assembly I happened to visit Konaka one day in the course of a speech-making trip. When Shimada Saburo (a well-known newspaper editor) and I called a couple of rickshaws to take us to the hall where we were to speak, to my amazement one of the rickshaw men turned out to be that same bald priest of Jorenji who had once wielded such authority. . . . Unwilling to take advantage of this change in his fortunes and let him pull me like a beast of burden, I told Shimada to go on ahead, paid the fallen priest the fare he would have earned, and made my way to the meeting on foot.

In later life Shozo often had reason to reflect on the narrow horizons of the people of Shimotsuke, the pettiness and inability to unite even in times of crisis that according to him marred the otherwise idyllic life of this fortunate province.

To cope with Hayashi's new tactics, he and his father now worked for the most part underground, Shozo himself spending a good deal of time in Edo trying to ferret out Hayashi's plans by making up to disaffected samurai in the fief headquarters. At first, he recalls, this was not easy. Apart from anything else, the city-dwellers were very ready to despise a squat, rough-looking countryman with a thick accent. To bolster his confidence, he told two of the Rokkaku samurai whose acquaintance he made how he had escaped attack by robbers in the city streets one night by throwing his lantern in their faces and running away before they recovered. His friends merely laughed; anyone but a coward, they explained to this simple country soul, would have run his attackers through without a thought. In his own way Shozo took the lesson to heart. When the three of them came across a mad dog outside the Rokkaku mansion a night or two later, he whipped out his sword before either of the samurai had made a move and cut it in two.[1] After that, he remarks, they began to show him a grudging respect.

During one of his visits to Edo, a series of small engagements was fought not far from his home between government troops and guerilla bands of samurai under orders from the powerful rebel clan of Satsuma. A message from his mother warned Shozo that whatever his reaction to national events — the country was approaching a state of civil war — he must stay in hiding in the capital if he wanted to be of use where he was most needed, in the fight for justice in their own fief: if he were to come home, Hayashi would have him arrested for complicity with the guerillas.

Already rumours were being put about that Shozo was a secret supporter of the Emperor's cause, which in Shimotsuke, solidly loyal as it was to the Shogunal government, would be little short of treason. In the sense in which Hayashi intended it, the allegation was quite untrue. Shozo did have an instinctive, emotional reverence for the Emperor and the Imperial institution, which he retained all his life; but as a countryman brought up in a small fief closely associated with the central feudal government and with no record of any Imperialist agitation, he no less instinctively supported the administrative authority of the Edo regime.

A few months later, indeed, he was to prove his impartiality on

---

1. This is the only recorded instance of Shozo wielding, or indeed wearing, a sword. In general, only samurai were allowed to wear swords. Peasants were normally forbidden to carry weapons of any kind but exceptions were sometimes made in the case of village headmen, in whose families the privilege might then become hereditary. (See above, p. 16.)

national issues by organizing accommodation and medical aid for both Imperialist and government troops who marched through Konaka within half a day of each other. At this stage, events directed his life for him. No 'ideas' informed his actions yet, nor any other motive than an immediate antagonistic response to the corruption and greed of those in power in his own fief.

When the fighting in Shimotsuke had died down, Shozo did return home to Konaka. He and his father sent in another bitterly-worded petition describing Hayashi as 'a 'robber' and the young lord of the fief, somewhat more charitably, as 'deficient in counsel', to fief headquarters; this time, both were summarily dismissed from their posts, Hayashi now feeling himself strong enough to treat these recalcitrant peasants with less restraint. Two of their chief supporters were also arrested; one was freed instantly by a crowd of villagers who chased the fief constables away with mattocks and sticks.

The struggle grew more intense as it drew to a close. Sometime during 1867, as the central government was on the verge of breakdown, Shozo and others took the bold step of petitioning the headquarters of the Imperial forces at Shizuoka for the removal of Hayashi. Astonishingly, at a time when great national issues were at stake, this plea from a group of peasants was heard: Hayashi and his chief henchmen were at last arrested. But the wheel was still turning. A month later others who stood to lose by Hayashi's eclipse had secured his release. Two headmen of the anti-Hayashi party were arrested in turn.

As determined as ever to carry on the struggle, and wondering how it was that he himself was still at liberty, Shozo made his way secretly to Mito, an important town not far from Shimotsuke, intending to enlist the help of an influential group of samurai supporters of the Imperial cause known as the *Tengu-to* or 'Society of the Goblins'.[1] But the Goblins were too intent on preparations for a campaign against government forces to listen to him.

Frustrated once more and unable to consult with others of his party, he slipped back to the capital, to hand in yet another petition — directed this time to a branch of the Rokkaku family he believed was sympathetic — demanding the rearrest of Hayashi and the release of the imprisoned headmen. The plan was that the recipients would use their influence with other relatives who were closely associated with the new government that had just replaced the Shogunate in Edo. In fact they did no such thing. The petition was sent straight to the fief headquarters. Shozo himself was at once arrested in the month of May, 1868, four months after the formal proclamation of the Restoration of Imperial Rule.

---

1. They were given this name by their conservative opponents within the Mito clan. In Japanese, 'goblin' is synonymous with 'braggart'.

Feud in a fief

His 'trial' began next day. An official of the old regime conducted the hearing, in the presence of the young lord of the fief and of Hayashi, the latter extravagantly dressed and openly exulting in the humiliation of his most recalcitrant opponent. Ordered to state his side of the case, and not in the least intimidated by the traditional arrangement of the court, according to which the prisoner sat on the ground bound with rope, facing but below his inquisitors, Shozo delivered a long, fierce indictment of Hayashi for his six years of embezzlement and misgovernment. At a second session the following day he was beaten across the knees with an abacus and ordered to apologize for his insolence. His only reaction was to repeat his charges in the same tone.

Then for some reason, perhaps because amid the uncertainties of the newly emerging political and social scene the magistrate hesitated to take action, even to placate the formidable Hayashi, against a prisoner who defended himself and the cause of the peasants he represented with such obstinate effectiveness, the hearings ceased. Shozo was incarcerated in a cell so tiny that he could stretch his legs only by lying on his back and pointing them at the ceiling and his trunk only by 'putting my hands on the floor in front of me and lifting my bottom like an angry tiger'. A small hole in the floor served as a toilet. Afraid of poison, he rejected prison food, surviving for thirty days by licking a stick of dried bonito that a friend had had sent in to him.

How he weathered such treatment is barely imaginable. He himself attributed his survival to a combination of youthful stamina with an above-average share of simple obstinacy that would allow neither submission nor compromise when he believed himself to be in the right. (At least this pigheadedness made up a little, he remarks, for his lack of learning and arithmetic.) Certainly the strain would have told even more severely if the magistrate in charge of the case had not been replaced after little more than a month.

The new official, a samurai member of the family Shozo had hoped would intercede on his behalf with the new government, gave him a guarantee, which after some initial distrust he felt able to accept, that his food would not be tampered with. A third hearing took place soon after, but no verdict was forthcoming. Weeks and months passed. In the temporary paralysis of administration that followed the setting-up of the new regime, Shozo's case seemed to have been forgotten. From time to time the sounds of fighting in the streets penetrated his cell, as Imperial troops fought scattered engagements with supporters of the old order.

There was no further pretence of a trial. At last, 10 months and 20 days after his arrest, Shozo was called before the court again, not for a further hearing, but to be told he had been convicted of 'disturbing the peace of the fief, betraying the trust of his position, plotting in a nefarious manner and submitting presumptuous petitions', crimes which 'beyond doubt merited the severest penalty'. 'By special favour', however, in place of the punishment he deserved he was sentenced only to perpetual exile for himself and his family from the territory of the fief. . . .

This sentence was not the conclusive blow for Shozo that it seemed. Very soon afterwards all fiefs and their boundaries were abolished anyway. Even before Shozo's conviction, many who had been bribed or cowed into supporting Hayashi had become so disgusted by his oppressive regime and by Shozo's prolonged imprisonment, that they had switched sides. But this was not all. In an unexpected display of 'impartial' justice, simultaneously with Shozo's conviction Hayashi was dismissed, this time without hope of reprieve, and exiled together with his lieutenants. For the 'justice party', as Shozo called it, apparent defeat had turned into total victory.

Emaciated and bent, but with his spirit unbroken, hardly able to believe in the sudden reversal of his fortunes, in February 1869 Shozo hobbled out of prison into the brave new world of Meiji Japan.

3
Murder on a frontier

After years of underground intrigue and months of near-torture in his prison cell, the shock of freedom must have been almost too much to bear. There was no question, though, of a comfortable period of recuperation at home. The struggle had left the Tanakas heavily in debt, for one thing; and Shozo's sentence of exile from the fief had for the time being to be obeyed, which added to the family's difficulties.

But the admiration his courage had earned him showed itself now in practical sympathy. When he set aside a third of the family property to raise money for the repayment of their debts[1], reserving the other two-thirds for the maintenance of his wife and parents, his creditors insisted on over-valuing his fields, so that he was able to pay back all the capital sums with ease; the interest they waived, though he in turn insisted on giving them IOUs for the full amounts due.

To support himself, Shozo found work teaching writing to children in a village just beyond the fief boundary. His 'school' was housed in the one-room shrine of a fertility spirit — which also became his own temporary home, where he settled in with nothing to his name but a single cotton kimono. Parents of his pupils lent him a charcoal stove, some bedding, and a saucepan or two.

For a while he revelled in the new life, enjoying its tranquillity and independence so keenly that even the pangs of hunger went unnoticed when, after a few desultory attempts at cooking for himself (his wife was looking after his parents at Konaka), he gave up the bothersome task altogether. In his own words: 'Between a drink of water in the early morning and gazing with delight at the evening moon, I forgot all about the three meals men customarily eat'.

When three days passed without any sign of his having taken any food, the neighbours began to worry; and soon they had arranged a roster among themselves to cook his meals. One slight inconvenience, the absence of a toilet in the shrine, was soon remedied. Shozo procured an empty soy-sauce barrel, set it in the field behind the

---

1. All the money he had saved from his indigo business went on repaying some of these debts. Shozo did not grudge the money, calling it in later life his 'entrance fee to the university of society'.

worship-hall-cum-schoolroom, and had his pupils plant shrubs around it in a discreet ring. This, he says, served his purpose admirably — save only for the mild embarrassment, in rainy or snowy weather, of 'having to hold aloft a borrowed umbrella while in action'.

From time to time friends or acquaintances called to offer him openings in the small new enterprises that were beginning to mushroom as the country slowly returned to stability under the new government. As with countless other young Japanese of the day, Shozo's ambition was twofold: to be of use in the great leap forward, as the country set out to modernize its institutions, and to restore his family's fortunes, whatever the cost to himself. But he saw too, again like so many of his eager contemporaries, the need for much study if he was to make his way into the new world.

It was an invitation to study in the capital that finally persuaded him to give up his idyllic existence in the shrine. The invitation came from one Oda Takizaburo, who after graduating five years before Shozo from Akao Koshiro's temple-school in Konaka, had sat at the feet of Otsuki Bankei, a prestigious Confucian scholar and advocate of Western learning. Oda had secured a post in the bureaucracy — the aim of many of Japan's most able young men, then as now — as an inspector of schools. For Shozo, it must have seemed that a more auspicious mentor could hardly have been found to help him on his way. So he handed over his little school, saucepans and all, to the nineteen-year-old grandson of his old teacher Akao, and set out for Tokyo to take up residence in Oda's household as a paying guest — or so he thought — with ample time to read and attend lectures in the small schools with which the city abounded. He celebrated his departure with a poem:

> On every side
> The cocks are crowing;
> Eager to serve
> Our Emperor, I too
> Set out at dawn.

The reality betrayed his hopes. Oda, he found on arrival, had been dismissed from his post. When Shozo handed over the money for half a year's rent in advance, which he had got together by selling old pieces of calligraphy from his family's modest store of heirlooms, his landlord promptly went out and spent it all that same night on a drinking bout with friends. Oda's affairs, he discovered, were in chaos. Yet he could hardly leave right away. Not only had he at least *paid* the rent for six months; Oda was his *senpai*, an older man from his own district to whom he was bound to owe a certain respect; and in any case he had nowhere else to go. So he stayed, and with his usual gritty tenacity of purpose set himself to put the Oda household in order. Dismissing the maid, he did most of the domestic chores himself — cleaning, shopping, drawing water from the well next door, preparing the bath — till there was scarcely an hour left in the day for the study that had been the object of his coming; in less than a month the twenty-seven year old ex-village headman and political prisoner had turned houseboy.

Oda's querulous wife did not help matters. When Shozo's country appetite and broad frame, now almost fully restored to health, demanded at least five bowls of rice at a meal, she would never serve him with more than two; his peculiar position in the household prevented him from asking for more.

As often as not he would go to bed hungry and exhausted, to spend the night in wondering anxiously how he could extricate himself with dignity and make a new start elsewhere. There were compensations: now and then he would manage to slip away to hear a lecture; on a simple human level, the maid next door where he went to draw water took pity on his shabby state and offered to do his washing for him. Others too sympathized: among them the kindly proprietor and servants at a nearby inn at which he had often stayed during the Rokkaku struggle, who were astonished that so dynamic a man should have sunk (in their estimation) so low.

Self-pity was the last emotion to which Shozo was likely to succumb. Experience had already taught him that a man must take responsibility for his own actions, and that outward circumstances need not dictate his state of mind. His only comment, after describing how they stared at his unkempt figure: 'But for my own part I was sorry for them, that they felt it necessary to be sorry for me. They were only looking, after all, at a man who had chosen to go his own way.'

Not surprisingly, since it was usual for men from the same province to lend each other a helping hand whenever possible, another offer from a Shimotsuke *senpai* soon came his way. Hayakawa Shusai was a friend of Shozo's who had recently been appointed to an official post in the newly-established prefecture of Esashi[1], in the far north of the main island of Honshu. The Governor of Esashi was also a Shimotsuke man.

When Hayakawa suggested in December 1869 that Shozo should accompany him to Esashi, Shozo accepted eagerly. In the Japan of those days, Esashi was awesomely remote, a 'frontier' region of dense forests and icy mountain slopes; but even in the back of beyond, with two such influential friends he could hardly fail to get a foot on a firmer ladder than Oda had been able to provide.

With one or two junior officials, Hayakawa and Shozo set out from Tokyo on the long journey northwards early in February 1870. An hour before they left, an apparently trivial incident took place which was later to have a strange, and for Shozo a malignant, sequel. A

---

1. The present-day Iwate prefecture.

Shozo and Satori Hikojiro examining poisoned plants

young married woman called to see him at the inn where he had been staying the night with Hayakawa. She brought with her a *wakizashi* or dagger which Shozo had given some years before to her father, a former official of the Rokkaku administration who had supported Shozo in the struggle against Hayashi. Dismissed eventually from his post, her father had emigrated to Hokkaido; his daughter having meanwhile married a Tokyo man, he deposited the dagger with her before he left, with firm instructions to seek out Shozo and return, with his grateful thanks, the weapon for which he would no longer have any use. By an ironic quirk of fate, in view of what was to follow some months later, Shozo took the dagger and the chance that had led the girl to find him on his last morning in the capital, as good omens, and left in high spirits.

The journey of some three hundred and fifty miles, through the slowly melting snows of early spring, took fifteen days. Towards the end, one of the members of the party contracted malaria; Shozo gave him his one and only spare kimono for a blanket, arranged for the patient to be carried in a special chair while the others continued to walk and nursed him when they stopped. Not only were the roads connecting the northern provinces with the capital appalling, but there was as yet no regular postal, let alone telegraphic, system in operation. Hayakawa and Shozo were quite unprepared, accordingly, for the shock that awaited them on their arrival in the small town of Esashi. Both the Governor, to whom Hayakawa owed his appointment, and his Chief Secretary (another Shimotsuke man) had resigned and left the prefecture a few days before.

The role of political patronage, particularly in these first years of the modern era, was such that Shozo must have felt his chances of employment in Esashi had dwindled almost to nothing. Even Hayakawa, already an experienced official, was worried as to whether the new Governor would take him on. But for Shozo, at least, there could be no going back, for all his money had gone on the journey, and he would have to find work to survive.

For two weeks the question was taken out of his hands. The malaria patient had grown worse, and needed Shozo to nurse him past the climax, in the little inn where they had found temporary lodging on their arrival. As soon as he could be released from this responsibility, Shozo applied at the prefectural offices for a job as janitor at a new school for Chinese Studies that had been opened just before his resignation by the previous Chief Secretary.

Before his application could be answered events took control again, and this time the outcome was a welcome surprise. Hayakawa's appointment had been confirmed after all, and once installed he had succeeded in procuring for Shozo a post as *fuzoku*, a kind of probationary officer in the prefectural administration. Understandably, Shozo's delight was intense. 'My spirits rose to the skies ... I resolved to do all in my power to fulfil whatever duties might be assigned to me. There was no room in my mind for any other thought.'

This determination was immediately put to the test. The day following his appointment Shozo was posted to Kazuno, an isolated district hemmed in by mountains more than a hundred miles to the north-west of Esashi town. The region was in chaos. It straddled the former border between two rival fiefs and had been the scene of violent fighting not long before. Bands of samurai still roamed at will, plundering defenceless villages. Communications in the still snow-bound valleys hardly existed, nor was there any map of the area. The take-over of the two fief territories by the new administration had only just begun; an exceptionally poor harvest the previous year had led to widespread famine.

Setting out to investigate from the new District Office at Hanawa Village, Shozo felt he might have been travelling through 'occupied territory', systematically devastated by an enemy, instead of a prefecture newly established under the reforms of Meiji, the Era of Enlightened Rule. Dead bodies lay unburied by the roadside. Cattle were being slaughtered by the thousand for lack of foodstuffs, and the peasants themselves were barely managing to exist on a diet of millet and fern-roots.

Faced with such appalling conditions, Shozo threw himself into the task of alleviating them with such initiative, efficiency and staying-power as must surely have marked him out even among the many outstanding public men of Meiji, if the fates and his own uncompromising personality had allowed him to make a career permanently in administration, commerce or industry.

At his insistence, large quantities of rice were brought in without delay from the neighbouring prefecture of Akita. Almost at once, as soon as the snows had melted sufficiently, he began to organize the distribution of plots of virgin land to the poorest peasants; a complex operation in itself, since these lands had never been surveyed, and applicants were expected to supply their own sketch-maps of parcels of land in which they were interested. In all these cases, Shozo himself was compelled to devise an accurate method of surveying both the land and the all-important streams and springs, and of marking hundreds of boundaries hitherto defined only by custom.

Disputes, which because of the disorganized state of the district were very numerous, came to him for settlement. Often old customs inhibited action. When a peasant was called before an official, whatever the business involved, tradition had it that he must appear in cumbersome formal dress, bringing with him a present of freshly-caught fish. Corruption flourished. Shozo noted a typical instance during the summer when several prefectural officials were invited to a river-fishing spree by the owners of a small copper-mine. Inspection of the mine followed the agreeable party; the officials congratulated the owners on the tranquil state of their enterprise, 'a clear sign of the benefits of the spread of Imperial rule'.

Not long after the outing, rumours began circulating that copper was leaving the prefecture untaxed. Officials from the taxation department were planning another trip to the mine to examine the accounts, when a large consignment of saké suddenly arrived from the owners to blunt their reforming enthusiasm. Numbers of young and idealistic public servants were little by little bought off in this way; others, older and more cynical, merely took advantage of the remoteness of Esashi from the seat of the central government in Tokyo to do as little as possible about anything.

Yet another obstacle for the less corruptible spirits such as Shozo was the almost impenetrable dialect spoken by the mountain folk with whom they had mostly to deal. The solution proposed by Shozo's chief was simple: to take a local girl as concubine-cum-language teacher. Acting at once on his own advice, he all but ordered his subordinates to do likewise. Under protest, Shozo acceded. Somewhat quaintly, he explains in his own defence (in a matter in which most of his colleagues were so little troubled by pangs of conscience that they mocked him for his scruples) that in addition to the need for domestic help because he was working so hard for such long hours, he had to have assistance in dressing and undressing. Muscular trouble contracted in prison and brought on again by the severe climate of the north, he explained, had made it impossible for him to bend his arms sufficiently to get into a kimono . . .

Of the pressure at which he was working, despite this physical disability, there can be no doubt. Between June and October alone, apart from all other duties, he judged over 200 cases brought before him as district magistrate. A letter written to his parents in September (which includes a complaint that he has not heard from them ever since his arrival six months earlier, in spite of the recent establishment of a rudimentary postal service) describes his labours in some detail, along with much information about the life of the region, the state of its agriculture, the price of horses. It ends on an optimistic note: 'Next spring, when the warm weather comes, I hope to come home for a few days. Expect me then!'

But before he could make that spring journey which he and they must have awaited so eagerly, a destiny more unpredictable than most intervened in his life a second time. Nearly four years were to pass before he could visit his home again, and by then his mother would be dead.

* * *

At the end of 1870, the head of the District Office to which Shozo was attached returned for a prolonged period to the prefectural town of Esashi. Kimura, the next in command, was left in charge. The return of winter aggravating Shozo's muscular complaint so severely that he could hardly stand or sit without assistance, he was given leave early in the New Year to visit Azukisawa, a small mountain spa that could be reached on horseback.

The hot-springs proved unexpectedly beneficial. Immeasurably fitter after only four days of steeping himself in the healing waters, and worried about having left his work so long, he returned to 'anawa on the evening of January 8th. Next day so much urgent business awaited him that he had no time to call on his chief. Halfway through the night of the 9th, he was woken by a panic-stricken messenger with the news that Kimura had been savagely attacked and lay dying in his bed.

Shozo stumbled through the snow to the other house — it was not a couple of hundred yards away; the messenger had come to him first because he was the nearest.

Kimura was still just conscious enough to be able to greet him when he arrived. Bathing the gashes in his head with white of egg and binding them as best he could, Shozo sent for a doctor and despatched constables to search neighbouring houses and to block the few tracks leading out of the village that were passable. But no trace of the attacker was found and when the doctor came Kimura was already dead. A meeting at daybreak of all the little band of officials stationed in Hanawa agreed that Shozo and one other should compile a report on this bizarre murder.

No further clues were forthcoming. The report duly drawn up and forwarded to prefectural headquarters at Esashi, Shozo turned at once to cope with a huge backlog of 280 applications for grants of government land, all of which entailed the making of detailed surveys.

Physically much improved, he plunged back into work with his usual intensity. The seventeen-year old concubine/nurse/housekeeper was no longer with him. On his return from the hot-springs spa, deciding he no longer needed her services, he had sent her home; when some weeks later she asked to be 'reinstated', he refused, saying merely that he was 'too busy'.

The future too looked brighter than ever before. A message had recently come from Esashi, complimenting him on the excellence of his mapping and survey work, with a strong hint that very soon he would be appointed to a more responsible post at prefectural headquarters; Hayakawa had perhaps put in a word to reinforce the reputation he was gaining by his own efforts. Shozo could hardly help feeling he was on the way to a solid and worthwhile career.

By driving himself and others to the limit, he managed to work off the backlog in two months. After such strenuous labours and in the expectation that he would be summoned any day to Esashi for new duties, Shozo allowed himself to relax a little. But a summons of a very different kind was on the way. Early one spring morning — the very day after the last set of outstanding land applications had been dealt with — he was putting freshly-cut irises in the vase in front of the little shrine to his ancestors in the living-room, when six constables clumped in to arrest him for the murder of Kimura.

What lay behind this melodramatic reversal of Shozo's fortunes never came to light. But a likely guess can be made. The conscious dignity of officialdom must have suffered severely from both the murder itself and the apparent inability of all those concerned to find the criminal; a scapegoat of some kind was called for. It was known that Kimura and Shozo had often differed, sometimes to the point of shouting angrily at each other. This was hardly surprising, given Shozo's headstrong and unyielding temperament, and the difference of twenty-five years in age between the two men. What was conveniently ignored was that these clashes, like all Shozo's quarrels, were as brief and quickly forgotten as they were intense; at bottom Shozo respected the man whose greater experience, he afterwards willingly admitted, was a necessary corrective to his own impetuosity.

There was no evidence, at any rate, that Kimura had borne any grudge or interfered in any way with Shozo's prospects of promotion. But if an arrest *had* to be made, circumstantial evidence was available which pointed directly at Shozo. Inevitably, when he had been binding Kimura's wounds, a few drops of blood had stained the white *hakama* skirt he had thrown on over his nightdress; no one had drawn attention to this at the time, but someone must have noticed and remembered — someone jealous, perhaps, of Shozo's ability[1] — the tell-tale stains, and Shozo could not deny that they had ever existed, even if he had wanted to, for traces of them still remained.

Even more incriminating was the alleged discovery of more blood on his dagger, the return of which had given him such pleasure on his last morning in Tokyo. Told of this, Shozo was flabbergasted; as a precaution immediately after the murder, he had shown the dagger to his colleagues, so that they could see for themselves that it was spotless. But as it was presented, the case against him seemed unassailable. Only one witness might have helped — Kimura's young son Kumakichi, who had opened the door to Shozo on the night of the murder. But he had gone three hundred miles to the south to join his

---

1. More complex motives than jealousy may have been at work. Throughout Japan, during the early years of the Meiji administration, there were numerous feuds between factions within the bureaucracy, originating from different samurai clans. Kimura's murder was probably occasioned by some such vendetta; and Shozo's isolated position as a mere ex-peasant, with no samurai connections to protect him, would have made him an obvious choice for a frame-up by the real killer, who was never discovered.

mother in Shizuoka; far enough in those days for him to be to all intents and purposes inaccessible, even if the authorities would agree to summon him, which for the time being at least they refused to do.

At a preliminary hearing in Hanawa Shozo was beaten with a lash twenty times for arguing with the prosecutor about the evidence and as many times again for refusing to confess; but such torture, in his phrase, 'only made me the angrier'. Bound with ropes, his feet imprisoned in *ashikase*, two thick boards with matching semi-circular holes the size of the ankles, he was carried in a prisoner's sedan-chair over the mountains to Esashi. On the way the party crossed the still snow-covered pass Nanashigure ('Seven Showers').

Man of action and defiant principle that he was, a vein of lyricism, giving easy and natural expression to his own feelings of joy or suffering, and readily linking those feelings with the forms of nature to humorous or deeply moving effect, was as marked in Shozo as in most of his countrymen. His poetic comment on the crossing of Nanashigure Pass, cooped up in his prisoner's chair:

> *Over Seven-Shower Pass*
> *With hands bound*
> *And no sleeve free*
> *To dry my shower*
> *of tears!*

At Esashi, there was some pretence of a trial. For a moment Shozo's hopes were raised. The doctor who had examined Kimura's body testified that the wounds must have been inflicted by a *blunt* dagger. The weapon produced in court, with the bloodstains, was certainly blunt — and equally certainly it was not Shozo's, which was exceedingly sharp. Shozo suddenly recalled that at the end of a saké-party one evening just before his arrest, a colleague had taken his dagger by mistake, to bring it back in its sheath (or, as was now obvious, another dagger like it, but blunter) a few moments later with profuse apologies. But to his chagrin, his old weakness betrayed him: he could not remember who it was that had made the exchange. Furious at his protestations of innocence, the Esashi prosecutor ordered the 'abacus treatment' to be administered while he questioned his prisoner further.

This crude form of torture consisted in making the victim kneel on a bed of small wooden blocks, each one tapering at the top to a sharp curved edge like that of an abacus bead, and then placing across his knees a heavy piece of stone, which would now and then be shifted from side to side in order to ensure constant renewal of the pain. In Shozo's case the 'treatment' was prolonged — according to one account he was driven unconscious sixteen times — but it failed to break his spirit, though he was shocked into realizing how completely he was in the power of a man with not the slightest concern for justice. 'I was tortured if I failed to answer him, and tortured if he didn't know how to answer *me*.'

Baffled, the prosecutor sent Shozo back to his cell, and there he remained. Summer and autumn came and went. Some of his feelings he recorded in poems:

> *Every evening*
> *Visiting the window*
> *Of my prison cell,*
> *You make me lonelier still —*
> *Moon of Miyagi moor!*
>
> *Chirruping*
> *In the prison yard,*
> *In their voices the sadness*
> *Of the passing year —*
> *Autumn insects.*
>
> *Here, on Miyagi moor*
> *I may leave my bones;*
> *Yet the dawn moon's faint gleam*
> *Will reveal*
> *My sincerity.*

Winter in prison in this northern town proved the severest ordeal he had yet had to face, harder to bear than the insolence of the warders, who had decided that Shozo was the most brutal kind of assassin. Four prisoners with whom he shared cells died of cold. For months the primitive state of the postal system frustrated his attempts to send for warm clothes from his home in Shimotsuke, though once he was lucky enough to be given a kimono belonging to a prisoner who had died of dysentery.

The spring of 1872 brought some mitigation of his hardships, however. First there was a visit from his father and brother-in-law, news of his arrest nearly a year before having at last penetrated to Shimotsuke. With Tomizo as living evidence of Shozo's respectable background, the attitude of the warders improved noticeably. Then in March, with the abolition of Esashi Prefecture, came a sudden transfer from Esashi to Morioka, the capital town of the new prefecture of Iwate. The Governor of Iwate, who during the years preceding the Restoration of Imperial rule in 1868 had himself served a term in a provincial jail for his Imperialist sympathies, had an unusual concern for the welfare of prisoners under his jurisdiction; as a result, to Shozo's astonishment, the warders began to 'behave quite kindly'.

As for the trial for which he was still waiting, nothing more happened for two whole years. Nothing, that is, save for a brief confrontation in court with his former concubine, from whom the prosecutor failed abysmally to extract anything to Shozo's disadvantage. But under the improved conditions Shozo was almost happy.

How he spent his time during this period he does not say, except that he thought much about a prisoner's need for peace of mind (fortifying himself, no doubt, with wisdom from the Chinese texts he had struggled to learn as a boy) and developed a private method of concentration to improve his memory, a method about which he merely says, unfortunately, that 'it would take too long to describe'.

This latter course of self-training had wider implications. It taught him, he recalled later, the need for single-minded action, the folly of dissipating one's energies in divergent interests — a simple enough maxim, but one which he was to observe with such fidelity as to lay him open in later life to mockery and to charges of fanaticism, even of madness.

Another winter passed in Iwate prison, made memorable by the receipt of his first parcel of warm clothes from his mother. New Year 1873: several small miracles followed in succession. *Tatami*, the comfortable Japanese flooring of thick rush mats, were installed: after two years of sleeping on wooden or earthen floors, for Shozo the change was 'a move from hell to paradise in a single night'. For the first time a list of prison rules was promulgated, allowing the prisoners certain privileges: flowers were to be permitted in cells, food and books could be sent in from outside. Thanks to well-wishers in the town, who provided him with two eggs a day and a quantity of reading matter, Shozo began to study 'politics and economics'. The names of the books he does not specify, apart from a 'life of Wellington', Rousseau's *Du contrat social*, and Nakamura Keiu's famous translation of Samuel Smiles' *Self-help* — the inspiration of so many earnest young men of Meiji Japan — long passages from which he would repeat aloud in his cell to cure himself (with complete success, as it turned out) of a slight stammer that had troubled him since boyhood.

With regard to the crime of which he was accused but neither convicted nor sentenced, all through 1873 still nothing happened. Another winter passed. Then at last, one morning in April 1874 the Governor of the prefecture, no less, called Shozo before him, and told him, without any prior hint of what was coming, that he was free.

Ironically, investigation of his case had been delayed more than a year because several senior officials of the prefecture had themselves been imprisoned after disturbances following the abolition of the Nanbu fief and the establishment of the prefecture of Iwate; but if the machinery of justice in the new era had been slow to move, in the end at least its wheels had turned to good effect. Cross-examination of Kimura's son in Shizuoka had established that the murderer, whom the boy had seen before his escape, could not have been Shozo, and had confirmed Shozo's statement as to the origin of the bloodstains on his *hakama* skirt. More surprisingly, one of his colleagues who had agreed on the night of the attack that Shozo's dagger was spotless had come forward belatedly to testify to that effect.

The abruptness of his release stunned him. After just over three years of prison life he was in no state to face at once the long journey home. A local official named Nishiyama who had kept him supplied with eggs (they had met at Oda's in Tokyo) took him in to recuperate for a while.

Soon he was out and about, fulfilling the Japanese proprieties by paying his respects to the graves of men to whom he had been bound by ties of obligation — Kimura, for instance, and Hayakawa, who had died suddenly while in harness at Esashi — and formally thanking the friends who had sent him books and other comforts.

Meanwhile his uncle arrived to fetch him home — with the news that his mother had died two months before. A friend in the Iwate prefectural office had given him a letter addressed to the former Governor of Esashi which would almost certainly have brought about his reinstatement in officialdom; but his uncle's insistence that Tomizo wanted him home weighed more with Shozo than this prospect of immediate reemployment, and the letter remained undelivered.

So it was that early in the summer of 1874 he came home from prison a second time with no prospects and only his character intact. If he had needed a reminder that once again he faced the challenge of building a new life entirely from scratch, a gruesome entry in the village registry at Konaka would have provided it. Three years before, his name had been struck off the register with the terse annotation 'executed'; the erasure had stood ever since, till it was hurriedly corrected when the village clerk heard Shozo was on the way home.

4

'Totchin'[1]

The years of Shozo's second imprisonment saw drastic reforms in many aspects of Japanese life, as the modernizing administration got into its stride. So much had changed so quickly, he says, that at the age of thirty-three he was made to feel like a new-born baby. All the feudal domains had been abolished, the Western calendar adopted, a railway opened between Tokyo and Yokohama, the educational system reorganized, conscription introduced.

In politics, the united front of the young samurai who had engineered the Restoration had already broken: Saigo Takamori, Itagaki Taisuke and other leaders had resigned in protest against the decision not to mount an expedition to Korea with Japan's new army, and a petition had recently been submitted by a number of ex-Councillors of State for the establishment of a popularly-elected parliament.

The times could hardly have been more challenging, not least for someone of Shozo's robust character and unique experience. For the time being, however, the need to find some means of support for his father, his wife and himself precluded any other interests.

An opening came when a saké-brewer in the neighbouring village of Akami took pity on Shozo and offered to take him on as his *banto* or assistant, living in, to mind his shop. Shozo was overjoyed. His comment has the weighty moral tone of a Meiji Japanese, and an ex-headman into the bargain, reared on the Chinese classics; a trifle pompous to our ears, perhaps, but conveying nonetheless the sincere feeling of one who had learnt by ordeal that a man's contentment need in no way depend upon his material condition or social status:

This was good fortune indeed, straight from heaven. The learning of the greatest scholar, if he does not understand the day-to-day affairs of ordinary men, is worthless. Assured that no better opportunity to study this everyday world would present itself, I readily consented.

The business of the everyday world was impinging closely enough on his own life even before he took up his new employment — in the

1. See below, p. 43

shape of the IOU's he had insisted on handing to his creditors after the Rokkaku struggle. An innate horror of owing anything to anybody had been reinforced, curiously, by his reading in prison of a similar almost fanatical scruple on the part of the young Wellington.

With his father's permission (still necessary, though by now Tomizo had handed over to Shozo the headship of the house) he sold what few disposable possessions the family still retained to rid himself of the burden; but they fetched no more than a tenth of the sum required. He need not have worried. Without exception, and in defiance of all his protestations, his creditors returned the IOU's. From the constraint of 'this other prison', as he felt his debts to be, he could now at last feel free.

So much for obligations contracted in the past. To ensure that from now on he would incur as few as possible, though he would be paid little but his keep, and Katsu was too busy in the fields to be able to earn more than a pittance by her sewing and other work, he drew up the following four-point 'household constitution':

1. *Notice of any debts to be posted in the family eating-place, so as to keep every member constantly in mind of them.*
2. *All household articles to be used for at least three years. Nothing new to be bought unless it was unavoidable.*
3. *All members of the family to rest on Sunday.*
4. *A family council to be held whenever there was a question of any extra expenditure.*

Since Shozo himself, in accordance with Japanese custom, would be staying most of the time in the house of his master the saké-brewer, leaving his wife and father on their own, a doctor was sought out to live in the Tanaka house, care for the ageing Tomizo, and in the rest of his time provide medical attention for the villagers as need arose. All this arranged (the doctor-lodger he found stayed eleven years), Shozo departed for the saké-shop in Akami.

His duties there were of the humblest. Apart from minding the shop, he was required to deliver casks of saké to customers, collect them when empty, chop firewood for the brewing operations, and — at least at first — keep accounts. Of the last responsibility he was relieved when his master, who had adopted modern methods of book-keeping recommended by the great pioneer of utilitarian learning, Fukuzawa Yukichi, discovered the primitive state of Shozo's self-taught arithmetic.

Not since his brief spell teaching children calligraphy in the shrine after his first imprisonment had Shozo felt so carefree, with nothing more serious to disturb the placid succession of his days in the shop than an occasional problem engendered by his 'household constitution'. Once his wife Katsu appeared with a surprise present of an apron and kimono she had made him from new cloth. Furious at her shameless breach of Article 4 of the constitution, Shozo punished her for this bout of wifely indiscipline by sending her back to her parents in disgrace for three days.

On another occasion the discovery on a brief visit home that the *tatami* mats in one room had been renewed without his knowledge led to a similar outburst — which was deflated by the quiet rejoinder from Katsu: 'It was your father's decision'. For as Shozo shamefacedly recalls, ' "Father" was sacrosanct. I couldn't punish *him*!'.

But it was not to be expected that such a man as Shozo would remain a shopboy for ever. The wonder is that he stayed with the brewer so long. No doubt there were differences between them from the start; but it was two years before the break came. A man leading a packhorse called at the shop one wet day and ordered a drink, leaving the horse out in the rain. Shozo angrily refused. How could he serve a man, he bellowed, so disloyal to his master as to put his own comfort before that of his master's horse and the safety of his load? Unfortunately the brewer was within hearing. A shop-assistant of such views, he decided not unreasonably, was 'ill-adapted to business'; and Shozo was dismissed. Like any other apprentice learning a trade, till then he had worked for his board and pocket-money only, leaving it to his employer to put aside whatever 'wage' he might think his 33-year old apprentice deserved. Now, when he had to leave, the brewer was not ungenerous. Or so at least thought Shozo, with his ready gratitude for any piece of good fortune however small:

To my astonishment he presented me with forty-eight yen[1] as payment for my two years' work — an unlooked-for blessing indeed. The money enabled me to rest a little and get quite fit again, and to start a night school. I was delighted beyond words.

Some time in 1876, therefore, Shozo exchanged shopkeeping for a third stretch of teaching, until some more appropriate prospect should present itself. The young men, not the children, of Konaka were his pupils. What he taught them he does not say, but they must have been glad to sit at the feet of a fellow-villager whose experience of the new Japan had been so adventurous.

As it had been feudal politics that ultimately prevented Shozo from following his grandfather and father as lifelong headman of a Shimotsuke village, so now the larger tensions of national politics intervened to put an end to his final round of schoolmastering — and in the event, to give direction and purpose to the remaining thirty-six years of his life.

In January 1877 Saigo Takamori led his 15,000 strong rebel army out of their base in southern Kyushu in a determined bid to topple the central government, from which he had resigned just over three years

---

1. Shozo's starting salary as a junior district officer in Esashi Prefecture had been 8 yen a month.

before. Many sympathized with Saigo, not least out of admiration for his powerful and generous personality, the epitome of all that a samurai should be; but if the nation's will to reconstruct and modernize its institutions was not to be emasculated by civil war, the rebellion had to be put down, and put down it was, though it took the entire force of the new Imperial army, plus reserves and police, nearly nine months to do so. In these circumstances, any overt sign of sympathy with Saigo and his cause was likely to be dangerous. One day during the 'south-west war' as it was called, a district headman named Takada happened to call on Shozo. Among other things they discussed the war, on the basis of reports in a Tokyo newspaper Takada had brought with him. How sad it was, Shozo remarked, that Saigo had to be described in the paper as a 'rebel bandit' — he was a man of honour, and must have had reason to act as he had done. These words were reported to the police, who promptly put it about that Shozo was of 'unreliable' character: young men were advised not to attend his classes, till finally the night school was forced to close for want of students. Shozo was once more out of a job.

The old question faced him as insistently as ever — what work could he find that would restore the family's fortunes; or more realistically, that would keep them alive and out of debt. The 'south-west war' had quickened his interest in politics, which had been roused in the first place by his experience on the receiving end of misgovernment, his prison reading, and especially by the demands now being made by some opposition leaders for a parliament.

After Saigo's defeat and suicide in September 1877, numerous enthusiasts for representative institutions flocked from all over the country to Shikoku, home of the 'liberal' statesman Itagaki, in search of inspiration and leadership. Most of them, in spite of their temporary intoxication with Western-derived notions of popular government, were merely disgruntled samurai who wanted a greater share in government for their own clans (which officially no longer existed), and believed that with Saigo dead, Itagaki offered the next best flag around which to rally.

Shozo too was eager to visit Shikoku. Closer contact with the realities of power and with the lives of ordinary people had given him a sounder basis for his incipient interest in democracy than these samurai could claim. For him, a parliament was essential because in the aftermath of a bitter civil war, with a financial crisis and continuing political instability, only a representative assembly could restore public confidence in the country's future. The young samurai leaders who had masterminded the Restoration of Imperial rule were unquestionably men of genius; but when they fell out among themselves, genius only aggravated the damage.

One curious factor in driving Shozo into politics — betraying, perhaps, a lingering trace in him of peasant superstition — was the fulfilment of a prophecy he had made in conversation just after the civil war ended. Takada had called on him again, no doubt to check on his political views. Questioned on the death of Saigo, Shozo replied: 'The country has lost one of its foundation stones. Before long it will lose the other.' He had in mind Saigo's fellow-clansman and the leading figure in the government at the time, Okubo Toshimichi, who as Home Minister had had overall responsibility for the quelling of Saigo's rebellion. Why should anything happen to Okubo, asked Takada. Shozo's explanation was cryptic:

I answered, that is the principle of things. One should not speak only of such matters as they appear outwardly.

In a little over six months, Okubo was dead, assassinated on a Tokyo street. An entry in Shozo's diary in August 1911, written from a very different perspective near the end of his life, records ironically the effect on himself:

It was conceit — conceit at the accuracy of my earlier prophecy, that confirmed my resolve to devote myself entirely to political reform.

The idea of a visit to Shikoku had to be abandoned, however. Shozo could not afford it. But he was more and more determined to find some method of procuring the degree of financial independence that would free him for political work.

The method he hit upon was simple but daring — so daring in fact did it seem to his countrymen friends that when he naively urged them to follow his example they laughed in his face, even those who like him had never succeeded in making good the sacrifices they had endured in the Rokkaku struggle. All *he* knew of business, they declared, was the addition and subtraction he had learned in the saké-shop. But the last laugh was his. The paper currency was being increased; prices were starting to rise rapidly.

Using his authority as head of the household, Shozo sold their storehouse and every possession of every member of the family that was not absolutely essential, and with the ¥500 thus raised bought up every scrap of land he could find an owner willing to part with. Within a few months land prices had risen as much as 10 times before starting to level off. Selling off some of his purchases, Shozo made a profit of over ¥3,000. By early in 1879 a modest income for him and his family had been assured.

This speculative success did not turn his head. Already he had been elected to the district council, and had used this position to send to the prefectural governor, for forwarding to the central government, a 21-item petition for the democratizing of local government. (Like many other petitions at the time, it was blocked by the governor.) That his vocation lay now in the well-trodden arena of politics, he was clear. But as with so much else in his life, his manner of taking it up was memorably eccentric.

According to the logic of the lesson he believed he had learnt in prison — that for himself, at least, any achievement worth the name could only come from total concentration on a single activity — commitment to public life would by definition demand the abandonment of all thought of private gain or ambition. Filial piety dictated that so drastic a step on Shozo's part should be agreed to by his father, even though the latter had 'retired' from the headship of the family. So he wrote his father (who of course was living in the same house) a formal letter, asking permission to carry out his plan. The main points of this remarkable document were as follows:

> That Shozo would give no more thought to working for private profit;
>
> That he should spend a minimum of ¥120 a year 'on the public good' for 35 years;
>
> That the son and daughter he and Katsu had adopted (they themselves were childless) should be sent away for readoption after having been adequately educated;
>
> That 'Shozo had forty million countrymen and friends — twenty million of them his guardians, and twenty million his children. Heaven should be his roof, and earth his bed.'

Shozo could be realistic as well as rhetorical, though, and did not expect, in view of the years of financial stringency their previous political involvement had brought on the family, that his father would easily give his consent. But in this he was mistaken. To his surprise Tomizo did not turn a hair, but congratulated him on his intention, merely asking whether he was sure he could carry it out. Then he wrote down the following verse — a Zen priest's *kyoka* or 'mad poem'   and handed it to Shozo:

> *What's the good*
> *Of Buddhahood*
> *Beyond the grave?*
> *Better strive*
> *While still alive*
> *Your soul to save!*

Shozo was encouraged beyond his hopes. He solemnized his decision by a three-day purificatory fast, concluding it with a vow 'to the deities of heaven and earth' that he would abide by the principles he had adopted.

So, resolved to make frugality a rule of life and to be always content with simple clothes and simple food, I gave myself up to politics.

To the spirit of this vow he was to remain entirely faithful for the remaining thirty-five years of his life.

*   *   *

According to one of his recent Japanese biographers, Shozo's letter to his father marks the great divide in his life. Till now, in the main, it had been other men's actions, impinging on principles which lay too deep within him for conscious formulation, that had determined his own: from this point on, with clearer objectives, he strove more consciously to rise above *mujo*, the flow and mutability of things.

This view tends to obscure a second, more profound change in Shozo's modes of thought and action which has attracted less attention than it merits from Japanese writers — the rejection, in the last decade of his life, of politics in the conventional sense in favour of a far more radical, apparently impractical (and to us strikingly modern) view of man, nature and society. But this avowed self-dedication to 'public life' in 1879 certainly shaped the course of his life, including those final years of non-violent resistance and ecological pioneering, as much as any other single action.

The first phase — ten years in prefectural politics at a time when to respectable country folk, at least, politics itself was an eccentric, almost disreputable activity — cannot have been easy. Shozo's summary is characteristic:

For ten years I achieved not one single thing. With my father worn down by age, my family poor, and myself so often away from home, people spoke of me as a good-for-nothing, an incompetent, miserable fellow. Yet in all the hectic comings and goings of my political life my father took pleasure.

But his own subsequent account of the period belies this modesty. The 'hectic comings and goings' were to include among other things the third and (in the event) for Shozo the most triumphantly successful of the trials-by-ordeal mentioned earlier as landmarks in his career.

Shozo's first enterprise, prior to standing as a candidate in the next election for members of the Tochigi Prefectural Assembly, was to join with a small group of like-minded spirits in Tochigi (the capital town of the prefecture) to found the *Tochigi News*.

The thrice-weekly paper, one of the first of its kind in Japan, was to stand for popular rights and representative government. The manner of its launching, if not the enthusiasm of its promoters (none of whom had any experience of journalism) left something to be desired. No advance advertisements were distributed, no deliveries arranged; only a single notice hanging outside the one-room office announced to the world 'First issue of the *Tochigi News* on sale here.' Not surprisingly, only fifty copies were sold.

The method Shozo adopted next day was also a little unorthodox, though it clearly reflected once again his own paternalistic, headman's background — calling on all the District headmen in succession, he badgered them to buy up stocks of the paper with their own money and distribute it free to the people 'in order to promote their knowledge'. The majority, he claims, agreed without demur. Needless to say, for the first few years of its existence the paper rarely paid its way, and financial difficulties were dealt with as resourcefully as those of circulation.

Once in the early days Shozo and a friend were deputed to call on a well-to-do relative of one of their colleagues, to borrow ¥50 for immediate expenses. The relative, Yui by name, refused point-blank. For once Shozo's unwashed state (living in the cheapest of lodgings, now and for the rest of his life he cared nothing for appearances, or even for cleanliness) came in useful.

Yui showed no sign of acceding to our request, though he called for some saké to console us for his refusal. All of a sudden I felt something biting my neck. I picked it off; it was a louse the size of a grain of wheat. When I went over to the verandah, the better to examine my undershirt, I found a little army of the creatures marching in two lines down the hem. Using a method of disposing of them that I had learnt in prison, I took up a teacup from the table and squeezed them one by one against the side with my thumb. They made a noise like beans bubbling in a pan. 'What on earth are you doing?', Yui asked. When I told him, he handed over the ¥50 at once, and we left. . . .

Others who heard from Yui of his uncouth visitor were happy to lend him money for the paper before he crossed their threshold.

Despite many crises, the *Tochigi News* survived and prospered. In 1881 the group were able to bring in a journalist from Tokyo, Nomura Motonosuke, as editor-in-chief and 'president' of the paper. Nomura, a member of a well-known association of young progressives — he himself was only twenty-three — had been working as 'petitions officer', handling all news of petitions for parliamentary institutions submitted to the government, of the leading liberal newspaper in Tokyo, and lecturing in his spare time on Bentham and J. S. Mill. He and Shozo had met for the first time the previous year, when Nomura gave a political lecture in a temple in the town of Ashikaga, north of Konaka. After the meeting was over, Shozo and his friends went with Nomura to the inn where he was staying overnight, for some hours of further discussion. Next morning Shozo alone, his enthusiasm undimmed, pursued Nomura by rickshaw to the village from which he was due to take the return boat to Tokyo, and in a riverside teahouse fired off questions at the learned young expert till the very moment of his departure.

Nomura's impressions of his questioner are of special interest, since they are the earliest of which any written record survives. Shozo struck him (and his opinion was later confirmed by intimate friendship) 'not as a man of profound learning, not as a genius in the ordinary sense of the term', but as a *nessei naru seishinka*, a man of quite extraordinary 'sincerity' and force of character.

The word *seishinka*, as Nomura says, was often used during this period, for the early years of Meiji bred many 'men of forceful character'; but whereas in the majority this forcefulness showed itself only in a magnificent courage, reckless and not without an element too of brutality, in Shozo the courage was combined with an equally out-of-the-ordinary sensitivity, a meticulous care for detail and for the feelings and problems of more ordinary men. The years were to bear out the accuracy of this assessment of Nomura's.

Some months after this first meeting, Nomura returned to Tochigi on a prolonged lecture tour arranged by Shozo. The many meetings at which he spoke were typical of hundreds of others taking place up and down the country as the 'movement for popular rights' approached the peak of its short period of vitality. Billed as 'educational' meetings, to deter the police from interfering, they were held in every conceivable location: temples, shops, wayside shrines (at one of which an old woman threw in a coin as she passed, misled by the speaker's fervid eloquence into thinking his address was a sermon), farmers' storehouses, silkworm-sheds. The police did not in fact leave the meetings alone, despite the ostensibly harmless topics of the lectures. But compared with later years their attentions were mild; though they followed Nomura everywhere, some became quite friendly, and one even resigned in order to join the movement.

In spite of his youth and obvious ability and enthusiasm, Nomura's début as editor and president of the *Tochigi News* was not easy. A crisis erupted on his very first day, when the paper's creditors arrived in a body to dun him for their money; it was barely averted by Shozo, who by day-long 'rushing around' (a phrase that recurs with increasing frequency in his biography) managed to raise ¥1,000 from friends and supporters.

A few weeks later the machines ran out of paper in the middle of a printing: the paper-merchant, still not paid in full, had cut off supplies. Shozo was at his lodging, on the point of leaving for a meeting of the Prefectural Assembly, to which he had recently been elected. Taking off the expensive formal kimono he was required to wear as an Assemblyman, he put on his nightdress (his other clothes being already in pawn), raised enough cash on the kimono to pacify the paper-merchant for a day or two, and proceeded by way of several back-streets to the Assembly. . . . He was rather proud of this exploit, but not for long:

That evening Takahashi Seitaro, the office janitor, called. I told him how I'd saved the situation with my 'quick change'. He laughed. 'It's no more than we've a right to expect from the bosses. But what about a mere janitor like me — I've pawned things more than once to help the paper through! You've no business to boast!'

I was profoundly ashamed.

Often there was no money for Nomura's salary, which got him into trouble at the temple where he was lodging; or for the compositor-mechanic who was living in at the office. Income from advertisements was almost non-existent, and bills were difficult to collect, as many villagers who read the *Tochigi News* found it hard to get used to the idea of paying for it at regular intervals. To meet all the paper's commitments, Shozo — fund-raiser in chief, by virtue of his energy and persuasiveness — had constantly to devise new expedients.

As its circulation increased, so did the fervour of its political articles, which brought risks of another kind. Several times during the ten years Shozo was associated with the paper, fines were imposed and members of its small staff arrested and imprisoned, mostly for short periods, one for five years. But Shozo's courage was infectious. Thanks largely to his pertinacity, the *Tochigi News* withstood all such buffetings, to play a prominent role in the development of provincial journalism as well as of democratic political consciousness.

At about the same time that he had helped to launch the paper in 1879, Shozo began his career in politics proper. After defeat on a technicality (one of the ideographs of his name had been printed wrongly on the voting papers) in the Prefectural Assembly elections of December 1879, two months later he was elected in place of an Assemblyman who had resigned. Within a few days he was present as an observer at a national conference in Tokyo of provincial officials. It was with these appointed officials, under the prefectural governors, that real power lay; the functions of the Assemblies were still severely limited, though not nugatory. The prestige of the former may be judged from this extract from an Imperial Message sent to the conference on its last day:

'At the time of Our accession, with the assistance of Our divine ancestors, We restored Imperial rule, established prefectures and districts, and carried out reforms without parallel in history. Though We were then of tender years, you, Our loyal officials, laboured day and night, never ceasing to care for the nation and serve the people. Your efforts have helped to lay the foundation of constitutional government, and thus to realize Our purpose, nourished from Our boyhood. To you We have entrusted the administration of local affairs. If there are samurai who are yet without work, ensure that they are provided with employment; if there are farmers and merchants who have not profited by learning and culture, instruct them, and deepen their knowledge; if there are those in whom the heat of political argument obscures their understanding of affairs or tempts them to adopt extreme political views, admonish and reprimand them, so that they may change their ways'.

Assemblymen from twenty-four prefectures, meeting in Tokyo at the same time as the bureaucrats, took the opportunity to send a petition for the creation of an elected Diet to the Genroin or Senate.

For the next ten years, till his resignation from the Assembly in

Shozo showing a poisoned plant to the Diet

order to stand for the national Diet, Shozo's political position depended on a deep belief in three things: the efficacy of representative institutions as a guarantee of fair government and social justice, the importance of a formal constitution to underwrite those institutions, and the benevolence of the Emperor. The second and third of these three articles of faith remained with him all his life; where parliamentary government was concerned, experience was later to force him into scepticism. For the moment, however, 'representative government' and 'a constitution' were his twin battle-cries.

In August 1880 he organized his own political association, the *Ketsugokai* or United Association, for disseminating these notions: two months later he and nearly 700 other members signed their own petition to the Senate. The wording may seem impossibly naive today, but it well conveys the almost childlike faith of those earnest would-be democrats of the 1880s:

'We humbly believe that His Majesty leads a frugal life, and that He is gifted with great insight and wisdom. He rises early and sleeps late, never relaxing for a single day, reveres Heaven, and cares for the welfare of His people. This none will deny. Yet why is it that the light of His virtues does not shine more brilliantly? The reason, we fear, is the lack of a constitution and a national parliament. A parliament would unite high and low; and if high and low are united, the true Imperial benevolence would instantly be revealed, the lament of yesterday would be transformed into the happiness of today, and past poverty transmuted into present riches. Thus the establishment of a parliament is the will of His Majesty and the earnest desire of His people'.

Naive though Shozo's own political attitudes were, they were far more deeply rooted in his character and experience than those of the majority of his colleagues, whose ideas of *minken shiso*, the philosophy of popular rights, were in the main derived from books, and therefore more liable to wilt, as they did conspicuously during the next two decades, in the face of authoritarian pressures.

Public office did not lessen Shozo's readiness to denounce arrogance on the part of authority. In March 1881, when Fujikawa, the new governor of Tochigi, gave a dinner for the popularly elected Assemblymen, he treated his guests with what seemed to Shozo less than proper respect. In a protest hardly imaginable in a country where formality is carried to such extremes, Shozo calmly turned his chair round and sat with his back to the table. 'The evil custom of revering officials and despising the people', he notes, after a brief description of the incident, 'was thereby somewhat abated.' But less eccentric activities — endless lecture-tours with his colleagues in every part of the prefecture, and humdrum constituency work — kept him fully occupied during these early years, earning him a good reputation as an elected representative.

The Imperial Edict of October 11, 1881, announcing that a parliament would be established by 1890, stimulated the formation of political parties opposed to the ruling oligarchy: Itagaki's so-called 'French-style' Liberal Party in the same year, and Okuma's 'English-style' Progressive Party in April of 1882. In reality the government was merely making sure it would keep popular representation, if it had to come, to a strict and comparatively ineffectual minimum but for a time the enthusiasm of the popular rights men burgeoned.

A founder-member of the Liberals, Shozo at once set about organizing branches in Tochigi Prefecture. His unusual mixture of commonsense and stubborn adherence to principle, however, led him to transfer his allegiance within six months to Okuma's Progressives.

The Liberals' inaugural conference had approved his proposal for a merger of the existing liberal-minded newspapers in Tokyo to form a single financially viable paper, to be committed to the party's views, and Itagaki had agreed too that he himself should not serve as president of any new paper as well as of the party; but the first proposal was later thrown out, and a new paper *was* started with Itagaki as president.

Scrupulous in his own rejection of all private gain, Shozo — in this never realistic — expected others in public life to think likewise. He wrote to Itagaki accusing him of degrading the dignity of a politician, let alone that of the president of the Liberal Party; and when no satisfactory answer was forthcoming, resigned at once to join the Progressives.

Japanese politics have always thrived on factionalism, and with the Liberals already well-established in Tochigi, and the Progressives forging ahead rapidly with the aid of Shozo's powerful eloquence at meetings and in the *Tochigi News*, competition between the two not very dissimilar groups was intense. Humour, and sometimes danger, flavoured their rivalry.

Liberal Party supporters made use of the ideographs of Okuma's name (O-kuma = great bear) and his birthplace (the remote southern island of Kyushu) to protest against his alleged over-intimate connection with business interests; in several towns a huge bear of wood and straw was paraded through the streets bearing the placard:

DANGEROUS WILD BEAR
CAUGHT ALIVE
IN THE
KYUSHU MOUNTAINS

WAS PAYING
¥250,000 A YEAR
TO MITSUBISHI
FOR PROTECTION

The model ended up in a ceremonial public burning.

A progressive meeting was about to start in a restaurant in Tochigi when thugs hired by the Liberals burst into the room firing pistols into the air. Shozo leapt to his feet, bawling 'If you mean to destroy the Progressive Party, kill Tanaka first!'. Unprepared for such defiance, the interrupters withdrew in haste. 'It'd take more than a gun to down our Tochigi *chindai!*' shouted someone. (Tochigi *chindai* = Tochigi garrison commander.) This is said to have been the origin of 'Totchin',[1] the nickname — affectionate or sarcastic, according to the user — by which Shozo came to be known, in the Diet and throughout the country.

Towards the end of 1883, however, unpalatable realities began to overshadow such trivial incidents as these. The appointment of Mishima Michitsune as Governor of Tochigi in October heralded the third — the shortest, but in some respects the most bitter — of Shozo's confrontations with autocratic power.

---

1. Formed from the To- of Tochigi and the *chin* of *chindai*.

5

Democrat versus developer

Mishima Michitsune, a samurai of the powerful Satsuma clan, had played an active part in the Restoration of 1868. Since 1874 he had acquired notoriety as a provincial governor in whom patriotism and the restless energy of a born 'developer' were combined with a ruthless disregard for the impact of his measures on the lives and feelings of the citizens under his control. On assuming the governorship of Fukushima in 1882 he had initiated an ambitious programme of roadbuilding, designed, in his own estimation, to civilize the largely mountainous region by opening it up to traffic and trade.

In a poor prefecture like Fukushima, forced labour and heavy taxation were the inevitable concomitants of the civilizing process. Mishima resorted to both without scruple. There was widespread and active opposition to his plans, and over 2,000 adherents of the Liberal Party were arrested, including many members of the Fukushima Assembly; some of the latter being subsequently sentenced to long terms of imprisonment.

If the maximum benefit were to be extracted from Mishima's roads, it was only logical that sooner or later they would have to be extended into Tochigi, the prefecture adjoining Fukushima to the south-west, and for Mishima the word 'later' had no place in his vocabulary; pressure was brought to bear on Fujikawa, the governor of Tochigi, who in February 1883 introduced a budget inflated by proposals for a three-year roadbuilding project to link up with Mishima's in Fukushima. On the ground that they would impose an impossible financial burden, the Assembly promptly threw out these proposals — twice. Fujikawa reacted equally decisively by dismissing the Assembly and declaring his proposals adopted and no longer debatable.

This display of personal rule was nothing very much out of the ordinary; prefectural governors in general at this time paid very little attention to the elected Assemblies. But Fujikawa's methods evidently struck the central government as unsophisticated. Before the summer of 1883 was over, it was given out that he would be transferred to Shikoku, and replaced by none other than Mishima himself, who —

conveniently for the building of the roads planned to connect the two prefectures — was to act as governor of Fukushima and Tochigi concurrently.

The announcement caused consternation in Tochigi. Some of Mishima's jailed opponents in Fukushima had already been executed, convincing anyone who still had doubts of Mishima's brutality. Political activity in Tochigi dwindled to almost nothing, out of fear of a coming clamp-down; well-to-do families, afraid of having to make huge compulsory contributions to public works — one of Mishima's favourite weapons — began to move out of the prefecture. Shozo's fighting instincts were aroused.

Hard-working and popular as he always was as an elected representative, both in the Prefectural Assembly and later in the Diet, it may be doubted whether his talents could ever have found their fullest expression amid the mixture of paperwork and factional intrigue that play so large a part in such institutions in Japan, as elsewhere; nor, with his authentic peasant and headman background, can he ever have felt entirely at home in the Progressive Party, which despite its name was closely associated with business interests. (In any case, the heart had gone out of both Progressive and Liberal parties by 1884. Economic depression, plus a series of severe government measures aimed at inhibiting all organized opposition, including censorship, restrictions on public meetings and numerous arrests, made it impossible for them to function effectively.) But no one could have been better fitted to stand up to Mishima's bullying.

The two men were built on the same scale — outspoken, uncompromising, fearless, with seemingly endless reserves of physical strength — and would have made formidable allies if their goals and motives had not been so totally different. As it was, Shozo took the lead in resistance even before Mishima arrived to assume office. His first thought was to organize a campaign to have Fujikawa stay on, for despite the latter's cavalier treatment of the Assembly Shozo felt he had for most of his term 'shown some respect for the popular will' by honestly trying to keep taxes low, and his very lack of finesse made him easier to oppose than the more sophisticated Mishima. His efforts were in vain.

Officials in the prefectural offices who had previously expressed disgust at Mishima's savage methods in Fukushima refused to say a word against him now that he was shortly to become their own chief; most supposedly 'liberal' citizens followed suit. When Shozo arranged a farewell party for Fujikawa[1], to his disgust only half the invited guests turned up, presumably for fear of incurring Mishima's

---

1. It may seem oddly inconsistent, particularly in the context of Japanese manners, that Shozo should have been ready to organize a party for a man whose arrogance he had so ostentatiously snubbed two years before. But grievances never lingered for long in his memory, nor did inconsistency ever bother him, except when the most fundamental principles were involved.

future disfavour by accepting an invitation from a known opponent.

When I saw how few had come, tears came to my eyes — tears of anger at the shallowness of human feelings. Why could they not bring themselves to greet the Governor when he is leaving, I thought — district heads, section heads in the prefectural offices, shopkeepers; these insignificant mice, these maggots of men!

Again, his next words are characteristic:

I felt all the more keenly my own responsibility in the coming struggle, and resolved the more firmly to discharge it.

as is the fair-minded addition

However, three district headmen had already resigned, unable to bear the thought of serving under Mishima. Some at least of our officials were men of character and courage.

Mishima took over as governor of Tochigi in October 1883. Immediately he went into action.[1] His main projects were two: to move the 'capital' of the prefecture from Tochigi to Utsunomiya (which would involve building new prefectural offices, new roads, new schools and a new prison), and extending the Fukushima roads down through the mountainous northern district of Tochigi Prefecture. His nominees were placed in posts such as that of the chief superintendent of police, and police powers given to district officials. Gifts were exacted from the well-to-do. An unpaid labour force of 6,000 was mobilized from the villages, with a fine of an average of three days' normal earnings imposed on each village for a man called up but not presenting himself — and a threat in the background of a general corvée for all males between the ages of 15 and 60.

Utterly determined to carry through plans he believed to be for the country's good, Mishima made these dispositions with amazing speed and thoroughness; profiting, no doubt, by his experience in Fukushima, where he had not moved fast enough to crush the opposition before it could crystallize.

Before the projects themselves (which had not been publicized) were actually launched, he invited the Standing Committee of the Prefectural Assembly to a 'get-acquainted' dinner at a Tochigi restaurant. Their suspicions aroused by the lavishness of the entertainment, the Committee members insisted before partaking of it on each of them paying for himself; and after this unusual beginning to

---

1. The following message reported to have been addressed by Mishima on his arrival to district heads, police chiefs and other prefectural officials may not be authentic in every word, but certainly conveys the gist of his attitude:

My main policy is the furtherance of public works. These must be started at once, with no more warning than a flood or a landslide, or a flash of lightning overhead that gives a man no time to cover his ears before the thunder. You will ensure that work is initiated as I direct, on the same day throughout the prefecture. . . . Contributions must be collected, and a labour force raised and set to work night and day without rest, so that all projects may be completed with the utmost speed. If there is delay, the people will have time to complain: they will refuse to obey orders, hold meetings, and appeal to the law, thereby obstructing all progress. This is the lesson I have learnt from my experience in Yamagata and Fukushima.

an official party, all went well. Till very late in the evening, that is, when Mishima had left. A policeman burst in on the proceedings, apparently to arrest Shozo — perhaps in the expectation that he would be drunk. One of the guests, a police inspector and henchman of Mishima's, who *was* · drunk, suddenly became confusedly loquacious, now congratulating himself on the ease of this arrest compared with the trouble they had had in Fukushima, but swearing the next moment that the policeman should be dismissed in the morning for having been so thick-headed as to intrude on the party. Equally embarrassed by this threat from his superior and Shozo's insistence that he do his duty, the policeman prudently withdrew. Shozo followed up his advantage by requesting the inspector to repeat his previous remarks ... whereupon the inspector apologized, and the party broke up.

Mishima had strategems up his sleeve more effective than this kind of 'comical, childish trick', as Shozo called it. Next day he called the Committee together again, apologized very politely for having treated them the previous evening with less than due respect and suggested they should make a tour of inspection of the site of one of his projects in the mountains. Rather surprisingly, the bait worked. The moment these recalcitrant representatives of the people, escorted by a number of helpful officials, were safely out of the way on their two-week trip at the public expense, Mishima put all his plans into action.

In Utsunomiya, designated by Mishima as the new prefectural centre, chaos reigned for several weeks. Houses were demolished without warning and with only minimal compensation, to make way for new roads and buildings. A few bold spirits attempted defiance. When labourers with picks and mattocks arrived early one morning to demolish a house that stood at the entrance to the site for the new offices, the owner, an elderly samurai named Honda, confronted them with a spear; his ancestors had won his land at the spear's point, he shouted, and only by force of arms should it be taken from him. Even he gave way, however, when his compensation was tripled.

The ceremony for appeasing the spirits of the soil on the site levelled for Mishima's own offices provided another touch of black comedy. Mishima threw a party on the site to celebrate after the ceremony proper, inviting his supporters and many Assemblymen, including those now back from the decoy-trip of inspection. Most accepted: Shozo refused. On the day, he and two friends climbed a small hill immediately behind the site and sat there bawling abuse at Mishima and his guests, who responded in kind, so that the party ended in uproar. 'A childish enough protest, it can't be denied,' Shozo wrote, 'but amid the general rottenness and venality some such "antiseptic" gesture was essential.'

Building went ahead with incredible speed. It was directed like a military operation by Mishima in person, who drove his labourers by the most effective method — working among them himself, head wrapped in a sweat-cloth, digging trenches and humping soil in a bamboo basket. In less than two months the new prefectural offices were completed. Mishima planned a spectacular formal opening, to be attended by a government Minister and two State Councillors from Tokyo, and several hundred other civil and military functionaries. In this he was frustrated by the Assembly.

The ceremony in question was such that on this occasion at least he could hardly act as if the representative body did not exist; and by now discontent was beginning to solidify. Three times the Assembly, by refusing its sanction, forced Mishima to postpone the ceremony, though a triumphal archway had already been constructed, and special clothes bought for several score of geisha who were to have entertained the distinguished guests.

Harsh though the effects of Mishima's administration were in the two main towns of Tochigi and Utsunomiya, the Assemblymen were especially incensed by the even more overt cruelty of his handling of the peasants on his roadbuilding schemes. Shozo spent much of the spring and early summer of 1884 collecting evidence of the barbarous methods employed, which reached a climax in what became known (in the usual delicately vague Japanese terminology) as the Otome Village Incident.

Hearing rumours that violence had broken out at the village, which lay on the route of Mishima's main north-south road, not many miles from Tochigi, Shozo at once rode off to see for himself. Most of the villagers, he found, had fled from their houses in terror, leaving only their animals behind. Before starting to drive a road through the area, Mishima had summoned the headmen of Otome and other affected villages to the prefectural offices, surrounded them with police, and compelled them to sign a document assenting to his plan. This formality completed, the villagers were pressed into road-making gangs. Most of them made a precarious living as rickshaw-pullers, or as boatmen and fishermen on the nearby Tomoe river, earning not more than about 8 sen a day; yet not only were they paid nothing for their forced labour, but a fine of 25 sen was exacted for each day a man absented himself. Not surprisingly, many turned up late for work, after fitting in other jobs in order to make ends meet.

As an example to the malingerers, the police arrested, bound and flogged the headman of Otome — to be attacked themselves by infuriated villagers, who succeeded in rescuing the headman temporarily. Officialdom could not take such a defeat lightly, and soon afterwards a reinforced band of police rampaged through the village with naked swords, beating and kicking everyone in sight, including the headman's wife, who was stripped and beaten, and making a total of 73 arrests.[1]

Such was the situation when Shozo arrived to investigate. Incensed at this latest example of Mishima's inhumanity, but too experienced to take precipitate action, he spent some time collating reports of the disturbances, then left for Tokyo. There, through the good offices of an influential friend in the Progressive Party, he obtained interviews first with an Under-Secretary at the Home Ministry, then with the Minister himself, Yamagata Aritomo. Probably these interviews were instrumental in securing the central government's intervention against Mishima three months later: an Assembly petition to the Executive Council (later re-formed into a Cabinet) was arranged for Mishima's dismissal. The Under-Secretary with whom Shozo had pleaded made a personal visit to Utsunomiya (a very rare event at the time for such a senior Tokyo official), and though he was carefully entertained by Mishima, reported honestly to the Council on the strength of popular feeling against Mishima in the prefecture.

The end was not yet. In September 1884 Mishima laid a motion before the Prefectural Assembly asking it to approve a nominal supplementary budget — ostensibly to cover additional expenses incurred in his public works programme. In reality this was a ruse to force through the Assembly the legalisation of his extortions during the preceding ten months, so that the way would be cleared for his third attempt to organize the grand opening of his new buildings in the new 'capital' of Utsunomiya. Though present for the debate, Mishima emphasized his contempt for the Assembly by snoring ostentatiously.

In a voice whose denunciatory vehemence was later to become something of an institution in the Tokyo Diet, Shozo roared his protest to the chairman: Mishima woke up and left, whereupon the motion was rejected unanimously, and once again Mishima had to postpone the opening ceremony. Before it adjourned, the Assembly appointed its chairman and vice-chairman to convey an indictment of the Governor to the Executive Council of Ministers in Tokyo.

That evening Mishima sent the head of his Public Works department to the inn where Shozo was discussing the latest developments with the chairman and his deputy. Assembly debates were one thing, the messenger had been deputed to say, and personal relations another; the Governor would appreciate it if they would join him right away at another inn for 'a friendly and confidential talk'. Shozo and the others refused, though the same messenger came

---

1. I do not wish to obscure Mishima's achievements as a roadbuilder. (He no doubt deserves the following tribute in the Japanese Travel Bureau's Official English-language Guide to Japan: 'Attempts were made from time to time to make the Shiobara spas more accessible, but it was not until the governorship of Viscount Mishima, a vigorous advocate of good roads, that anything was done to popularise them'. Thus even foreign tourists have cause to be grateful to this development-minded governor.) But they were bought at a high cost in human distress, and it was this that struck Shozo most forcibly.

back twice to urge them again to accept.

Just after he had gone for the third time, two Assemblymen burst in, urging them not on any account to go. They had heard, they said, of a plot to have the three men murdered. A group of thugs had been hired by Mishima; they were to pick a quarrel with the three on their way to the proposed meeting with the Governor, lure them to a back street and kill them outright. Several suspicious figures, probably the hired assassins themselves, were already hanging about in the shadows outside. Shozo and the others were wondering what to make of this when another official came to renew Mishima's invitation. Again they refused, with the two Assemblymen warning them against leaving the building. The official hurried out. A moment later there was a growl of '*Why* won't they come?' outside, after which the 'suspicious figures', who must have overestimated the amount of saké they needed to get up their courage, came in out of the dark and crowded into the adjoining room. Their loosened tongues instantly confirmed the warning the two Assemblymen had brought. The Assembly vice-chairman was as equal to this occasion as Shozo himself.

Removing the partition door between the rooms, he called out, red-faced with anger, 'Don't disturb yourselves! My friends and I have been too busy with public affairs to have time to eat — if you have a meal for us, serve it now!'

Probably this challenge would have defused the situation anyway, but even so it was lucky that just at that moment several more Assemblymen appeared on the scene; and the assassins, now thoroughly intimidated, slunk away.

Convinced by now of the danger to his life, Shozo slipped out of Utsunomiya the following morning and made his way to Tokyo. The journey took three days. Within a week some of his friends had collected money for his support — others had been arrested immediately after his disappearance and cross-questioned as to his whereabouts — and sent it by one of their number to his hiding-place in Tokyo, with the warning that he should lie low in the capital till things were safer.

Encouraged by this demonstration of support, Shozo gratefully accepted the money, but not the warning: there could be no excuse for his remaining inactive, he insisted, if others were to suffer on his account. So he started back home at once, to resume the collection of evidence to be used against Mishima. The task was not easy: despite the widespread hatred of the Governor, many who had suffered most from his barbarous methods were too timid to give evidence willingly against him. Police were constantly on Shozo's track, so that this elected representative of the Tochigi citizenry had to move everywhere with the furtiveness of an escaped criminal. One incident flavoured this tedious game of hide-and-seek with a touch of sardonic humour:

I was walking along the new road near Okubo when I saw a cloud of dust rise in the distance, and immediately afterwards heard the clatter of a great many wheels, apparently coming in my direction... I lay down in a clump of bushes at the roadside, and waited for whatever it was to pass... Fifty or sixty rickshaws came into view, carrying a few officials and thirty or more geisha, the brilliant reds and yellows of their dresses making the whole procession as gay as a rainbow. A peasant I spoke to in the fields afterwards told me the officials were from the Ashikaga district office, on their way with a crowd of geisha from Ashikaga and Kiryu to the opening ceremony at the new prefectural headquarters in Utsunomiya. Evidently they hadn't heard that the ceremony had been cancelled again....

Here was I, a member of the Standing Committee of the Prefectural Assembly, having to hide in the bushes from a collection of petty bureaucrats and geisha girls! Society's a strange thing, I thought, sighing and smiling at the same time. Then I went on into Yanada District, gathering evidence from Otani, Osa, Tanuma, Inamura and other villages.

At the end of September, Shozo crossed into Gumma Prefecture, where he imagined the police would not follow him, and put up at an inn in the little town of Tatebayashi, just across the border. But Gumma was to offer not even a temporary respite. Exhausted, he fell asleep immediately — but was woken by a stranger before nightfall and warned to leave the inn at once. Five days before, a small band of Liberal Party activists had attacked a police station not far away with bombs, in a naive attempt to start a revolution. The attack was futile enough, but it alarmed the central government as well as the provincial authorities.

This was the first serious case of 'terrorism' in the modern period,[1] and what was worse from Shozo's point of view, it appeared that the bombs had originally been intended to blow up the government Minister invited to attend the opening of Mishima's prefectural offices; Mishima had at once put it about that Shozo was one of the ring-leaders in the Kabayama Incident, as it came to be called,[2] and the police search for him had spread into Gumma and elsewhere. Of all this, as he moved by stealth from village to village (where by now the corvée had interrupted the circulation of such newspapers as normally reached them), Shozo had been totally unaware. At first he refused to heed the warning. There would be danger wherever he went, he knew, but too much work still remained to be done for him to bother about the risks. However, the earnestness of the stranger's reply convinced him, despite its oddity:

---

1. Of the twenty-one conspirators arrested and later tried in Tokyo, seven were executed, and all the remaining sentenced to long terms of imprisonment.
2. From Kabayama Hill, on the top of which the conspirators raised their flag of revolution.

'What you say is admirable', he answered, 'but if you do not accept my help you will most certainly be in serious danger. Our castle here in Tatebayashi was once called Fox Trail Castle. An old fox led the way in marking out the moat inside which the castle was built. I am your old fox: follow me now, I beg you.'

The old fox led him to a doss-house in one of the darker back streets.

A woman brought some food; Old Fox went out again. After a while I heard a low voice, calling outside, 'Tanaka! Hold out your hand!' It was pitch-dark, but I thought I recognized the voice; so I opened the window and put out a hand as I was asked. Imagine my surprise when I felt banknotes dropping into it. 'From Matsumoto', said the voice; then I heard footsteps hurrying away. Matsumoto was the doctor in charge of Tatebayashi Hospital.

The pace of the hunt quickened. Arriving after dark at a pre-arranged rendezvous back in Tochigi where he was to receive documents from two helpers who had been taking statements on Mishima's activities of the prefecture, Shozo was brusquely received; both the men he had expected to meet had been arrested, and Fukuda, the owner of the house, had only just returned from the police station, where he had been questioned all day as to Shozo's whereabouts. Only Fukuda's daughter-in-law took pity on him, throwing him a pair of sandals and some money from a window as he turned to go. Another meeting arranged for a day or two later was no more successful.

At the house of a well-to-do landowner (Mishima had incurred the hatred of every class) Shozo waited for 'Old Fox', who had promised to bring him a further batch of incriminating evidence. Three days passed after the appointed time, and still there was no sign of his anonymous friend. News reached his host that more and more of Shozo's associates were being arrested.

Shozo decided it was too risky to wait any longer; he set off again, this time for Tokyo, to use the indictments of Mishima he himself had collected in one more direct appeal to the central authorities. As wily in outwitting the police, perhaps, as his self-chosen nickname implied, Old Fox did turn up, barely an hour after Shozo had left. But it was too late and too dangerous, to try to catch up with Shozo. Before he had gone far, someone recognized him as he was walking through a village and called out his name. As ill-luck would have it, a policeman overheard, and began to shadow him. Shozo boarded a train for the capital: the policeman followed. Not far from Tokyo, however, a flood had washed away a railway bridge, so that the passengers had to be ferried across the river in small boats; seizing his chance, Shozo escaped across the fields.

His trials were far from over. To his astonishment, when he arrived some hours later at an inn on the outskirts of the city and sat down to rest, after handing over some of the muddier of his clothes to be washed, the innkeeper, to whom he was unknown, started to commiserate with him on 'the arduous work men of your profession have to undertake'. From what he went on to say, the implication quickly became clear.

A round-up of Liberal Party 'radicals' had been taking place in the area, as elsewhere in Tokyo — five students who had called at the inn the previous evening had been arrested on the premises, and the innkeeper and his maids had assumed that Shozo was just another policeman engaged on the disagreeable task of searching out 'dangerous elements'. Weary though he was, Shozo could hardly stay till they were disillusioned.

When darkness fell I went on further into Tokyo. Presenting myself without warning at Akabane's house (Akabane was assistant editor of the Tochigi News) *in Ushigome, I said I was tired out, and asked if I could sleep there. Akabane himself wasn't at home. His wife was in the last stages of pregnancy; big enough to burst, she looked. Had I been in Tokyo all along, she asked. The police had searched their house the day before, apparently. Then she showed me the* National Daily. *'It says you were arrested yesterday. Broken out, have you?' I told her I had just come from Tochigi, in the hope of getting an interview with the Foreign Minister:*[1] *I wasn't ready to be arrested yet. But would she let me sleep a bit? Without any fuss she took me into the kitchen, showed me the lie of the land outside the back door, and was leaving me to lie down by the stove, when in walked Akabane. The police were in the neighbourhood again, he said. It was no good my staying....*

Akabane escorted him to a tiny inn some distance away, in a quarter where the police were less active. It was very late. The landlord began to ask awkward questions. Here, too, it was unsafe to stay. Out on the streets again, Shozo spent what remained of the night in rickshaws, clattering from one side of Tokyo to the other, sleeping in fits and wondering in the intervals whether his plan of calling on the Foreign Minister might not end in what he had so far managed successfully to avoid — his own arrest — because 'the Minister was not a personal acquaintance'.

One hardly knows which to wonder at most — Shozo's naivety, his courage, or the sheer resilience that could keep him intent on his mission despite physical exhaustion and a long series of setbacks.

By the morning he had wisely decided against an immediate attempt to see Foreign Minister Inoue. Instead, he called — incredibly, in the circumstances — at the official residence of the

---

1. Inoue Kaoru, a former samurai of the Choshu clan who had studied in England. Among the chief problems facing Inoue at the time was that of revision of the 'unequal' treaties with the Western powers, for which there was widespread clamour in the country. Shozo had intended to ask Inoue how the government, when it ignored the barbarities committed in its own name by men like Mishima, could devote so much attention to the need for treaties implying equal status with 'civilized' Western nations.

Chief of the Tokyo Police. Fortunately, perhaps, that officer was not at home; but Shozo, undeterred, left with a secretary a copy of his detailed indictment of Mishima's misdeeds, and went on to the offices of the liberal *Yokohama Mainichi* newspaper, hoping to get help from his friend the editor in securing a meeting with the Foreign Minister.

Shimada Saburo (founder and chief editor of the *Yokohama Mainichi*, and a former secretary to the Senate) was less than enthusiastic. Since so many of Shozo's sympathizers — and even some of his relatives, including most recently his married sister — had been arrested and ill-treated when they could not or would not reveal Shozo's whereabouts, simple human feeling demanded, in Shimada's view, that to save them further harassment he should give himself up. At first Shozo resisted the suggestion, on the ground that all his friends had all along been as ready as he was to face the consequences of their political views. Eventually, however, Shimada persuaded him, and he set out for Metropolitan Police Headquarters — but not exactly to give himself up.

I was received very politely, and shown into a room with comfortable Western-style chairs. After a moment a superintendent officer came in: what might my business be, he asked. I replied that I had come to Tokyo to see the Foreign Minister; but it had come to my notice that the police were looking for me, and had arrested many of my friends in the course of their search. Here I was, I said: why did the police want me? Then you are giving yourself up, he answered. No, I said — I had committed no crime to give myself up for. But I would like to know why the Governor of Tochigi was making so many people suffer on my account ... I showed the superintendent the newspaper cuttings I had brought from the Mainichi, *with details of all the arrests.*

He was very glad I had come, anyway, was all the superintendent said by way of reply; five days before, a request had come from Tochigi for my arrest, and they had been hunting for me ever since. What was the charge, I repeated. He didn't know, unless it was in connection with the Kabayama Incident — their only duty was to arrest me and send me under guard to Tochigi. That's ridiculous, I said: the law's writ did not run in Tochigi. My task was to resist Mishima by exposing his lawlessness. If I were sent back, it was mirror-plain he would have me killed. Then I began to list Mishima's crimes in detail, producing the evidence I had collected.

Shozo's list was a long one.

Before I was halfway through, the superintendent interrupted me. Police Headquarters had no authority to deal with such matters, he said, so there was no point in my going on. They might have no authority, I told him, but I had the right to put the case before him, whether he chose to listen or not....

I went on, but obviously he wasn't listening. 'How can you possibly send me straight into the clutches of such a public enemy?' I complained. 'Don't you know,' he said with great solemnity, 'that no corner of our whole Empire of Japan is without the protection of the law? Of this I give you my guarantee.'

'I shall hold you responsible for it,' I said.

With that I made him promise to let me keep the documents, and agreed to let myself be sent into enemy territory.

Police accompanied Shozo back to Tochigi next day. His feelings were complex. Angry with himself for having — as it seemed — let himself slip into Mishima's clutches so easily, he still had enough faith in the validity of the Japanese notion of 'responsibility' to believe that the superintendent would honour his guarantee — that he would be permitted to forward his documents to the right quarter, and that before long he would be able to defend himself in a public trial, which could only (according to his thinking) result in his release and Mishima's disgrace.

When he arrived at Utsunomiya prison, after relatively considerate treatment on the way, the omens were not good. Vindictive warders harassed him, sometimes with physical violence, sometimes with a show of contempt, such as dropping their burning cigarette-ends into his food while he was eating. All his requests for a public trial were refused. As soon as Assemblymen began to visit him in prison, he was moved to a dank and dirty jail in Sano, thirty miles away.

With Shozo, the most active and dangerous of his opponents, safely locked away, Mishima was to all appearances victorious. By way of celebration, he went ahead immediately with his oft-postponed ceremony for the opening of the prefectural offices; it was held at last on 22 October, in the presence of no less than Prince Sanjo, President of the Council of State. In his speech Mishima quoted, with egregious complacency but scant regard for the accuracy of the analogy implied, from the opening of the song 'On the joy of the people in the growing opulence and dignity of King Wu' in the Chinese Book of Odes:

When he planned the commencement of the marvellous tower,
He planned it, and defined it,
And the people in crowds undertook the work,
And in no time completed it.
When he planned the commencement, (he said) 'Be not in a hurry;'
But the people came as if they were his children.[1]

But as with the Esashi affair, the reversal of fortune was to come suddenly, and this time far more speedily. Almost to a man, the members of the Assembly had boycotted the opening ceremony. Some, however — no doubt encouraged by the publication in a

---

1. Legge, *The Chinese Classics*, Vol. IV, p. 456.

national newspaper of a letter Shozo had smuggled out of prison to his father and relatives, urging them not to relax their opposition to Mishima on his account — had called on Prince Sanjo beforehand with what purported to be letters of felicitation and of apology for their inability to be present at the opening. In fact, they were systematic indictments of Mishima, along the lines of the documents Shozo had read out to the police superintendent in Tokyo.

These repeated expressions of protest, reinforcing dramatically Shozo's earlier plea to Yamagata, and confirming press reports of Mishima's disastrous unpopularity, must have tipped the scales against him. Three weeks later, in the middle of November, he was abruptly dismissed, along with many of his subordinates, and — in a public humiliation rare in the extreme for such a senior official of the Japanese bureaucracy — demoted to a post of relative insignificance in the Home Ministry.[1]

Shozo was released the following month. For weeks he was fêted in towns and villages all over the prefecture. The police found the sudden change difficult to get used to; they attended many of the welcome meetings held for him as if he were still officially 'dangerous' and even tried to break some of them up.

Administratively, thanks to Mishima's single year of office, the prefecture was in chaos, with shortages of food, depressed wages and constant outbreaks of banditry. But the cause of it all had been removed; and as if to underline Mishima's total defeat, the prefectural buildings of which he had been so proud were razed to the ground in a fire early in 1885.

The stubborn resistance of a few had conquered in the end. But for the majority, factionalism and a cringing fear of authority transmitted through generations of submission to autocratic rule had made any overt protest unthinkable. Of this Shozo was very clearly aware.

In a politically conformist society, the very rigidity of his determination was bound to make him a lonely figure. Sometimes he lamented the 'childlikeness' of the Shimotsuke peasantry (who still made up the bulk of the population of Tochigi) and the smallness of their preoccupations. Yet never, either in the struggle against Mishima or in later, more protracted 'campaigns', did he show any trace of bitterness or complaint that where he led others could not always follow.

Without this special kind of tolerance, even his extraordinary moral courage might have won respect, but not the affection and

---

1. The demotion was only temporary, however. The following year, Mishima was made Chief of the Tokyo Metropolitan Police, a position of great power, which he wielded with such severity that the Tokyo populace nick-named him *Oni-sokan*, 'demon police-chief'. In a proclamation issued when he was about to enforce Prime Minister Yamagata's harsh Security Ordinance of 1887, he announced that he 'would suppress alike all arsonists, robbers, Liberals, and Progressives'.

sympathy that he was able to inspire in many who found his stand on many issues too uncompromising for 'reasonable' men to countenance. And for the moment, at least, he was 'Totchin' indeed, undisputed hero of the prefecture. The nagging question remained, however: what kind of long-term political career could he build on his lengthening series of confrontations with autocratic power, however successful they had been so far.

6

'Gift of a priceless jewel'

The four years from Mishima's dismissal to the promulgation of the Constitution in 1889 and the launching of the Diet in the following year were among the most tranquil of Shozo's life, if by tranquil is meant devoid of spectacular drama. Certainly they were busy enough — constant public activity hardly ever left him time to visit his wife and father, a state of affairs which continued for the rest of his life — but for a man whose experience and character set him apart from the ordinary run of politicians, the daily round of routine Assembly work and political meetings up and down the prefecture was bound to seem in some degree frustrating.

Enthusiasm for the 'popular rights' movement was waning; not, in the case of Tochigi, because of official repression (the effects of the Security Ordinance[1] of 1887, which resulted in the banishment of 600 'liberals' from Tokyo, were hardly felt outside the capital) but because the government promise of a Diet had satisfied the politically naive majority of its supporters.

Shozo himself could not help looking forward with intense eagerness to the granting of the Constitution and representative government as the guarantee of a new era of 'respect for the people's will'. Till then, political controversy would remain largely in abeyance.

In the spring of 1885, the Assembly elected him its Vice-Chairman; but he declined to serve, preferring to devote his time to helping in a multitude of ways all over the prefecture in the restoration of normal life in the aftermath of Mishima's misrule, and in the consolidation of his own Progressive Party support.

A plan to impeach Mishima was abandoned when the fire at the prefectural offices destroyed incriminating documents. But there

---

1. The intention of the Ordinance was to prevent 'agitation' during the negotiations with Western powers for the revision of the unequal treaties. The government was afraid that opposition politicians would attempt to convert the popular discontent with its conduct of the negotiations into a campaign for more thorough-going democratic representation under the forthcoming Constitution, which was then being drawn up behind closed doors. The Ordinance remained in force till 1891.

were other more positive steps to be taken to commemorate the end of Mishima's term.

At the end of the year Shozo led a delegation to Ito Hirobumi (Prime Minister in the recently-formed first Japanese Cabinet) to propose the granting of greater control over prefectural finances to elected Assemblies. To his satisfaction (but not greatly to his surprise, for it was Ito himself who had originally proposed Mishima's appointment to Tochigi, and according to the Japanese code he must have felt responsible for the resentment his protégé had aroused) Ito agreed at once. This peaceful triumph set the seal on Shozo's reputation in his native prefecture.

Already in September a national newspaper, in compiling one of the lists with which the Japanese delight to classify memorable persons and places, had named him as one of the Ten Famous Heroes of Tochigi. Then, in February 1886 came his election to the most prestigious non-official position in the prefecture — the chairmanship of the Prefectural Assembly. With life in most of the prefecture now restored to something like normal, this time he was ready to accept the post, and served as Chairman till his election to the Diet in 1890.

There is little of special interest to recount from the intervening years. One curious incident of which a record survives seems to belong to this period. It may be apocryphal (anecdotes about him abound) but there is a ring of truth, too, in the note it strikes, of a simple directness as delightful as it is rare in a man of nearly fifty, and of a restlessness, too, in his new position of political respectability:

Tanaka Shozo called on Fukuzawa Yukichi (the great scholar of the Japanese 'Enlightenment', advocate of 'practical learning', and founder of Keio University).

'What is your business?' asked Fukuzawa.

'I should like to enter Keio University,' answered Tanaka.

'Have you a job back home?'

'Yes. I'm Chairman of the Prefectural Assembly.'

'Excellent!' said Fukuzawa, and suggested they should lunch together. After the meal he resumed his questions.

'What is your religion, by the way?'

'One that's not very well-known in Japan as yet — in fact, it has only one believer.'

'And what might this religion be?' asked Fukuzawa, mystified.

'Tanaka-ism,' replied Tanaka very seriously.

Fukuzawa burst out laughing. 'That's odd, it's the same with me — I'm a Fukuzawa-ist!'

When at last the oligarchs, working behind closed doors under the direction of Ito, had drawn up the Constitution promised in 1881, the government announced that it would be promulgated by the Emperor at a ceremony in the Imperial Palace on February 11, 1889. Chairmen

The River Watarase, before pollution

of Prefectural Assemblies, Shozo among them, were invited to attend, as representatives of 'the people' to whom the Constitution was being graciously granted.

For Shozo, with his still unshaken belief in the sincerity of his country's leaders and the beneficent concern of the Emperor for his people, the prospect was one of undiluted joy, of the dream of years about to come true. Something of a shock was awaiting him, however, when he arrived in Tokyo a few days before the great event. The official arrangements for the ceremony, in an unwitting exposure of the spirit in which the constitution-makers had worked, provided only for the prefectural Chairmen to 'respectfully observe' (*haikan*) the proceedings, not to 'attend' them. In a country where subtle differences of rank and precedence carry such weight, the implications were obvious.

Astonished and furious that he and his colleagues — the only popular representatives invited — should be so snubbed, Shozo led a protest delegation to Yamagata, the Prime Minister. He gained his point. The seating plan was altered, so that the Chairmen were no longer downgraded as humble 'observers'.

With this tiny victory won for the spirit of democracy, Shozo's delight in the occasion was complete. The night before, he wrote to a friend back home, he could not sleep for joy. Of the three poems with which the letter ends, the first two testify to the depth of his gratitude for the granting of the Constitution:

> *What joy,*
> *What cause for thankfulness —*
> *This gift*
> *From our Lord to his people*
> *Of a priceless jewel!*
>
> *Our Constitution —*
> *Most precious of all*
> *Our Empire's treasures.*
> *Watch over it, preserve it,*
> *Through ages eternal!*

The third, a cacophonous outburst in which there is nothing 'poetic' except the traditional 31-syllable form, was perhaps prompted by memories of Mishima's provincial dictatorship, a reign of terror which he was sure would be unthinkable under the Constitution:

> *Be sure of this,*
> *That all who violate*
> *This Constitution*
> *Are criminals, traitors,*
> *Rebels, bandits!*

In these poems, the spontaneous response to a ceremonial event, there was also a prophetic element. It was on the basis of the simple but intense emotions expressed in them — reverence for the Constitution and unrelenting fury with those who in his view contravened its spirit — that during the next two decades Shozo was to challenge the government, the orthodox concepts of national development and, finally, even the parliamentary process itself.

Attendance at the ceremony whose significance he saw in such terms presented problems for one who thought of himself still as 'a peasant of Shimotsuke'. Normally careless of dress, but conscious now of the grandeur of the occasion and of his own dignity as the sole representative of the nearly 100,000 citizens of Tochigi, Shozo asked the prefectural office to provide him with the Western frock-coat and trousers that he would be expected to wear.

The suit they supplied, however, turned out to fit him so badly as to be unwearable, and Shozo, who had never put on western clothes in his life, had to turn for help at the last minute to the Chief Secretary at the Home Ministry in Tokyo. Fortunately the latter was able to procure something suitable, and dignity was preserved. Shozo showed his appreciation by sending the Secretary ten bottles of beer — the only present, he remarked years afterwards, that he ever made to an official.

Arrangements went ahead for the setting up of the Diet provided for in the Constitution. Shozo resigned from the Assembly to stand as a candidate for the national body, and on 1 July, 1890, in the first parliamentary elections in the country's history, he was elected by a large majority to represent his native district of Aso.

The Diet met for the first time on 29 November. The deliberations were hectic and bitter. The session was short (the Constitution provided for ordinary sessions of only three months per year); the new parliamentarians had expected a much larger share of real influence than the ruling oligarchs, the authors of the Constitution, were prepared to allow them; and tension was increased from the start by Prime Minister Yamagata's openly contemptuous attitude to the Diet and its members.

In a confused and frustrating parliamentary situation, Shozo attracted attention from the first. In part this was due to his impressive physical presence — no one could mistake the short but broad and rock-solid figure, defiant of convention in a shabby black kimono — and unusually powerful voice. The *Tokyo Nichi Nichi Shinbun* wrote on 5 December:

'The election of a Chairman for the whole House on the 2nd was the subject of angry debate. Spectators found themselves staring again and again at Representative Tanaka Shozo, who kept bawling at the top of his voice, *Mr Chairman — Tanaka Shozo, Representative 277 — aren't you going to allow anyone to speak but Suehiro and Oe? Mr Chairman —* '

But despite this propensity to shouting, which he retained nearly all his life, there seems no doubt that Shozo — precisely because of the depth of his veneration for the Constitution and for the Emperor in whose name it had been promulgated — took his duties as a parliamentarian more seriously than most of his fellow-members.

The range of topics on which he spoke in the first two sessions, questioning or castigating the government, is formidable, and includes: corruption on the part of the Communications Minister, the 'cowardly inhumanity' of the notorious Security Ordinance,[1] which was applied to children of 15, the inordinate wealth of the Finance Minister (Shozo demanded he should finance the building of warships out of his own pocket, 'as the Queen of Spain sold her ornaments to help Columbus'), the futility of censorship, the threat to education of the new tendency in schools to impart only facts (when some Diet members called his speech on this subject 'out of order', he retorted with peasant earthiness that they were all 'a bunch of ignorant maggots'), the 'insincerity' of the Foreign Minister, who bought nearly 3,000 acres of potential farming land ostensibly for agricultural development, then kept it undeveloped for his own selfish enjoyment.

All his speeches, whatever their frequent lack of conventionally polite language (he was often ordered from the chamber, and would readily apologize later for his manner, though never for his matter) were delivered with extraordinary passion, conveying an impression of his total commitment as a parliamentarian to whatever issue was at stake, however trivial it might sometimes seem to others. With such a deep sense of responsibility as a servant and guardian of the Constitution, he saw nothing odd in treating Prime Ministers as naughty children — or, as his involvement in the single greatest issue of his parliamentary and subsequent career grew deeper, as 'bandits' and 'criminals'.

That issue crystallized with a politely-worded question put by Shozo in writing to the Minister of Agriculture and Commerce on 17 December, 1891. In his speech on the following day, he wanted to know why, when Article 27 of the Constitution guaranteed that 'the rights of property to all Japanese subjects shall not be violated', and the Mining Law clearly gave the Minister authority to suspend mining operations 'if they endangered the public good',

The poisonous effluent from the copper mine at Ashio in Kami-Toga District, Tochigi Prefecture, has been allowed to inflict heavy losses and hardship each year since 1888 on villages in every district on either side of the River Watarase, where it flows through Gumma and Tochigi prefectures. The effects of the effluent are steadily worsening. With fields being poisoned, drinking water

1. See p. 58, n. 1.

contaminated, and even the trees and grasses lining the dykes being threatened, no one can tell what disastrous consequences the future may hold.

Why has the government done nothing for so long? What measures does it propose to compensate for losses already incurred, and to prevent their recurrence?

Thus began one man's fight against pollution, to end only with his death twenty-two years later. But before describing the vicissitudes of this long struggle, for which above all Shozo's name is now remembered, it is necessary to give some account of the development of the great copper mine at Ashio.

7

Pollution: the prelude

The immense copper deposits in the mountains at Ashio, 15 miles south-west of Nikko, are said to have been first discovered in 1608. A Zen temple was the first owner of the site, and for many years extraction continued on a very modest, almost private scale, though in 1635 Ashio copper was used in the roof of the celebrated mausoleum of the first Tokugawa Shogun, Ieyasu, at Nikko.

For a time ownership passed to the feudal government in Edo. The mine served as one of several sources of copper for the coinage, as the imprint of the ideograph 'Ashi' on some coins of the period testifies; and some of its output was exported to Holland and China. Later it came again into private hands.

About 1790, when peasants living on the banks of the River Watarase, which has its source close to the mine, complained of pollution of their river by copper effluent, the Shogun's reforming Adviser, Matsudaira Sadanobu — more enlightened in this respect than his successors of the 1890s — at once ordered production at the mine to be stopped. It remained closed for more than 80 years.

The spectacular modern development of Ashio began when it was bought by Furukawa Ichibei in 1877. A village headman's son like Shozo, Furukawa, as dynamic and original a character in many ways as the man whose arch-opponent he was to become, had had early experience of finance and business. As a young man he had helped his uncle who was an accountant to the Nanbu clan in north-east Japan. Later he worked as a money-lender's dun,[1] and in higher positions in

---

1. In the early nineteen-thirties Furukawa was held up as a model of Japanese toughness and stamina. One curious story that was broadcast over the radio as a supreme illustration of his powers of endurance belongs to his years with the money-lender. When collecting money due, he would often refuse to leave until the cash was handed over. Once he stayed two days and nights in a debtor's house, sleeping on the floor in the kitchen, and assuaging the pangs of hunger by licking some strips of dried seaweed hanging from a hook on the wall — till the debtor explained that it was his habit to warm the seaweed over the fire and wrap it round his penis 'as a cure for the colic'.

He himself was evidently proud of such feats. For thirty years after the beginning of the modern period in 1868 he continued to wear his hair in the old coiled-up style of the feudal era, 'to help him keep the stamina he had trained himself to as a debt-collector'. When he finally did agree to have his hair cut short in the modern manner, it was in honour of his having received a Court decoration in 1900. Marquis Inoue (the Foreign Minister to whom Shozo had intended to appeal in 1883, and throughout his life a prominent linkman between government and industry) wielded the scissors.

two companies. When one of these companies collapsed in 1877 — Furukawa seized the chance to launch out on his own. With capital borrowed from Inoue Kaoru, then a high official of the Ministry of Finance, Shibusawa Eiichi, who was later, like Furukawa himself, to become one of Japan's best-known and most influential businessmen, and Shiga Naomichi, steward to the aristocratic Soma family,[1] he bought the neglected Ashio mine.

In the course of two and a half centuries of intermittent exploitation, over 8,000 holes had been bored into the sides of the great copper-bearing mountain. Most of them were now unused; 'house of ghosts', the mountain was nicknamed, though it must have looked more like a giant abandoned beehive. Furukawa set to work to develop his acquisition with a thoroughness and disciplined energy as great as that of any pioneer of industrialization in his or any other country. His success was phenomenal. Production rose as follows:

1877	45 tons
1883	641 tons
1884	2,268 tons
1885	4,057 tons
1891	7,486 tons

The demand for copper expanded at a continually increasing rate, particularly with the rapid growth of electrification in the late 1880s; and as the country's largest single domestic source of copper, Ashio's prosperity was guaranteed.[2] But from the first Furukawa was aiming at foreign as well as Japanese markets.

In June 1888 Furukawa concluded what must have been one of the most daring export deals ever undertaken, for the supply to a French syndicate of 19,000 tons of copper over a period of 2½ years — on current production figures, more than the total anticipated output of

---

2. Though Shiga Naomichi never became prominent in his own right, the fact that Furukawa borrowed from him turned out to have interesting consequences. Naomichi's grandson was the celebrated novelist Shiga Naoya. Naoya (1883-1971) is the only literary figure who is known to have been deeply concerned over the Ashio pollution issue when it reached the proportions of a huge public scandal in 1902. For his time, he was something of an Angry Young Man. Unfortunately, and in large measure because of his grandfather's early investment in the mine, his indignation remained stillborn. See below, p. 138, n. 1.

2 By the early 1890s, Ashio was producing 40 per cent of Japan's copper. Copper was also the country's third most important export commodity, after tea and silk.

Pollution: the prelude   67

the mine for the same period.[1] The target was met in full. The miners, of whom by this time there were 3,000, were driven hard and paid well: according to Japanese who visited the Furukawa-created town of Ashio, off-duty they sported gold watches and 'looked like officials or company executives'.[2] Furukawa, and the nation with him, could well be proud of this nineteenth-century Japanese industrial miracle.

But for exploitation at such breakneck speed of the rich deposits at Ashio a heavy price had to be paid in terms of 'ecological damage', to use the present-day term. (Not that the owner or managers of the mine, unshakeably confident in the importance of its contribution to the advance of industry and 'civilization', ever admitted these effects; even when they deprived thousands of their livelihood, those who protested were always dismissed as 'agitators'.) The most obvious, and at first sight least important, aspect of such damage was the denuding of the wooded hills within a radius of several miles of the mine.

Huge areas of forest, sold by the central government to Furukawa for next to nothing, were felled to provide fuel for Ashio's ever-growing refineries; the chimneys of the refineries themselves gave off a thick sulphurous smoke that rapidly poisoned most of the remaining vegetation. In this respect Ashio was not, of course, unique. A publicity booklet printed by the mine's own press in 1908 quoted an American writer's description of the copper mine at Butte in Montana:

'It is a fearful place to live. I know men who tell me they have settled there in the certainty that they have thereby hastened their own death ... The town is flowerless, grassless, godless ... The smelting process has utterly destroyed the beauty of the landscape, evil gaseous smoke has killed all plant-life for miles round about; the streams are putrid with effluent, and the town itself seems buried under monstrous heaps of slag ...'

The publicist was quick to point out, however, that while the mining of copper must involve *some* adverse effect on the local environment, Ashio had of course escaped the worst evils of the

---

1. The story of the signing of this export contract shows something of Furukawa's own brand of obstinacy — and, from the foreigner's point of view, the difficulty of doing business with the Japanese at that time. Agreement having been reached after many weeks of negotiation between Furukawa and the English firm of Jardine Matheson, the contract was drawn up, and the manager of Jardine Matheson's Yokohama branch announced that he would sign on behalf of his clients, the French syndicate. Furukawa, however, refused to sign, on the ground that 'Jardine Matheson he knew, for he had dealt with them for several years; but he knew nothing of foreign parts beyond Yokohama', and would therefore only sign if Jardine Matheson themselves were described in the contract as the purchasers. Nothing would make him change his mind. Eventually the Jardine Matheson manager had to give way: his name was entered in the contract as 'the purchaser', while a representative of the syndicate, the real purchasers, signed as a witness. This eccentric insistence of Furukawa's stood him in good stead. Nine months later the French syndicate collapsed; but Jardine Matheson had to go on paying Furukawa.

2. Despite their gold watches, the lot of the miners themselves was in other ways very far from happy. But I am not concerned here with this side of the mine's history.

American example.

The truth was a good deal less simple. To begin with, the deforestation of the mountains round Ashio might not have mattered so much if it had not been for the fact that the rich plain of Shimotsuke, between the mountains and the coastal provinces, depended on those very forests for their continued fertility. Almost every year, after the melting of the high snows and the prolonged heavy rain of the wet season in June, the River Watarase would flood out over a wide area of both banks along its middle reaches in Gumma and Tochigi prefectures, its waters fertilized with the leaf-mould carried by innumerable mountain streams which came together in the forests above Ashio to form the river proper. Unlike most floods, these were welcomed as the main cause of the prosperity of the Shimotsuke peasantry. Never severe and quickly receding, they were in every way beneficent.

But now the systematic felling of the mountain trees began to upset the delicate balance on which that prosperity rested. As the dwindling forests lost their capacity to absorb much of the rain and melting snows and to contribute their life-giving mould to the streams, so the volume and potential danger of the floods increased. Even so, the damage to agriculture might have passed without comment in a country where natural disasters of many kinds had always been so frequent that resignation to them had been elevated into a virtue. By far the most serious of Furukawa's activities — in its implications for the farming towns and villages on the plain below — was the deliberate dumping of poisonous copper waste in the River Watarase itself, which flows through the town of Ashio directly opposite the main entrances to the mine.

Such dumping was never admitted by the mine management. Whenever in later years it was grudgingly conceded that some of the disastrous effects of the pollution of the Shimotsuke plain might have been due to Ashio, the official explanation would be in the first place that given an industrial operation of this magnitude and importance to the national economy, some effluent was inevitable, and in the second (somewhat inconsistently) that if there *were* harmful effects, they could only be caused by 'abnormally heavy' floods sweeping down into the plains the waste that had accumulated in the river-bed since mining operations began in the early seventeenth century.

A very different picture was given in an anonymous article published in a Tokyo journal in April 1900. According to the writer — a white-collar employee of the mine who had worked at Ashio for many years — the dramatic rise in output following the discovery of an immensely rich seam in 1882 led to some 6 per cent of the mine's entire production being discarded, as less readily refinable by the comparatively primitive methods then employed. The question arose of where to deposit this unwanted rock, in this region of close-packed precipitous mountains. At first the waste was dumped into several narrow ravines nearby. When within a very few years these ravines became too full for easy access, a proposal was made within the company to carry the waste by a specially-constructed railway to level uplands well away from the river and town; but the plan was vetoed, on the ground of expense, and the decision taken to dump the waste directly into the River Watarase.

With dynamite and pickaxe the surplus ore-bearing rock was reduced to rubble, which in turn was shovelled into the river whenever there was a prospect of heavy rain to wash it away downstream. Immediately before and during the exceptionally heavy rains of August 1890 and September 1891, over a hundred labourers worked night and day to clear accumulated tips of poisonous rubble.

Much milder rainy seasons during the next few years making this method of disposal less practicable, the tips reached unmanageable proportions, till finally the scheme for removing them by rail was adopted after all. But the unexpectedly violent flooding of the river in July and late August of 1896 proved too great a temptation. On 8 September, for instance, a huge, hastily-organized labour force tipped into the raging waters of the Watarase over 700,000 cubic metres of rejected ore.

The truth of this account is easily corroborated by checking it against the dates of the most deadly waves of pollution to strike the Shimotsuke plain, which correspond closely to the dates the writer gives for the massive dumping in the river. But of all this nothing was known at the time outside the mine itself. The owner and management were too busy, in their own estimation, to concern themselves with possible effects of this marginal activity on peasants 40 or 50 miles away; their workers were too loyal to the company to question its wisdom; and the mine was physically too remote from Tokyo to be in danger of many prying visitors. So for many years the dumping went on unhindered.

The first signs of the poisoning of the river in its middle and lower reaches appeared as early as 1878, a year after Furukawa's purchase of the mine, when it was noticed in several places that fish were dying from some unknown cause. These deaths gradually increased in number. Eels were found swimming so slowly that children could catch them with their hands; and more ominous still, both children and adults who waded out from the bank in the hope of securing their dinner in this easy way discovered afterwards that red swellings began to form between their toes if they stood in the water for any length of time.

In 1880 the governor of Tochigi issued an edict banning all fishing in the Watarase, 'on health grounds', but set up no investigation to discover why it was that the fish were dying so mysteriously. Such official indifference may seem hard to credit, when so many families derived their livelihood from fishing, and were bound to be severely hit by the ban, as in fact they were: a private survey of three districts made in 1890 found that the number of fishing households had sunk over the previous three years from 2,733 to nil.

With few exceptions, positive concern for the people's welfare was not a feature of provincial officialdom. Besides, the fishermen were after all in a minority, and most of their catches, anyway, supplied only the Tokyo markets — there was little local demand. The peasant majority, conditioned as they were by generations of relative prosperity, were puzzled, but not as yet greatly worried, by this interruption to nature's benevolent cycle: even the change in the colour of the water to an oddly light shade of blue was comfortingly attributed to riverside dyeing shops in the textile towns of Ashikaga and Kiryu further upstream.[1]

Slowly, as poisoned water seeped through irrigation sluices into fields beyond the river banks, some found themselves affected more directly. Late in the spring of 1886 peasants in the village of Kawasaki were dismayed when their fields of young rice and potato plants began suddenly and for no apparent reason to decay. Meetings were held; somehow the idea began to get about that it was the soil that was contaminated, and that the Ashio mine, hidden in the mountains nearly 40 miles away, might be responsible.

In the three years that followed, attacks of the strange blight occurred elsewhere. Sometimes it was so severe that cultivators, after spending all their savings on fertiliser in a vain attempt to keep them alive, were driven to abandon rice and corn and concentrate on mulberry trees, in the hope that their deeper roots would draw nourishment from below the layer of contaminated soil. But often even the trees wilted and died. In the afflicted areas, still confined to scattered pockets of land near the river banks, puzzlement gave way to hardship and deepening fear.

The situation erupted into crisis during the summer and autumn of 1890. At Ashio, as output had risen yet more steeply in the drive to fulfil the Jardine Matheson contract, so had the tips of rejected ore to be dumped in the river when the rains came. In August, a month after Shozo was elected to the Diet, the severest floods the Shimotsuke plain had ever experienced burst the banks of the Watarase and many of its

---

1. In fact some farming land does seem to have been contaminated as early as 1880 or 1881, but the effects on crops were as yet less dramatic than on fish. There was in addition a further reason why news about such pollution did not spread. The Governor who had issued the order banning the catching of fish was concerned about the problem; but not long after his order, apparently under pressure from the central government (and thus indirectly, no doubt, from Furukawa) officials throughout the prefecture were directed to refuse all applications for tax reductions in which the words 'mine pollution' appeared as a reason for the applicant's loss of income. Out of long habit the peasants accepted the official ruling (which remained in force for many years), and 'pollution' became, ironically, a 'dirty word' even among its victims.

tributaries,[1] to destroy crops over a large area in both Gumma and Tochigi prefectures and leave behind a layer of contaminated mud in which nothing would grow. One man was drowned while struggling vainly to repair a breach in a dyke — the first recorded peasant victim of the mine.

Shock, and the desperate but time-consuming task of salvaging what remained of damaged crops and property, delayed any positive reaction from the people of the area as a whole; but as time passed, the suspicion that the mine was to blame became a certainty.

In December 1890 village heads drew up a petition to the Governor of Tochigi complaining that the lasting devastation caused by the floods, far worse than any in living or recorded memory, had been due specifically to the presence in the water of large quantities of copper sulphate, and asking, though with the exaggerated humility expected by officialdom in such documents, that if the poisoning of the river could not be stopped the mine should be ordered to close, or the fertility of the whole rich plain might be permanently impaired. It was signed by 1,000 peasants. The Prefectural Assembly unanimously passed a resolution in similar terms, also addressed to the Governor. But the peasants at least, wisely, did not stop at petitions. For expert confirmation of their case, samples of contaminated soil and water were taken for analysis to the Geological Survey Office of the Ministry of Agriculture and Commerce. In a two-line note the Ministry acknowledged receipt of the samples, but added, unbelievably:

'It is difficult, however, for this Office to undertake the analysis requested.'

What pressures lay behind this polite rejection can only be guessed. Professor Kozai Yoshinao, of the Tokyo College of Agriculture, to whom other samples were submitted, was more forthcoming. His summary of a long and detailed analysis concluded unequivocally that all the samples contained dangerous quantities of copper compounds, and that these were the cause of the loss of fertility in the flooded areas.

A year later, on 2 February, 1892, the professor published (in no less authoritative an organ than the government Official Gazette) an expanded report along the same lines, based on the examination of soil from 50 and floodwater from 13 separate areas respectively. His conclusions were confirmed by another expert from the Agricultural College, whom the governor of Tochigi had consulted independently, by chemists from Tochigi Hospital, and by at least

---

1. At one place in its lower reaches the Watarase is very narrow, and its banks steeper than elsewhere. On reaching this point, the floodwaters from upstream were liable to go into reverse and sweep back upstream in a 'backflow', which would cause further flooding of many small tributaries on either side of the main river. This phenomenon was not natural but man-made. In major works begun by the feudal government and completed by its Meiji successor, the river had been deliberately narrowed at this point, in the hope of preventing floods from reaching the crowded metropolis See below, p. 143 n. 2.

two other Tokyo professors who had made their own tests.

By the middle of 1891, it was clear beyond reasonable doubt, in Tokyo as on the spot, that the Ashio copper mine was responsible for the poisoning of a considerable area of rich agricultural land. Moreover, if no countermeasures were taken the floods of August 1890 would obviously recur, with similar or even more disastrous results. Yet nothing was done either by the central or by the prefectural government. Neither rice nor corn nor rape (the last-named being of particular importance, since its leaves were a basic food in the country diet, and its seeds the main source of oil for lighting in peasant households) nor mulberry (essential for raising silkworms, the common resource of the farmer who could not support himself solely by his crops) would grow in soil still barren in the spring of 1891, eight months after the fatal floods had receded.

Bemused by the strange deadness of the earth, but working frantically to restore their only source of livelihood, the peasants tried to bury the poisoned topsoil, or heaped it into great mounds, making their fields look like prehistoric burial-sites. Neither method proved effective.

As soon as it became apparent that the land was not recovering when the floods withdrew, Shozo sent Satori Hikojiro, a student from Waseda College (forerunner of the present Waseda University) to the disaster area to make a succession of surveys on his behalf. When both the peasants' petition and the resolution of the Prefectural Assembly were ignored, he decided to raise the matter in the Diet; and this he did, armed with the results of Professor Kozai's analysis and up-to-date reports from Satori of the struggle the peasants were facing to survive, in the speech of 18 December, 1891, already quoted (p. 63).

The Minister at first made no reply to Shozo's question. On the 24 December, in the course of a debate on the Ministry's financial estimates, Shozo asked the reason for the delay, pointing out that under the Diet rules a Minister who could not give a satisfactory answer to a question immediately must explain why he needed more time. In a reply whose singular lack of urgency set the tone of what was to be the government attitude for nearly six years, Shozo was told:

'I am ready to reply at any time — indeed I have the papers with me today. Yesterday too I had it in mind to ask the Speaker for permission to reply, but the debate on the estimates was particularly lively, and I thought it better to wait, so as to avoid interrupting the discussion. I may perhaps give my reply tomorrow.'

But however ready he may have been, the Minister did not give his promised reply the next day, either. Again, this time with more asperity, Shozo demanded to know the reason. How was it, he asked, that the Minister could be so blind to the hardship the mine was inflicting on innocent people? Was he too blind even to read the regulations that vested in him the power to put an end to it? Or was the Minister perhaps letting himself be swayed by the fact that he was personally related to the owner of the mine?

This last question was not the gratuitous smear it might seem. From its origins in the early Meiji period, the modern Japanese politico-industrial complex has depended for its cohesion partly on interlocking relationships involving marriage and adoption, besides the more common links of shared school and background; and there can be no doubt that the government's dilatoriness was connected with the fact that the second son of Mutsu Munemitsu, the Minister Shozo was castigating, had not merely married Furukawa's daughter, but had been formally adopted by him as his heir.[1] The marriage and adoption merely cemented a friendship that dated back to the 1870s, when Furukawa had been *banto* or manager of the Onogumi Company and Mutsu the chief of the tax division in the Finance Ministry.

Still the Minister did not deign to reply. Five days later, after prolonged filibustering by members angry at the government's contemptuous treatment of the new legislature, the Prime Minister dissolved the Diet. The Minister's reply to Shozo was then published in the Official Gazette, where it could not be answered. It consisted essentially of three points:

1. It is true that there has been damage to agricultural land adjoining the Watarase river in Gumma and Tochigi prefectures.
2. An investigation is now being carried out by specialists into the cause of the damage, which is not yet clear.
3. The owner of the mine is adopting the necessary preventive measures, and has taken steps to stop the outflow of mineral matter by ordering ore extractors from Germany and America.

This was prevarication at its most skilful, designed to forestall further questions by diffusing a comfortable sense of official competence. 'Damage', if not 'pollution', was admitted, its cause was 'under examination'; point three suggests that machines are on the way which will stop any further trouble at its source. If there was any inconsistency in claiming on the one hand that the cause of the damage had yet to be determined and announcing on the other that the necessary measures were being taken to prevent it, attention was no doubt diverted from it by the reassuring tone of the whole statement (and, in the original Japanese document, by the vagueness of the terms employed).

In one respect the reply was blatantly deceptive. The primary

---

1. Another link of great importance was now being forged between government and mine. Hara Kei (the 'progressive' Prime Minister of 1918-21) was at this time Mutsu's private secretary. Later he became managing director and Vice-President of the Ashio Mining Company, and then, as Home Minister in 1907, presided over the last and most tragic act of the whole pollution saga.

purpose of the 'extractors' was naturally to increase the amount of copper recovered, not to prevent the escape of dangerous residue. Strictly speaking, therefore, they were irrelevant to the pollution issue. Furthermore, they were not installed until at least eight months after the publication of the Minister's statement; and in fact it was quite unknown what indirect effect, if any, these machines would have in reducing the poisonous content of the slag being dumped in the river. On the control of such dumping, the immediate cause of the 'damage' to the fields, neither the Minister nor the mine had anything to say.

Behind these evasions lay not only the Minister's own equivocal relationship with Furukawa, but a deliberate policy of falsifying the facts, based on a conscientiously-held view of the future of the nation and its industry, on the part of his officials. Wada, Chief of the Mines Division of the Ministry of Agriculture and Commerce, directed his subordinates to report that the evidence was insufficient to prove that effluent from Ashio has been responsible for the crop failures along the banks of the Watarase. A German expert in the Ministry's employ reported obediently that the cause was simply 'poor soil' — though revealing later in a private publication of his own that in fact he had had no more doubt than Professor Kozai that copper was to blame. A technical report by a Japanese geologist at the Ministry's Agricultural Testing Station was never published.[1] The reason for this apparent perversity on the Ministry's part was given with perfect frankness in the following sentence from an article by Wada in the *Tokyo Nichi Nichi Shinbun* of 10 February, 1892:

'Suppose for the sake of argument that copper effluent were responsible for the damage to farmland on either side of the Watarase — the public benefits that accrue to the country from the Ashio mine far outweigh any losses suffered in the affected areas. The damage can in any case be adequately be taken care of by compensation.'

Beyond question, Ashio copper was essential to Japan's industrialization. If there was to be a choice of priorities between industry and agriculture, agriculture must give way. For Wada — and for the majority of thinking Japanese then and since, at any rate until the 1970s — the issue was as simple as that.

The problem might have been solved on this basis, if Wada had meant what he said about compensation. But neither now nor at any time later did the government show any disposition to 'take care of' the damage in this way. Nor, though Professor Kozai's analysis was accompanied by detailed recommendations on the measures necessary to restore fertility to the poisoned soil, was any assistance in carrying out these measures offered to the peasants, whose unaided

---

1. Its existence was generally unknown till it was disclosed many years later by a Professor at the Agricultural College who had seen it.

efforts were quite inadequate to cope with the disaster.

This is not to suggest that the government or Furukawa willed the increased pollution of the next decade: it was due rather to an obsession with the necessity of industrial advance, together with the complacency of the metropolitan bureaucracy, who did not feel it incumbent upon them to visit rural disaster areas themselves. Like many of their samurai forbears, whose attitudes in practice often belied the honoured status theoretically accorded to the farmer in feudal society, they could not help regarding the peasantry as a remote, barely human species whose welfare certainly did not concern *them*. The instinctive assumption was, therefore, that any restriction of the mine's activities in the interests of mere peasants was unthinkable.

As a 'peasant of Shimotsuke' himself, Shozo saw things very differently. But however unsatisfactory the government's attitude as expressed in the Minister's statement, with the Diet dissolved, he was deprived for a while — and very nearly permanently — of the only platform from which there was any chance of effective protest.

The general election of 15 February, 1892 was 'the bloodiest in Japan's history'.[1] The police, and thugs hired by the prefectural authorities, did their best to intimidate the electors from voting for Shozo; but despite their campaign of innuendo and violence — his office was wrecked and several of his workers beaten up — he still managed to beat the government candidate by 733 votes to 634.

In May, 1892 as soon as the new Diet convened, Shozo returned to the attack. Why, he demanded, when Professor Kozai's report had been published, and corroborated by the work of another expert, Professor Tanba Keizo of the Tokyo Medical College, was the government still ignoring the disastrous situation in Shimotsuke? At least they could hardly claim now that the cause of the damage was not clear. The fishing industry of the entire area had been destroyed, and upwards of 4,000 acres rendered completely sterile, with crops severely affected over a much wider area; scores of miles of dykes had been weakened by the poisoning of the grass that had covered them, which would greatly increase the danger from any recurrence of the floods. To make the lot of the peasants even worse, in many places even drinking water had been contaminated. Yet the authorities were doing nothing, either to relieve distress or to prevent it in future. The law authorizing the Minister to close any mine operating against the public interest was clear; in the face of the abundant evidence that Ashio was the cause of the pollution, he could have no excuse

---

1. Borton, *Japan's modern century*, p. 100. Shinagawa Yajiro, the Home Minister, 'ordered all the prefectural governors and police, who were directly responsible to him, to support the government candidates in each district ... Twenty-five persons were killed and nearly 400 wounded. The election, despite the strong-arm police methods, gave the Cabinet only ninety-five seats as opposed to a total of 163 seats for the "people's parties".'

whatever not to act.

Since the previous Diet the Minister had changed, but government policy had not. The new Minister's statement of 11 June in reply to Shozo made official indifference to the plight of the rural population even clearer:

1. That poisonous effluent from the Ashio mine is one cause of the damage to agricultural land has now been established.
2. The damage, however, is not of such magnitude as to affect the public peace, and the Minister does not, therefore, propose to invoke his power to order the mine to close.
3. Government agencies have no powers to deal with loss and damage already incurred.
4. The owner of the mine is preparing to bring dust extractors into operation.
5. The owner of the mine is arranging for the construction, at his own expense, of 'sediment basins', which will be dredged from time to time to remove contaminated sand from the bed of the Watarase river. The government is satisfied that there will in future be no effluent in sufficient quantities to harm plant life.

If the Minister could be excused for the grudging, face-saving tone of his admission that pollution was 'one' cause of the damage, the deliberate twisting of the words 'public good' in the Mining Law into 'public peace' was harder to forgive — and for anyone who had followed the Ashio story, the phrase had a specially ironic flavour: it was 'public peace and happiness' that the peasants meeting in Azuma Village 18 months before had invoked in their plea to the prefectural governor to prevent an industry owned by one man from disrupting an entire community. The refusal to accept responsibility for relief showed a rare degree of bureaucratic callousness. Yet the government with its aloof self-confidence evidently believed that the vaguely impressive references to such technicalities as 'extractors' and 'the construction of sediment basins', though brief and devoid of concrete detail, would suffice to set at rest the fears of a few thousand provincial peasants. Copies of the statement were printed and distributed free throughout the afflicted area. Many undoubtedly did accept its claims as no more to be questioned than any other pronouncement of high authority.

Shozo was less credulous. In two long speeches on 13 and 24 June he denounced the Minister's statement as merely a device to allow the mine to continue working as before. The statement itself 'stank of copper'; the Minister and his department had been poisoned, debilitated so that they were blinded to the contamination of rivers and crops and could serve only the mine-owner's interests.

In a particularly bitter analogy, Shozo referred to the political issue which was uppermost in the minds of politicians and public alike:

the renewed attempts being made by the government to secure revision of the 'unequal' treaties with the western powers, who still retained numerous extraterritorial privileges for their nationals in Japan. If the government was so keen to abolish the stigma of extraterritoriality, why did it turn a blind eye to Ashio, where the law of the land was no more applicable, it seemed, than in any of the so-called foreign concessions, and the consequences for the Japanese people were far more harsh? The foreigners had their own guards and courts to protect them; the tax-paying farmers of Shimotsuke had no such protection or means of redress. Or was it the Minister's view, Shozo asked with bitter sarcasm, that even the 'public peace' would not be threatened until peasants marched on government offices with bamboo spears and banners of straw?

The speeches were well-argued and forcefully delivered, their very vehemence implying expectation on Shozo's part that the government *must* heed such a strong case; his faith in the influence of the Diet and in the sincerity of the country's leaders was not yet dissipated.

On one fundamental issue, it is true, Shozo had not touched: the conflict in a modernizing state between the claims of industrial development and those of agriculture. For more than a decade the Meiji government had assigned priority to the former, and to the country's rulers and intelligentsia, intent on the systematic creation of a modern industrial base, it was self-evident that when the two came into conflict, industrial needs were too urgent to be frustrated by local outbreaks of distress among the peasantry. To Shozo, however, the reverse was no less obvious. It was not merely that as a countryman he was closer than the Tokyo modernizers to the traditional scheme of things, in which — even if it had been honoured more often in the breach than in the observance — those who worked the land ranked immediately beneath the samurai, higher than merchants or artisans; his headman background, as the guardian of his villagers against the rapacity of the feudal authorities, the powerful sense of natural justice engendered in him by his earlier political struggles, the new notion of popular rights, and his devout belief in the Constitution as the protector of all Japanese subjects, combined to make it axiomatic that the welfare of citizens, no matter how obscure, must take precedence over the demands of any industry, however 'vital to the nation'.

Shozo was never antagonistic to industry or modernization as such but his conviction that people came first was so deeply and emotionally held that he never felt it necessary to discuss in a rational way the problems attendant on rapid industrialization. This made it all the easier for the government to persuade itself that he was at best a worthy but impractical eccentric, at worst a noisy mountebank whose rantings deserved no serious attention — and for the many influential figures who in later years lent their support to his cause, to abandon him when he refused all advice to modify his uncompromising stand.

So his Diet tirades remained unanswered. If they had any effect at all, it was merely to stimulate the government and Furukawa to proceed even more vigorously with a ploy they had already launched jointly, in the hope, evidently, of isolating and thereby silencing the troublesome Shimotsuke Dietman: mine officials toured the poisoned areas, offering farmers small sums of cash[1] if they would sign a document undertaking to make no complaint about pollution damage to their land and to refrain from calling for government action against the mine for three years — the period allegedly required for testing the extractors being installed at Ashio. Various methods were adopted to persuade them to sign, among them the hint, which was totally false, that the mine was likely to be exhausted before long, so that if the farmers did not accept this 'compensation' now, they would not have a second chance.

Official support for the mine was obvious when the Governor of Tochigi Prefecture (a central government appointee) nominated nineteen members of the Prefectural Assembly to serve on an 'Arbitration Committee' — a curiously-named body, since it made it appear that the farmers were in legal dispute with the mine, rather than the proven victims of its operation — the function of which was simply to persuade the farmers to accept the mine's offer.

At meetings up and down the prefecture, their elected representatives, who in the peasants' eyes had acquired all the prestige of *o-kami*, the 'upper ones', appealed at once to their patriotism, their need for ready cash, and — oddly — their moral sense. The closing of the mine, they were told, would be a national disaster, and was therefore out of the question. Any attempt to take Furukawa to court in the hope of winning higher compensation would involve years of legal wrangling, given the thousands of potential claimants, and in any case the expense would be prohibitive. The only sensible solution was the 'moral' one — to recognise the 'sincerity' implicit in Furukawa's approach and accept his cash offer, in the interest of the supreme traditional value of social harmony. The other item in Furukawa's document — the undertaking to make no further protest for three years — was of course played down, if not lost sight of altogether in frequent references to Furukawa's conscientious installation of extractors.

On occasion these approaches were met with a certain amount of peasant cunning, some villages deliberately suspending all attempts to recultivate their pollution-ravaged fields in order to force the mine to buy their submission at a higher price. But greed and the inherited assumption that whatever the 'upper ones' decided must be right

---

1. The sums were very small indeed. In one typical area the peasants received an average of less than 10 yen each, or about 6 yen per acre of poisoned land.

Pollution: the prelude

drove many, particularly the smaller landlords, to sign the Furukawa document; and not merely to sign, but to address obsequious letters to the Arbitration Committee, assuring its members of their 'tears of gratitude' to the Committee for its having 'helped to solve the problem in so entirely satisfactory a manner, and for having completely removed the threat of disastrous pollution from so many towns and villages.' The arbitration programme went forward so smoothly, in fact, that in September 1892 the governor thanked the Committee for its work and dissolved it. Officially, the problem of copper pollution no longer existed.

Shozo was not wholly silenced. He still doubted the efficacy of the much-publicised extractors, nor did he have any faith in the Arbitration Committee, suspecting on good evidence that many of its members were acting only out of a desire to ingratiate themselves with the Governor and with Furukawa. Many times during 1892 and 1893 he toured the affected villages, warning them that the agreements they had signed contained not the slightest guarantee either that their land would quickly recover or that future floods would not bring even severer poisoning than before and urging them to send representatives to Ashio to check the working of the extractors.

Yet in the general mood of complacency that 'something had been done', few would listen to him. In the Diet, likewise, his voice was crowded out by other preoccupations — the rising to its climax of the agitation over the revision of the unequal treaties, bitter squabbling among the political parties (much to Shozo's disgust, as he records it in a satirical verse — 'Such bickering!/Husband and wife inside the mosquito net/Farting at each other'), a rapid succession of parliamentary dissolutions and general elections, and, with the advent of 1894, increasing tension with China. When war finally came, the demand for Ashio copper rose steeply; before long Furukawa was decorated for his services to the nation. With the farmers bought off, officialdom busy with 'national issues' and Shozo elbowed by events off the centre of the stage, it looked as though the brief drama of pollution and protest was over.

But what had happened so far proved to be only the prelude.

Mounds of poisoned topsoil

8

Pollution: growth of a crisis

War with China broke out in the summer of 1894. In Japan there was widespread enthusiasm for the conflict and for six months most minds were preoccupied with news of the fighting.

Though out of the public eye, Shozo carried on with his parliamentary duties. But he differed greatly from the typical provincial Dietman of the nineties, who was inordinately proud of his status, fawned on the leader of whatever faction within his party he had attached himself to and complacently patronized his simple-minded constituents. His appearance was already eccentric enough. It was dictated, not by any desire to draw attention to himself, though indeed he was accused of this, as of many other things, but by a slowly deepening sense of the relative triviality of all such outward things. Sometimes it got him into trouble.

When he stepped off the special train carrying him and other parliamentarians to attend the extraordinary wartime session of the Diet in Hiroshima, a policeman, convinced that one so shabby must be a potential troublemaker, attempted to arrest him, explaining afterwards that this unusual Dietman 'looked like a 60-year-old student'. And perhaps not surprisingly it is with students that we find him as intimately involved during this period as with Diet affairs.

Abandoning the respectable inn that had so far been his base in Tokyo, he moved into a cheap students' lodging-house — to the great embarrassment of the other inmates. Then as now, Dietmen attracted a constant stream of visitors, and before long the students begged Shozo to take himself elsewhere, complaining that since his arrival the noise of all the comings and goings in the flimsy Japanese-style house had made it impossible for them to work. At first Shozo refused to budge. Eventually, however, a curious compromise was achieved.

A nephew of Shozo's, one Harada Sadasuke, who had a good position as a civilian official attached to the army, greatly admired his eccentric uncle and helped him quietly in all kinds of ways, from his first election to the Diet till the end of his life. Harada, knowing from experience that it was useless to offer Shozo cash, since he would immediately give it away, had recently deposited a sum of money in the bank in Shozo's name, from which Shozo could draw interest of 6 yen a month. Half of this sum he now promised to three students as rent for a little house, if he could share it with them. There were conditions, of course; Shozo still retained his shrewd head for a bargain. The students were to allow him to receive any of his constituents, who might spend the night in the house if they wanted; in return, he would pay over another 3 yen towards the cost of their communal food, which the students would cook. The question arose of naming the establishment. The House of Unity, suggested the students somewhat pompously; but Shozo persuaded them to call it The People's Club *(Heimin kurabu)*, in commemoration of the movement for popular rights, and to emphasize also that it was not a hostel with a director but a community where all had equal rights. For many years, long after Shozo had had to move elsewhere, the house provided a home for students from Tochigi Prefecture. One of the original members of the Club later recalled those first days:

'Now and again we'd have a drinking session, the four of us. We'd take it in turns to go along with an empty bottle to the place opposite the police-station and buy a bit of saké, and on the way back a single portion of loach boiled in soy sauce. Then we'd sit in a circle on the floor, drinking and poking with our chopsticks at the fish, enjoying ourselves hugely. As soon as Shozo got a little bit tipsy, he would start chanting songs from *One hundred and twenty-seven poems of the T'ang dynasty*. There he goes again, we'd say to each other. The noise! It was unbelievable. And he went on so long, it was impossible to study; but when we protested, he would get up and slip out as quietly as a mouse, taking refuge in the landlord's house next door. He would give up his own freedom rather than impose himself on us.'

When he needed to escape for a while from the press of Diet business and constituency visitors, Shozo had other retreats beside the landlord's house. One, which he used on the infrequent occasions when he had the money to pay for admission, was a commercially-operated bathing beach on the outskirts of the city. Another was the well-known Juntendo Hospital. The doctor he had installed in the family house at Konaka had once worked here, and thanks to his introduction Shozo had the freedom of the wards, which he would frequently use — not to recover from any illness, for he was in excellent health, but to withdraw for a few hours from the rush of public life and sometimes even to prepare his Diet speeches.

Not unconnected with these quiet times, perhaps, are the first signs in his diary of a new inwardness. Terse, often cryptic reflections, sometimes in poetic form, begin to appear among the record of daily events and observations on the political scene.

> God
> Can hear the sound
> Of one hand clapping.
> The sound of two hands
> Anyone can hear.[1]

> Polish
> The mirror of my mind
> Till it reflects
> All things
> Without distorting —
> All things.

The flood-like ch'i of Mencius,[2] loyalty and justice between ruler and ruled: these are the sound of one hand. The sound of one hand is the root of things; of two hands, the branch. Rice-plants in the paddy-fields are the root, trade and commerce the trunk, the saké-shop the branch....

Apart from the Buddha, there is no true humanity.... From 1886 to 1890 I slept. From 1890, little by little, my eyes have been opened. Now in 1895 I begin at last to take notice of religion....

Confucius said, Of three men you meet, one must be your teacher.[3] Must take note of common things, of the feelings of common people. As Newton discovered gravity by watching an apple.

Among his other themes is one that will recur with ever greater frequency: the ennobling effect of adversity.

> Only after a pummelling
> By the rain
> Are the maples
> At their best —
> Autumn brocade.

There is also a notable scepticism as to Japan's 'glorious' victory over China, which roused such enthusiasm among his countrymen. The Three-Power Intervention, by which Russia, France and Germany forced Japan to return the Liaotung Peninsula, ceded to her by China in the Treaty of Shimonoseki in 1895, and which inevitably caused bitter resentment in Japan, moved him only to the sardonic comment:

> What else but that
> Land taken
> At the spear's point
> Should be yielded
> To the spears of others?

1. The reference is of course to the well-known Zen *koan*. See (e.g.) Yampolsky, *The Zen master Hakuin* (New York & London, 1971), p. 163 ff.
2. See *Mencius* (tr. D. C. Lau, Penguin Classics), p. 77.
3 See below, p. 155 n. 1.

Released for a while from the pressures of his lonely campaign against government and mine, Shozo seems to have begun the attempt, even if only in a fragmentary way, to tie together the different strands in his experience, in a philosophic or religious search for which thus far he had had neither time nor inclination. At first, inevitably, he had recourse to the traditional wisdom he had imbibed in his youth from Buddhism and the Chinese classics, and which were to provide much, though not all, of the seedbed for the development later of his own more personal insights.

It was in this frame of mind, no doubt, that during the war he toured the country lecturing on the Confucian principle of harmony. Of the contents of these talks no record remains. Such anecdotes as survive from the journey picture the Shimotsuke peasant rather than the Confucian lecturer. We find him calling on old Tokutomi Kazutaka, father of the famous popular novelist Tokutomi Roka, and castigating him for not manuring his precious old pine-trees correctly; or painstakingly designing a kind of duffle-bag to carry his modest belongings. (Shozo thought the western suitcase ugly and inconvenient, and disliked using a Japanese *furoshiki* or cloth wrapper because when it was tied by his clumsy hands the contents would invariably fall out.) In fact, he was so delighted with the result of his bag design that at once he had the daughter of his landlord at the People's Club make several, one of which he sent to the prominent politician (later Prime Minister) and founder of Waseda University, Okuma Shigenobu. For this short spell, at least, his life was relatively peaceful.

* * *

However undramatic this period of Shozo's career may have been, he had not forgotten the polluted fields along the banks of the Watarase. Nor had Furukawa. Floods in the summer of 1894, though not as violent as those of 1890, had an almost equally calamitous effect, partly owing to the fact that Furukawa's denuding of the mountain slopes above Ashio and the consequent gradual silting-up of the lower reaches of the river with soil and sand washed down by the rains meant that the rains no longer needed to be exceptionally heavy for flooding to begin.

Conditions worsened: it rapidly became apparent that the extractors had entirely failed to reduce the quantity of poisoned rock dumped in the river. Taking advantage not merely of the general distraction provided by the war atmosphere, but also of the absence at the front of many younger peasants — who by now might well have resisted such pressures — Furukawa once again sent his emissaries among the villages with instructions to cajole or browbeat the farmers into signing another 'agreement'. The terms of this second document were such that had it not been for the intimidation with which it was accompanied and the extreme distress many farmers were undergoing, with much of their land rendered irremediably barren, it is hard to see how anyone in his right mind, even among the timid peasants of Shimotsuke, could possibly have put his name to it. The previous agreement was specifically cancelled (though it still had over a year to run), and in return for a cash sum that was in nearly every case less than that previously offered,[1] each man had to undertake that 'in no circumstances, whatever damage might be caused to his land in future, whether for short or long periods, by poisonous mine effluent of any kind, would he at any time make any request for compensation or other complaint or petition, either to the mine, to the government, or to the courts. . . .'

In addition to the previous lie that the mine might soon be exhausted and find itself unable to pay, the means of persuasion included the assertion that the emissaries were acting on instructions from the local administration. Sometimes this was true. The ties between the central government and the mine were closer than ever. Furukawa's old friend and relation by marriage, Mutsu Munemitsu, was now Foreign Minister, while Mutsu's protégé, Hara Kei, was managing director of the mine.

Overt collusion between government and mine was carefully avoided at the higher levels, the Governor of Tochigi, for example, making no attempt to promote this second round of agreements; but in the districts and villages, where there was less danger of adverse publicity, officials backed the mine's palpably dishonest offer with such unashamed vigour that even the chairman of the governor's former Arbitration Committee, angered by their blatant unfairness, called in the Prefectural Assembly for an edict to forbid the mine from discharging any contaminated rock into the River Watarase.

Other pressure was brought to bear through the bribing of influential villagers, as was confirmed in an unexpected way in a statement made by an old Shimotsuke farmer (whose father had been one of the few to resist Furukawa's machinations from the start) to a Japanese historian of the Ashio affair in the early 1960s:

'Father was friendly with a man who did part-time work at home for an envelope-manufacturer in Koga. One day this friend of his brought him a little present. . . . It was a lined notebook, with a list in it of all the big people the mine had bribed. It had come his way in a bag of paper sent him for turning into envelopes — from some Furukawa wastepaper-basket, I suppose.'

Subjected to blandishments or threats of such diverse kinds, many farmers again succumbed — about half of those whose land had been poisoned so far signed the new agreement, according to one account.

1. Sometimes it was as low as 20 sen an acre.

On signing, they received a letter from Furukawa which put his point of view sufficiently clearly, if not theirs. It contained these words:

'As a result of this contractual agreement between us, signed today, the Ashio copper mine pollution incident is now completely closed.'

Early in 1896 Shozo denounced in the Diet this concerted government-Furukawa attempt to bully the peasants into promising that 'neither they nor their children nor their grandchildren' would protest against a man-made evil that showed not the slightest sign of abating. But apart from an isolated individual petition or two to the Prefectural Governor and the Minister of Agriculture, little notice was taken of his speechifying in the prefecture, and less in the Diet. Meanwhile the war continued to its successful conclusion. Though the Treaty of Shimonoseki was signed in April 1895, the emotions it had roused dominated the public mind up to and well beyond the Three Power Intervention at the end of the year, which forced Japan to accept drastic modification of the treaty.

* * *

And then abruptly, with the heavy rains of August and September 1896, the pollution issue flared into life once more. The resultant floods were the worst the Shimotsuke plain had experienced since 1859, and most of the water carried the deadly poison.

This time not one prefecture but four were severely hit. Families who had pawned their last change of clothing to buy fertilisers that they believed might help resuscitate their dead fields saw their hopes washed away. Beside the greatly increased damage to the soil, many houses were wrecked; wells, ponds and streams, the only sources of drinking water, were poisoned, causing among other troubles outbreaks of an eye-disease which kept the women from the sewing by which they had been helping to keep their families alive, and giving rise to the bizarre spectacle of peasant fishermen who owned small boats rowing long distances over the floods in search of a bucketful of fresh water. For the first time there was serious danger to life as well as to livelihood. According to a public lecture given in December by a Dr Miyake, in certain areas even the atmosphere was contaminated.

Shozo went into action at once, hurrying round the flooded areas gathering facts and mobilizing support for petitions to the central authorities. After four months work, a small group he was instrumental in organizing estimated the farmers' losses at not less than ¥13,000,000:[1] over fifty thousand acres of agricultural land had been under water and thirteen thousand homes destroyed or damaged. Directly or indirectly, some half a million people were estimated to

---

1. Some idea of the value of this sum may be gained from the fact that the price of rice at the time was 10 yen a *koku*, the amount that would feed one man for a year.

have been affected.

The scale of the catastrophe goaded some at least of the docile Shimotsuke peasantry into action — young men in their twenties, for the most part, for whom the old virtue of resignation in the face of disaster had not yet become instinctive. Unryuji, a Zen temple in one of the worst-hit areas, became the centre of a spontaneous protest movement.

At a meeting held there on 2 November, 1896, 51 peasants from 19 villages (all had come on their own initiative, their communities being still too cowed and disunited to send formal representatives) adopted at Shozo's insistence a 'spiritual compact', committing themselves to fight the mine together. A petition to Enomoto Takeaki, the Minister of Agriculture and Commerce, the first of very many such, was drawn up, roundly declaring that it was now obvious that the extractors had been an intentional fraud, that the arbitration agreements had been nothing less than a crime on Furukawa's part, and that the mine must be closed forthwith, since the destruction of some of the richest agricultural land in the country far outweighed the benefit to the nation deriving from Ashio.

The group, still largely conditioned by 'feudal' thinking, tried at first to use the customary channels for submitting such a petition. But local officials would not accept it for transmission, claiming they were 'too busy'. The prefectural administrative headquarters, too, indifferent to the misery of thousands for whom it was responsible, refused to forward it to the Minister.

Undeterred and growing slowly angrier, the peasants delivered it themselves to the Ministry in Tokyo, where they were coldly advised that 'as the Minister had only recently taken office, the matter had not been thoroughly investigated; he would reply in due course'. Months went by, and no reply was forthcoming.

A petition to the Finance Minister for the remission of taxes for peasants whose land had been poisoned was returned with a note rejecting it, because 'the tax laws made no provision for poisoning by industrial effluent as a ground for remission'. There were other frustrations.

Police, openly intimidating, attended every meeting of the protesters; rumour insinuated that they were 'dangerous elements'. Yet despite the deliberate hostility of the local administration and almost total indifference on the part of the central authorities to suffering and destruction even on such a huge scale, feeling was growing too strong to be easily suppressed, while at the same time fuller reports of the extent of the damage and distress began to appear here and there in the national press. Much of this new publicity was due to Shozo, who after repeated visits to the offices of Tokyo's leading newspapers acted as guide to a number of their reporters on a five-day fact-finding trip round Shimotsuke.

On 26 February, 1897 Shozo launched a new offensive in the Diet. This time he was not alone: his question to Enomoto demanding the reasons for his Ministry's inaction attracted the signatures of 46 co-sponsors and 61 'sympathizers'. In a 20,000 word speech of sustained intensity he outlined the long history of the poisoning of the Shimotsuke plain and gave a vivid account of the suffering it was causing.

In an attempt to convince those — they were many — for whom the facts as he gave them were altogether incredible, and who therefore supposed him to be exaggerating for reasons of personal ambition, he produced samples of poisoned bamboo and rice-plants, and of a strange substance that resembled metal slag but was in fact the residue of a heap of contaminated rice-straw after burning. If the people had borne with this affliction so long, he explained, there were many reasons: for years the habit of generations had made them assume a natural cause for every disaster, they lacked any notion of their rights as citizens protected by the Meiji Constitution, communications in the area were poor, and there was no tradition of villages combining for joint action; the struggle for survival, as river and fields ceased to provide a livelihood, had left them neither time nor energy for protest.

If some members of the Diet were guilty of thinking of these fellow-countrymen of theirs as nothing but 'low peasants, cowardly and servile', how much more so were the agents of Furukawa and of the provincial government, who had deliberately taken advantage of their docility and readiness to obey the slightest word of the 'upper ones' to bribe them into a lifelong silence? But it was not only they who were at fault: 'When the nation's government is hated by the people and can no longer be trusted by the Diet, what is that but devaluation of the very concept of the nation? If the people are not protected by the law, they can have no duty to respect it; and when there is no respect for the law, no one can tell what trouble may lie ahead.'

Finally, in his first groping towards an explicitly ecological, conservationist outlook, Shozo attacked as fundamentally mistaken the policy of authorizing an enterprise such as the Ashio mine, in mountains bordering a vast and fertile plain, without stringent investigation of the probable consequences. As it was, poison was flowing over Shimotsuke 'like water spilt on floorboards'.

True to form, the government at first ignored this onslaught. But events were not to allow it to do so for long. A protest meeting in the Kanda quarter of Tokyo two days later, addressed by Shozo and (among others) Tsuda Sen, a former Genro ('elder statesman') and close friend of Enomoto Takeaki, helped to arouse public indignation further. The meeting itself was stormy. Fifty strong-arm men, hirelings of Furukawa, took up places in the middle of the hall; foreseeing their attempts to wreck the occasion, Shozo stationed a similar number of students between them and the platform, and a larger number of young men from the polluted areas in the four corners. The meeting attracted a lot of attention, partly because of its very turbulence. From now on a small but significant number of public figures joined their voices to Shozo's in urging the government to act — most notably Christian leaders such as Uchimura Kanzo,[1] influential journalists like Tokutomi Soho and Miyake Setsurei, and Konoe Atsumaro, Speaker of the House of Peers.

On 19 March Tani Tateki, a leading right-wing member of the House of Peers, distinguished for his role as a senior army commander in the years immediately following the Meiji Restoration, travelled to Shimotsuke to see the devastation for himself. Till that day he had persuaded himself that Shozo must be an impostor, a demagogue with a bent for oratory but no regard for the truth; a brief visit, such as no member of the government had yet seen fit to make, instantly convinced him otherwise.

In the fashion of the time he recorded his feelings by handing an extempore poem (commonplace in itself, but influential when it became known that its author had expressed himself thus) to one of the victims before he left:

> *Long famous for its name*
> *This Fertile Plain*[2]
> *Is so no longer.*
> *By the Watarase*
> *My sleeve is wet with tears.*

Shozo, as he hurried from meeting to meeting, organizing, encouraging, speech-making, must have been delighted by both the feeling and the wit in a similar poem sent to him personally by Katsu Kaishu, founder of the modern Japanese navy:

> *Who is it*
> *That fouls, unashamed,*
> *The pure waters*
> *Of the ancient river —*
> *Furukawa.*[3]

Along the banks of the Watarase exasperation grew as the government still gave no sign of what, if anything, it intended to do.

---

1. Uchimura expressed himself on the subject with his usual imaginative, sometimes even bellicose, pungency. On one occasion he wrote in a newspaper article that if he were Prime Minister he would station warships in the mountains near Ashio (how he would have got them up there is not clear) and bombard the mine (below, pp. 129-30). But his concern was wholly serious, and it is much to his credit and to that of his colleagues that they were in the forefront of the first wave of real public sympathy for the pollution victims.

2. An ancient name for the wider plain of which Shimotsuke is a part.

3 Unfortunately the wit, as so often in Japanese poetry, lies in a simple but not readily translatable pun. The word for 'ancient river', *furukawa*, is the same as the name of the owner of the mine; and here the word can be taken either as 'of the ancient river', or as 'Furukawa' — the answer to the question 'Who is it...?'

On 3 March, a few hours before Shozo was due to launch an association of Dietmen from the four affected prefectures to bring pressure on the authorities, over 2,000[1] peasants gathered before dawn at Unryuji Temple, and set off in their straw sandals to walk the 50-odd miles to Tokyo, to demand immediate action. At three towns on the way police turned them back, blocking the roads, but several hundred managed to get through to the capital next day, and assembled that night, exhausted, in Hibiya Park. Next morning an attempt to deliver a protest to the Speakers of both Houses of the Diet was broken up by police.

After another night, spent this time under cover at the great Honganji Temple in Tsukiji, fifty-five of the demonstrators were allowed into the Ministry of Agriculture to see the Minister. Enomoto listened courteously enough, but would only say that he would give them a reply 'before very long'. Others tried without success to enter the Foreign Ministry to protest against the pressure that the British, who had recently been importing quantities of Ashio copper, were rumoured to be bringing on the government to resist any interference with the operation of the mine. At last they dispersed, having first set up a makeshift campaign office in Tokyo and arranged for the printing of a handbill, which was widely distributed to the citizens of the metropolis during the next few days. This document gave the bare facts of the ravages caused by Ashio pollution; then, after begging any who could to visit the disaster areas, but not to let themselves be shown round by any official if they should do so, it ended with these words:

'Because of the mine, we have lost our property, our lives are in danger, we have been robbed of our rights. But the government ignores us, the law gives us no protection. Are we to be left to die? If there are any among you with a drop of pity, please help us. If not, give us death!'

On 14 and 15 May Shozo, with the support of fifty fellow-Dietmen, twice demanded to know when a government reply to his question of 26 February would be forthcoming and insisted on an assurance that when the Minister had anything to say he would say it in the presence of the questioner and not take advantage of a moment when he might be absent from the Chamber. (He was thinking of the government's tactic five years before, when his challenge had been answered only after the end of the Diet session.) Vice-Minister Kaneko gave such an assurance. It was broken almost immediately, for the long-delayed government statement was issued without notice on 18 May, after the completion of business and in the absence of many Dietmen, including Shozo.

This statement, issued over the names of the Home Minister and the

---

1. 5,000, according to a recent historical account compiled by a Japanese lawyer.

Minister of Agriculture, was a slight advance over its predecessors in that it accepted without qualification that copper-bearing waste from Ashio was responsible for the pollution of the plain on both sides of the Watarase. But in its subsequent claims that the floods were due solely to natural causes, that Furukawa had already paid adequate compensation, and that the extractors were in any case reducing the amount of poisonous waste; and its denials of any intimidation of the peasants either by representatives of the mine or by prefectural officials, the Ministers might have been acting as spokesmen of Furukawa himself.

A final paragraph, evidence perhaps of the beginnings of a belated but real debate within the Cabinet, noted that such 'incidents' were the 'inevitable concomitant' of the development of mining, whether at Ashio or anywhere else: recognizing there would be a conflict of interest between industry and agriculture, the government would 'give orders for studies to be made, with a view to taking appropriate measures after thorough consideration of the issues involved'. Which last, as Shozo pointed out later, was like promising to study medicine after you had killed a man.

Such a combination of whitewash and bureaucratic procrastination was bound to infuriate the peasants still further. Enomoto, the Minister of Agriculture, seems to have foreseen the possibility of such a reaction. Five days later, on 23 March, he himself went to inspect the disaster area, the first Minister to do so since the pollution scandal had broken five years before. The shock of what he saw, and probably also of shame at what he must now have realised had been the tragically irresponsible attitude of his Ministry, was violent.

Returning to Tokyo that night, he went immediately to consult the Foreign Minister, Okuma Shigenobu, a liberally-inclined politician, opposed to the bureaucratic oligarchs still dominating the government, and an influential member of the Cabinet. The two acted swiftly. Next morning, after an audience with the Emperor, they forced the Cabinet to a decision; and by noon that day special extra editions of the newspapers carrying the government's announcement were being advertised by bell-ringing newsboys in the streets of Tokyo.

The plan was far less dramatic, in fact, than the circumstances in which it was conceived might have suggested — it consisted merely in the immediate setting up of a high-powered Ashio Mine Pollution Investigation Committee, and of what further action might follow its deliberations there was no hint. Shozo was far from satisfied. That very day, just before Enomoto made his announcement in the Diet, Shozo had been deploring the lack in the government's earlier statement of any awareness of the rights of the peasants. 'They make good soldiers in their country's service, but poor pleaders if they are wronged, and have no money to bribe others into protecting them, while your mine-owner or crooked merchant avoids military service and uses his money to bribe the poor into "agreements".' Why could the government not see the suffering citizens, he asked, as well as the prospering mine? On past experience he had good reason for scepticism. The government's announcement had come on the last day of the current Diet session, so that it could not be debated. But that there was at least a powerful faction in the Cabinet which was genuinely concerned about many aspects of the pollution issue did become clearer as events unfolded during the next few weeks. Enomoto's visit had obviously turned the scales; and a dominant consideration in the mind of a government unused to drastic manifestations of opposition may well have been the necessity of avoiding further demonstrations like that of 3 March.

If this was the case, the announcement of the creation of the Pollution Investigation Committee came too late, apart altogether from the continuing blindness it showed to the human aspect of the problem. Some of the pollution victims who had spoken to Enomoto on his fact-finding visit of 23 March had guessed he was sympathetic, but he had given little of his feelings away, and had refused to say anything there and then of what action if any the government might be contemplating. Word of this refusal became known with extraordinary speed.

That same night over 4,000 peasants, wrapped in straw coats against the bitter cold and with survival rations of rice for up to five days, converged once more on Unryuji Temple, and by daybreak were well on their way to Tokyo. The police had got wind of what was happening and went to great lengths to stop it, cordoning off Unryuji Temple as the demonstrators gathered and later blocking the main route to Tokyo a few miles away with a force of nearly two hundred.

The peasants were in a desperate mood. In the dark they slipped easily through the cordon, and once on the road marched in tight formation spread right across the narrow road, overwhelming the police block by sheer force of numbers. Subsequently, profiting from earlier experience, they split up into small groups and took different routes. Clashes with the police and the *kenpei* (military police) increased in number and violence as they neared the capital; many were forced back. Yet as before, many hundreds got through.

On 27 December their representatives were permitted to call on the Minister of Agriculture for the second time that month. Enomoto is reported to have wept as they pleaded with him for relief; and next day he resigned — whether as a quid pro quo exacted by Furukawa's supporters within the Cabinet for the setting up of the **Pollution Investigation Committee**, or out of simple shame at his inability to offer the peasants any solid prospect of relief, was never made clear. There must have been a shortage of candidates to succeed him, too, for in one of the most curious combinations of Cabinet posts on record, Okuma became responsible for Agriculture in addition to Foreign Affairs.

Even Shozo could not but feel that there was at last a possibility of greater pressure being brought to bear on the mine, and perhaps even of help for the disaster areas. Okuma, leader of the Progressive Party, and a powerful figure in his own right, was known to be more liberal than his Cabinet colleagues. Public opinion was favourable.

The reopening of the Ashio issue had coincided with a new interest in social and industrial problems, as in the aftermath of the Sino-Japanese War unemployment grew and Japan began to experience some of the more unpleasant consequences of headlong industrialization. In the Diet, a pressure group of M.P.s committed to bringing pollution to an end had been formally launched. A number of leading citizens had formed a similar association, with a committee of ten to seek interviews with Ministers. Yet another group were distributing handbills throughout Japan describing the peasants' hardships.

Shozo himself, who was involved in most of these movements in addition to his continual trips to Shimotsuke to encourage the peasants' own campaign, had been vindicated. At a public meeting on 30 March, Tani Tateki voiced a now widespread opinion, in language that is not simply the hyperbole that came so easily to speakers of the Meiji era, but reflects the astonishment aroused in the Japan of those days by the phenomenon of the solitary campaigner for social justice:

'People were saying only recently that Tanako Shozo was an impostor, a madman. I say he is society's guardian god!'

By a fortunate chance something else happened that day which seemed to legitimize the whole campaign, for it suggested a positive interest in the pollution issue by one who in Meiji Japan had a better claim to the title of 'guardian god of society' than Shozo — an official visit to the disaster area, apparently at the command of the Emperor himself, by a Chamberlain of the Imperial Household.[1]

If there was hope for the future, the present reality was as grim as ever. The people of Shimotsuke themselves were by no means united behind the campaign. Furukawa was still obtaining signatures for his

---

1. One does not, however, need to be unduly sceptical to wonder how much of the true situation the Chamberlain was permitted to see. A well-known woman journalist of the day, Matsumoto Eiko, was told of the following incident by a minor official who had been in attendance on a 'very highly placed personage' when the latter was watching some army manoeuvres on the edge of the polluted area. The personage requested that he be served with fresh fish from a lake below the hill from the top of which he was watching the manoeuvres in question — to the horror of the local District Chief, who was responsible for his entertainment: the lake had been heavily polluted, and all its rich stock of fish had died. But rather than admit the fact, the District Chief hurriedly sent for a fish from elsewhere, had it wrapped in a net, and then dropped it for a moment in the polluted waters of the lake, from which it was then instantly 'caught' and served to the waiting personage. Perhaps the Chamberlain was treated with similar discretion.

agreements, in most cases from landlords, which helped to create the impression that the anti-Ashio men, who were mostly small or tenant farmers, were 'subversive elements'; this led to increased police interference with their meetings.[1] Military police were stationed at key points throughout the disaster area. Three of the peasant leaders were arrested and sent to prison for six months. They had called at the homes of some of those who had accepted Furukawa's bribes, to try to persuade them to change their minds; finding the owners apparently away, they had gone inside, but had found no one. Informers must have been watching, for a day or so later they were charged with 'house-breaking'.

The pollution itself continued unchecked. Cultivation was possible only in isolated pockets. Blindness showed a steep increase; babies and small children were dying of undernourishment, withering like young bamboo plants. The impossibility of growing enough food on his poisoned land to support his ageing parents drove one man to suicide. And as for the central government's attitude, the 'liberal' Okuma, like most Japanese politicians of the dominant parties from that day to this, maintained close connections with industrial interests, and even he could hardly have been expected to take instant restrictive action against a concern of such national importance and prestige as the Ashio mine.

For nearly nine weeks, while Shozo and his supporters worked feverishly in Shimotsuke and in Tokyo to keep the issue in the public eye, the Pollution Investigation Committee conducted its deliberations in total secrecy.

At last, on 27 May, came the publication, over the signature of Minami Teizo, Chief of the Mining Inspectorate in the Ministry of Agriculture and Commerce, of a Pollution Prevention Order, probably the first of its kind, and certainly one of the most drastic, ever to have been issued in any country. In a long list of curtly-worded instructions — there were 37 in all — the Order directed Furukawa to undertake a series of major preventative works, including the construction of 20 huge filter beds and sediment basins, the digging of deep moats around existing slag heaps to prevent them being washed away, and the introduction of numerous highly technical control processes.

Work was to be started within seven days of the issue of the Order; maximum periods for completion, varying from one month to five months, were precisely specified. All work was to be carried out under the supervision of Ministry inspectors. If any of these items were not complied with, the mine would at once be closed. Simultaneously

---

1. It may have been at this time that Shozo himself was offered by a Furukawa emissary 'an orange-box full of notes' (¥300,000, according to one account) if he would abandon leadership of the campaign. The offer was met, we are told, 'with a roar of disgust', and the emissary attempted no further persuasion.

with the Order a separate directive was issued restricting the felling of trees on the Ashio mountain slopes and ordering appropriate replanting in areas already denuded. On the face of it, the government had acted against a great industrial enterprise with remarkable severity and to all reasonable men it must have seemed that the end of the pollution scandal was in sight.[1] Such a view was however to prove tragically false.

* * *

Shozo was impressed by the apparent sincerity of the government's attitude. He was disappointed, of course, that the mine had not been closed outright; but Okuma had assured him personally in an interview on 1 June that closure would certainly be ordered after a year or so if the contamination of the Shimotsuke plain did not show a rapid decrease. The continued absence of any provision for relief to the victims — in the same interview, Okuma had insisted that any claims for compensation must be made through the courts, though in view of the poverty and ignorance of the potential claimants this was obviously an unrealistic proposition — was a severer blow. In these circumstances, and in the absence of any guarantee that the Order would have an immediate beneficial effect, he decided to continue the campaign, both in Tokyo and in the country. A Pollution Relief Association was formed in the capital to provide funds and material assistance. Continued publicity, and further personal calls on Okuma, brought some modification of the iniquitous situation whereby local tax officials were still refusing to accept claims for tax remission that contained the word 'pollution'.

Even so, remission was grudging in the extreme. Officials would claim they had seen young rice-plants growing — which was often true, for in some areas the effect of the poison would be delayed, producing a sudden withering of an apparently healthy crop — and maintain that any subsequent crop failure must be due to natural causes. Surveys carried out by Shozo and two assistants showed that

---

1. From the perspective of the 1970s we may indeed judge that Okuma deserves high commendation for having acted against what was after all an industry of vital national importance with a courage and decisiveness that have rarely been matched by any government, even in our more pollution-conscious times. (See, in this connection, the interesting articles by Nothelfer and Crane in Journal of Japanese Studies.)

It remains true, however, that the Pollution Prevention Order has the aspect of a panic measure, based on the sudden realization of the consequences of years of neglect of the problem, rather than on any seriously considered view of the absolute priority of agriculture for the lasting welfare of the nation. In so far as Shozo insisted on precisely this priority, it can be argued that in the last analysis he is more significant for us today than Okuma. His emphasis on the 'sacredness' of land and agriculture had its roots in the past. But what makes him unique, as I suggest elsewhere in this book, is that he straddles both past and future: nurtured in a society which had traditionally given a very high place, at least in theory, to farming, he speaks with equal clarity now to a generation which is slowly coming to see in the 'post-industrial society' and a return (at least in some measure) to an agriculture-based culture, not a pipe-dream, but a necessity to be welcomed.

poisoned flood water flowing into other rivers was now affecting parts of the Tokyo administrative area in addition to five outlying prefectures (Saitama, Ibaragi, Tochigi, Gunma and Chiba).

For many years, the circumstances surrounding both the drawing up and the implementation of the draconian Order to Furukawa were shrouded in mystery. Enough is now known, however (thanks to the publication of posthumous biographies of some of the protagonists in the Ashio drama, and of statements by ordinary individuals who because of their connection with the mine were aware of some corner of the complex web of facts but chose not to reveal their knowledge till long after the event) to make at least the outlines clear. The story that emerges shows how deceptive was the apparent solution imposed by the Order. It also proves, if nothing else, the immense difficulty of achieving a just settlement where such powerful interests are involved — a difficulty which has been demonstrated in almost identical terms by the experience of the Japanese pollution scandals of the nineteen sixties and seventies.

Before he resigned, Enomoto appears to have proposed closure of the mine as the only possible course, on the ground that no merely preventative measures could be devised that would guarantee the ending of pollution, and as a gesture to the peasants whose distress he had witnessed. Okuma may have taken a similar view at first.

On the Pollution Investigation Committee there was an almost equal balance between experts on mining and on agriculture: the mining engineers prevailed, however, by arguing that the closure of Ashio would imply restrictions on mining activities all over Japan — a threat which seemed unthinkable when the whole bent of the country was towards rapid industrialization. Against the hardships of the Shimotsuke peasants they could set the prospect of 16,000 unemployed if the mine ceased to function at Ashio, a town with no other industry or resources.

Throughout the period of the Committee's deliberations heavy pressure was brought to bear on the government by Furukawa. A group of his men met in almost continuous session for several weeks in a restaurant in Nagoya — where they were kept up to the mark by several visits from Furukawa himself and by the sumptuous meals he took care to provide on these occasions — to plan the day-to-day moves. Most of the actual lobbying was done by their leader, one of Furukawa's legal advisers named Kida.

As one of the still relatively few graduates of Waseda University, which Okuma had founded under another name in 1882, Kida was in an ideal position to plead his master's case with the other Waseda men with whom Okuma had surrounded himself — an advantage he used to the full — and his loyalty to Furukawa showed itself in an extraordinary pertinacity. The night before the publication of the Order, in a final attempt to mitigate its terms, he called on Okuma's friend, Goto Shinpei, chief of the government's Health Office. Goto would not see him, sending word that he saw no reason to admit an agent of Furukawa's at this late stage; Kida refused to leave, and sat on the doorstep till cockcrow, when Mrs Goto took pity on him and persuaded her husband to hear what he had to say.[1]

The Order as it finally appeared, therefore, was something of a compromise, falling short of outright closure but holding this threat in the background. Some Japanese writers, then and now, have held that since parts of the Order, notably that requiring the desulphurization of smoke, were apparently impossible to carry out with the technology then existing, the government must have intended all along to force the closure of the mine, but chose this indirect means so as to shift the responsibility on to Furukawa. Certainly Furukawa is reported to have been furious at the harshness of the Order. But if closure had been Okuma's real intention, he had reckoned without the combination of determination, cunning and an almost demonic energy that distinguished the old industrialist. Furukawa announced that despite the 'unreasonableness' of the Order he would carry out its requirements to the letter.

The extraordinary burst of activity that now began at Ashio suggested that he was keeping his promise. Work was rushed forward at once on all the projects, in the knowledge that for almost half the stipulated period for many of them the heavy summer rains would severely hamper operations that would in any case be made difficult in the extreme by the mountainous terrain, with communication only possible along the narrow, steep-sided ravines. A huge labour force, including all the Ashio miners[2] and hundreds of townspeople — every family not directly connected with the mine was pressed into supplying one male for unpaid service — worked day and night in two shifts, carving out the sediment basins. According to Furukawa's figures, no fewer than 583,000 man-days were worked, at a total cost of over a million yen. To a public easily impressed by the statistics of industrial 'progress', these figures were formidable indeed, suggesting that Furukawa had done away with the pollution hazard at enormous cost to himself. His success — for such it was generally taken to be — boosted still further his almost legendary reputation as one of the most dynamic of all the pioneering modernizers of Meiji.

But the figures quoted above were his, and his alone. Despite the clause in the Order requiring its provisions to be carried out under the supervision of government inspectors, no official report was

---

1. Kida was involved in one other of the many curious aspects of the pollution saga that make the Japanese records read like a detective-story. During this period, and for some years afterwards, Shozo made frequent use of a tiny inn in Tokyo called the Shinanoya, with whose landlord he was on excellent terms. From a life of Kida published thirty-two years later, it appears that this landlord was in Furukawa's pay, and would often visit Kida to report on Shozo's plans.

2 All mining was suspended for 40 days.

forthcoming to confirm that all the necessary work had been properly completed. This was surprising enough in itself: that the government's silence provoked little or no suspicion must have been due to Furukawa's prestige, the lack of scepticism among the public, and the remoteness and difficulty of access of the mine, which made journalists reluctant to visit it — together with the fact that the town of Ashio owed its very existence to Furukawa, who could therefore ensure quite easily that visitors were shown only what he wished them to see.[1]

Even more astonishing, however, is an incident that seems to have escaped notice altogether at the time. Almost immediately after the apparently satisfactory carrying out of the Order, the senior government official who had signed it, Minami Teizo, resigned his post as Chief of the Mining Inspectorate to enter Furukawa's employ as Manager of the Ashio mine. The inescapable implication — that Furukawa had been either unable or unwilling to carry out all the terms of the directive — is in the nature of the case impossible to prove; but irrefutable evidence that whatever measures had been taken were largely without effect was soon to be forthcoming, for the implementation of the Order was followed not by a decrease but by a catastrophic increase in the scale and severity of the pollution that had its source in Ashio. Four years later Shozo declared unequivocally that the Order had been 'an instrument of evil, merely fostering the delusion that pollution was at an end, and leading thereby to ever greater ruin of land and people'.[2]

---

1. A history of the mine published by the miners' union lists, as an example of the 'sights' that were provided for occasional visitors, a huge pine tree that grew alongside one of the new sediment basins. Extraordinary precautions were taken to ensure the continued health of this tree, as a symbol of the success of the anti-pollution measures, by massive and repeated applications to the soil around it of saké, and of a Japanese delicacy that is often served with it, dried cuttle-fish.

The anonymous article published by a former employee of the mine in April 1900 (See above, pp. 68-69) describes measures taken by Furukawa to discourage visitors from Tokyo and to influence those who still persisted in coming. The Mayor of Ashio was instructed to close certain inns, and to forbid the holding of meetings on pollution in the town's temples and theatre, while certain journalists from the capital were effectively silenced with lavish entertainment.

2 In this he was almost certainly being unfair to the government and to Furukawa. For five years, it is true, there was little or no improvement. But in 1902 the extent of the pollution did begin to decrease rapidly, and this must have been due, at least in part, to the government's measures of 1897, the effect of which was no doubt delayed by the layer of pollutants that had accumulated on the bed of the River Watarase during the many previous years of government indifference. (See below, p. 141 n. 1.) Until then, however, the continued suffering of the peasants gave Shozo every justification for his distrust of both government and mine.

9
'To kill the people is to kill the nation'

The floods of September 1897 were a little less severe than those of the previous year, but the floodwaters were as contaminated as ever. Lingering hopes of the effectiveness of the Order rapidly evaporated. A group of peasants who managed to visit Ashio that same month reported that one sediment basin close to the sources of the River Watarase was overflowing, and that the walls of another were cracked, without any attempt being made at repair. Ominously, too, the mountain slopes around Ashio were still being denuded of their forests, with little sign of the replanting that the government had decreed.

Shozo toured Shimotsuke as before, carrying out surveys of the extent of pollution and mobilizing opinion for fresh protests. Some 117,000 acres of farming land in the territory of 136 small towns and villages were found to be affected, with a consequent drop in land values of over ¥10 million. The death rate in the polluted areas had doubled. Petitions began to reach the provincial and central authorities in greater numbers and in increasingly desperate language, with little of the servility of earlier years. One such, drawn up in October 1897 by the headmen or mayors of 83 communities, accused the government of causing, by deliberate collusion with a single unscrupulous individual, the greatest man-made disaster not merely in Japanese but in world history. After demanding relief, it concludes:

'If our appeal is ignored, if nothing is done to restore our poisoned lands, if our rights as citizens of the Empire are not guaranteed, how can the life of the nation be assured and peace maintained?'

Another petition from the same group a few weeks later, bearing like the first the unmistakable stamp of Shozo's style and arguments, provided a long and detailed analysis of the history of Ashio pollution and the government's attitude before reiterating the demand for the

Poisoned fields in Yanaka

closure of the mine;[1] copies were sent to all Cabinet Ministers and to the Speakers of both Houses of the Diet. To this increased activity by the victims, however, there was little response in Tokyo.

In October Shozo was asked to testify before a special Pollution Committee of the House of Peers, but towards the end of the year a series of political crises deflected public attention. Okuma resigned in November from his two posts of Foreign Minister and Minister of Agriculture in protest against the autocratic methods of Prime Minister Matsukata; and Shozo, who because of his constant concern with pollution had never paid much attention to party factionalism within the Diet and was therefore trusted by an unusually wide spectrum of Dietmen, was much involved in coordinating the efforts of opposition groups to bring down the Matsukata government, which finally fell in mid-December. Marquis Ito, no liberal by any standards, took over the premiership, and for the fifth time in eight years the Diet was dissolved.

Both Okuma's departure and the broader political upheaval were harsh blows for the anti-pollution campaigners. Something of Shozo's mood at the time, alternating between his usual pugnacious disregard of obstacles and the beginnings of disillusion with Tokyo politics, can be glimpsed from the first entries in his diary for the year 1898, as can the contrast between the massive support he was continuing to receive from the victims themselves and the fickleness of public sympathy for them in the metropolis:

2 January 1898. New Year poem —
No kimono —
Who cares
If I have only rags?
I too can dance
At the start of the year.
Visited Okuma at Oiso. Quite a crowd there. Started talking about pollution, but it didn't go down well, and they turned me out.[2]

5 January. Spoke at anti-pollution rally at Tatebayashi in

---

1. It also listed the reasons why the pollution scandal had not received the national attention it deserved. These were 1) the microscopic nature of most of the contaminating material, which was identifiable only by academic specialists; 2) the slowness in most cases of the process of soil-poisoning, which made it less sensational than, for example, the short-term hardship inflicted by a flood pure and simple; 3) the lack of any national experience of this kind hitherto; and 4) the dearth of people who combined knowledge of the facts with the courage to publicize them.

2. In an interview given years later, after Shozo's death, Okuma recorded what may be his version of the same incident.

'Tanaka detested people who struck him as too clever or cunning. Once he called at my country house when Mochizuki Kotaro was dining with me. The moment he saw Mochizuki he turned crimson and roared out, "Turn that fellow out this moment, or I'll hit him!" "You may not fancy him," I said, "but he's my guest, after all; you behave yourself!" In the end it was Tanaka who had to be turned out. He was a fascinating person, though.'

The two accounts, by the middle-of-the-road statesman and the irascible, uncompromising, ex-peasant campaigner, are not necessarily incompatible. Okuma, who had known Shozo since 1881, admired him greatly.

Shimotsuke, with Takahashi and Enjoji from Tokyo. Audience of 5,000.

6 January. Spent the night at Shimada Yoshiharu's. He said the pollution business looked very difficult, and asked me how things were going. 'Every struggle has its ups and downs,' I told him, laughing. 'From July to November last year I was all alone. Suddenly in February of this year I found myself with three or four thousand supporters, and then from June till October they dwindled to only three or four, never mind the thousands. That's how it's been since then. More than once I've had to go it alone, and maybe success is too much to ask.'

Through most of January and February Shozo travelled up and down Shimotsuke, based on the campaign centre at Unryuji Temple. On 25 February between two and three thousand peasants left Unryuji for Tokyo in the third attempt at a mass demonstration in the capital. Several police moves to block the march in its early stages were frustrated.[1]

A major confrontation took place on the morning of the second day, after the marchers had spent a wintry night in the open. Police chiefs tricked their leaders into the compound of a temple at Iwatsuki, a small town in Saitama Prefecture, and harangued them all the morning, but with little effect, on their duty to return home and not 'break the peace'. On the mediation of the townspeople, who had received the marchers kindly and provided many of them with a hot meal, a compromise was reached: seventy-five of the marchers were to be allowed through to Tokyo and the rest would go home. But this meant in effect that the teeth of the demonstration had been drawn and no notice was taken of it in the capital.

Shozo had taken no part in the march, chiefly because to do so would lay himself open to the charge still being levelled against him from time to time — that he was using the pollution issue for personal publicity.

Such discretion was more than ever necessary at this time, as a general election was in the offing. When it came, Shozo was re-elected once again, taking over 70 per cent of the votes in his Shimotsuke constituency. Three days later he made one of his rare calls at his home in Konaka. If he was tempted to any feeling of complacency at his election victory — his fifth — it was dispelled by a visit that evening from Noguchi Shunzo, one of the most energetic of the young peasant leaders, who told him he had no right to relax for even a day

---

1 A police warning that the pontoon bridge by which the marchers were about to cross the River Tone was damaged and unusable was found to be false: the police had merely detached the controlling motor-boat from the pontoons and moored it nearby. Two young marchers dived into the river and repositioned the motor-boat, the small police guard being helpless against the huge crowd waiting on the bank. Elsewhere, the marchers slipped through woods and across fields to avoid the road-blocks the police had hastily thrown up with wooden stakes driven into the muddy country tracks.

when so many were in distress. This rebuke, from a man half his age and with only a tiny fraction of his experience in combating injustice, Shozo met with that instant recognition of sincerity in others that was the obverse of his fierce intolerance of the hypocritical and the arrogant. He merely notes in his diary:

I was filled with shame. Noguchi doesn't go home, though his child has died, his wife is pregnant, and the poison is ruining his fields. He takes no thought for his own affairs.

He rejoined the campaign at once, speaking at thirty-five places within a few days. His encouragement was badly needed. Extreme poverty and exhaustion had taken their toll, and unity among the peasants was as precarious as it had ever been. Understandably, if short-sightedly, innkeepers, tradesmen and owners of small businesses in the towns of the Shimotsuke plain showed little sympathy with the rural victims; from their point of view, the reputation of the whole area as 'polluted' was merely bad for business and the less said about it in public the better. And always, waiting in the wings, were Furukawa's agents with offers of more 'agreements'.

At times Shozo himself was all but overwhelmed by the difficulties and by the absence of any real progress. He too was near to physical exhaustion. References begin to appear in his diary to what he called his 'brain sickness'.[1] A letter to Noguchi Shunzo written in early April shows him coming perilously and uncharacteristically close to self-pity — and then jerking back to the old determination:

I've had a fierce cold since mid-March, but have managed to keep myself going with saké. All this journeying and speechifying in the snow, it tells on a man, I suppose. . . . I don't look ill, but I'm too heavy, and my mind isn't working properly. Brain-sickness, alas. I'm finding things very difficult. And it makes our whole campaign seem so ridiculous, somehow. . . .

A man need only tackle one big task in his life; everything else he must leave to Heaven. This affair of the mine strikes at 300,000 people and at the very foundation of the country. You and I need have no regrets at staking our lives on such a struggle. . . .

The summoning of the 12th Diet session in mid-May 1898 provided Shozo once again with a chance to raise the issue on the national stage — a chance of which he took immediate advantage, with a 31-point written 'question', co-signed by 94 other Dietmen, and a two-and-a-half hour speech of explanation, condemning Marquis Ito's government for its indifference to pollution and accusing officials of treating protesters 'like animals'. How, he asked, in a question he was later to repeat with increasing urgency, was it seriously possible to

---

1. Some have thought that this may have had its origin in the venereal disease he contracted in his youth (see above, chapter 1). It seems at least as likely that, as those who were closest to him have testified, the phrase was a home-made description of what he felt to be his condition in these periods of extreme weariness.

speak of 'the nation', when the rights of so many were trampled on without redress?

This speech, and another four days later, were overshadowed by developing friction on other issues between the government and the opposition parties: in June the Diet was dissolved yet again, and Ito's Cabinet resigned, to be replaced on his recommendation by Japan's first purely party Cabinet, led jointly by Okuma and by Itagaki, who had been the most prominent advocate of representative government before the establishment of the Diet. Liberal-minded people could be forgiven for expecting that this innovation at the top would bring with it a real change in governmental attitudes to social problems, of which pollution was the gravest. Shozo shared these hopes. The new Ministers headed the party[1] to which he himself still owed at least nominal allegiance. That they respected his own toughness and sincerity, even if they did not fully understand his thinking, was acknowledged by the offer from Okuma of a post in the new administration, that of Chief of the Metropolitan Police.[2] In fact, however, the new government was hamstrung from the start by factionalism within its own ranks, nor could any pressure be brought to bear from below, since the Diet had been dissolved and its members were facing another general election in August.

Enthusiasm for popular rights, too, had waned since the heyday of the movement a dozen years earlier: Okuma's and Itagaki's supporters, by now predominantly bourgeois, were no longer so far removed in outlook as they had once been from the conservatism of Ito and the other Meiji oligarchs who had held the reins for so long.

In the general election Shozo won his usual easy victory. In his diary there is no self-congratulation, only a keener self-questioning, and the note of frustration with the political merry-go-round grows stronger.

This morning I saw clearly this truth. No matter how clever a man may be, if he has many aims, he will achieve none of them: no matter how foolish or ignorant, if he concentrates on one thing only, he can hardly fail.

My zazen[3] *is 'running around'. My self-training isn't sitting in silence, but journeying by boat and rickshaw or on horseback along rocky roads. All this is zazen. Zazen doesn't have to be done only in silence, nor even sitting. Deeds are my zazen, and I do it everywhere. . . . Since this Cabinet was formed I have achieved nothing. In Tokyo politics I am an imbecile. All I do is go from village to poverty-*

---

1. The Constitutional Party, formed by Okuma and Itagaki out of the old Progressive and Liberal parties.

2. The circumstances in which the offer was made were as piquant as the offer itself. To deliver the message, Okuma's emissary had to call on Shozo at the People's Club where he was staying at the time in a tiny 'bed-sitter', along with his student friends. Needless to say, the offer was not accepted.

3 Silent meditation as practised in Zen Buddhism.

stricken village along the river bank. A duck waddling among the reeds... I've discovered something. Politics is easy, as easy as dealing with pollution is difficult. Astonishing and terrifying, the ease, the superficiality of politics these days.

Meanwhile he was still encouraging the peasants in Shimotsuke to keep up their flagging campaign. A petition to the Finance Minister in August pleaded to know why, when the victims of an earthquake in 1891 and of a tidal wave in 1896 had been compensated from government funds, no such official compassion was forthcoming for the casualties of man-made progress. It was not that the facts were not well-known. An article in the *Yomiuri* newspaper on 31 July, for instance, had described the debilitating effect of the years of pollution. Hisano Village, for example, its five hundred households no longer able to support their village office and primary school because of the loss of local revenue, had virtually ceased to function as a community. But the petition was ignored.

Early in September nature intervened once more, stepping up the crisis to a new level of severity. Two days of torrential rain caused at least one of the sediment basins at Ashio to burst its bounds, and since nothing had been done, despite vaguely reassuring statements from the prefectural authorities, to dredge the Watarase or raise the level of its banks at points of greatest danger, the flooding was immediate, widespread and lethal. Crops that in prolonged good weather had begun to grow in pockets of less badly contaminated land were destroyed. Among the peasants resignation turned again to open anger.

Shozo called on the Ministers of Agriculture, Finance, Home Affairs, and Education — the new Diet was not due to be summoned for nearly three months — to demand action. He was not welcome: the Ministers were too preoccupied with maintaining the government's precarious hold on office. In a poem Shozo expresses his wonder that human beings could be so insensitive (it happened to be the week of the Chrysanthemum Festival, when Tokyoites of all conditions flocked to admire the latest spectacular examples of this most traditional of Japanese flowers):

> *Many there are*
> *Who grow the blossoms,*
> *Many who view them.*
> *But do they know, or do they not,*
> *The spirit of flowers?*

Another poem defiantly accepts the isolation resulting from his persistent championing of an unpopular cause:

> *Tiring of the world,*
> *Hiding away, shunning its slander —*
> *What hope then?*
> *Only action, without thought of self,*
> *Brings joy.*

The peasant victims themselves were almost at once to challenge him by *their* actions to face squarely the issue of whether, in the face of Establishment apathy, protest through the conventional political channels still had any chance of success, and if not, to decide what other form of self-less action, if any, might still be open to him on their behalf.

On the afternoon of 26 September Shozo, once more exhausted to the point of illness from travelling and speaking, lay asleep in the room at a small inn that served as the Tokyo office of the anti-pollution campaign. Just before three o'clock a telegram was delivered. It had been sent from the town of Tatebayashi, not many miles from Unryuji Temple on the banks of the River Watarase, and read simply:

> TEN THOUSAND LEAVING TATEBAYASHI NOW.

That a big meeting had been planned for the previous evening at Unryuji, Shozo knew: this huge new mass march, on a far larger scale than any of the three previous demonstrations, was unexpected, and had obviously grown spontaneously out of the fury and frustration of the peasants as they had gathered at the temple and sensed the power of their numbers. That evening and next day five other telegrams followed, reporting the whereabouts of the spearhead of the march, together with the single word ADVANCING.

Shozo's first thought was of the danger of a major clash between the police and the marchers. In visits to the Ministers of Agriculture and of Home Affairs he reiterated the urgency of the need for relief, and asked them to direct that no attempt should be made to stop the march by force.

A further telegram on the evening of the 27th brought the news that the marchers had reached Koshigaya, some 15 miles from Tokyo, where they would be spending a second night in the open, sleeping by the roadside or in temple compounds. Knowing the mood of the peasants as he did, and being therefore the more worried about the outcome of a march on the capital without precedent in the modern or indeed in any other period of Japanese history, Shozo decided he must go to meet them before they entered the city. He and one helper, therefore, left the inn in two rickshaws at one o'clock on the morning of the 28th. After a stop at an inn at 5 a.m., 'so that the rickshawmen could eat', they made contact at seven o'clock with the marchers in the village of Fuchie,[1] which the vanguard had reached after leaving

---

1. Now part of Tokyo's Adachi Ward.

Koshigaya at dawn. Hundreds of tired and hungry peasants, old men of over seventy among them, were thronging through the narrow street, angrily rejecting orders to disband from a force of police and forcing them little by little to retreat. To gain time, Shozo appealed to the marchers to turn aside and rest in the yards and gardens of houses along the road. But the gardens quickly filled up, and still the column was flowing unchecked through the village.

At Shozo's suggestion the leaders now agreed to halt the demonstration and assemble as many of the marchers as possible in the compound of a large Shinto shrine, where Shozo would address them. Through the shrine gates they crowded, nearly 3,000 of them. As they settled down, Shozo learned of the earlier stages of the march. The government in Tokyo might have changed, but the authorities' recipe for dealing with such demonstrations was evidently the same as before, only more so: a cordon had been thrown around Unryuji at the start, with more military police in evidence than ever before, the pontoon-bridge and ferry-boat removed from the River Tone crossing,[1] villages en route forbidden to offer them food or shelter, or even to lend them pots to cook rice on the road; the marchers had been harassed at every turn by police with naked swords, and kicked and beaten when they lay asleep by the roadside at night. In the face of all these discouragements more than half of the 10,000 who had started from Unryuji two and a half days earlier had had to turn back.

That afternoon, flanked inevitably by police, Shozo spoke to the weary but still determined crowd. Governments and Ministers had changed so frequently, he reminded them — there had been ten Ministers of Agriculture in nine years — that the tragic human consequences of pollution had been too little understood by those in authority. Now at last, however, they had a government not of aloof oligarchs but of politicians, men of his own party, whose concern for their welfare was real. It was 'our' government, and he himself would ensure that their case was listened to. But if the proper relief measures were *not* speedily taken, he himself would march with them to the capital, and die at their head if need be. For the moment, to continue to march as a body would only increase the risk of bloodshed. He appealed to them, therefore, to return home quietly after choosing ten representatives to help him in bringing pressure to bear on the government.

To this request the peasants agreed, though they insisted on electing fifty representatives instead of ten. One might have expected them rather to reject his advice; the record of successive governments

---

1. The march might have ended altogether at the river crossing if Noguchi Shunzo (the young man who had castigated Shozo for visiting his home during the crisis) and others had not held at bay a squadron of sword-brandishing but evidently not very intelligent policemen while peasants from a village a little way downstream provided boats to replace the bridge and ferry-boat the police had removed, enabling large numbers to cross safely before dawn.

over the past seven or eight years gave little hope of a quick and genuine response. But through his long association with the world of the 'upper ones' in Tokyo Shozo had acquired in the eyes of the still feudal-minded majority of peasants a degree of authority which was almost irresistible, compounded as it was by the force of his eloquence and personality.

On his side, the paternalistic attitude carried over from his upbringing and experience as a village head — that he knew what was best for the peasants, and that when he spoke his mind they must of necessity do as he told them — still survived, with its corollary that higher authority must heed him when he spoke as the people's representative. He misjudged, too, the degree of liberalism or social concern in the newly-formed Constitutional Party, which was the power-base of the Okuma-Itagaki government. For all these reasons his halting of the march in mid-progress, when the resolution and sense of unity among the marchers had risen to a peak it had never reached before, may have been the most serious error in all his long fight against pollution. Certainly some of the more politically conscious peasants were unconvinced as they listened to him. If in the end they too gave in, it was out of an instinctive and profoundly Japanese respect for the 'sincerity' of his promise of total commitment to their cause, whatever the cost, if the methods he recommended were to fail.

In part, this 'sincerity' was an aspect of Shozo's paternalism, for it signified acceptance of unlimited responsibility for the welfare of those he considered himself to represent. Both qualities had their roots deep in his formative years, but the one did not depend wholly upon the other. Viewed from the perspective of his whole life, Shozo's spiritual growth had scarcely begun; from now on, while the paternalism was slowly to fade, the sincerity would find a deeper ground of its own. In a sense, the pledge of dedication he gave to the crowd in the grounds of the shrine that afternoon was ultimately to determine the course of the rest of his life.

The fifty representatives duly went on to Tokyo. For two days no Minister would see them. On the third day, when the Minister of Agriculture granted them an interview, he would promise nothing. A visit by Shozo to party headquarters to demand that other Ministers should receive them had no effect. Everywhere he was rebuffed and misunderstood. Ironically, some said he should be offered a provincial governorship for his success in keeping such an unheard-of demonstration away from Tokyo, while others accused him of simple exhibitionism. No way seemed open. 'Our' government collapsed from internal squabbles at the end of October, without the Diet having met once since it had taken office; Okuma was succeeded as Prime Minister by one of the most inflexibly conservative of all the Meiji leaders, General Yamagata.

Shozo's 'brain-sickness' returned. In his diary entries for October despair is faced squarely, and by that alchemy which usually only the artist and the mystic can command, made to yield its opposite:

> *If it is to be death,*
> *Then die! If life,*
> *Live on!*
> *To have been born*
> *In this world*
> *Was joy indeed.*
>
> *None now*
> *Have tears to shed:*
> *No cry is heard*
> *This autumn day*
> *But the cicada's.*
>
> *Sea and sky —*
> *If I make them mine,*
> *Bitterness fades.*
> *Floating or sinking,*
> *There is no wind,*
> *No waves.*

The blacker the world grows, the whiter one must be . . .

The thirteenth session of the Diet was opened on 3 December. After preparing the ground by bombarding various Ministries with petitions, and submitting an 80-point 'question' in the Diet itself, in a speech on 10 December Shozo delivered his most violent onslaught yet on the government. In one respect it was also sensational. Undeterred by the formidable character and prestige of the new Prime Minister, General Yamagata, he accused the army of 'treason' in having sent its own *kenpeitai*, the military security police, against unarmed peasants on a peaceful march to the capital to claim their constitutional right to the protection of life and property.

Fearing army reaction, the Speaker, Kataoka Kenkichi (who, ironically, had once been a leading figure in the popular rights movement) demanded that Shozo withdraw this charge. He refused. On the 12th, in a brief appearance when Shozo was not present, the Vice-Minister for the Army called for it to be expunged from the record. When next day Shozo demanded a proper reply to his charge, only to be told by the Speaker he was out of order in referring to business already dealt with, he exploded. Why, when the Vice-Minister had been allowed to speak in his own absence, was he not allowed the right of reply? The House, he insisted, must give its verdict on which of them was the liar, himself or the Minister . . . Kataoka ordered him to leave the Chamber. His party subsequently suspended him for a week 'for unbecoming conduct'.

Shozo's immediate reaction was bitter. In a new version of his poem of a few weeks earlier, he wrote:

> *Die, if you have to.*
> *Kill me, if you must.*
> *In a dead world*
> *What cause for grief*
> *In being killed?*

And for once there is a note of disgust with his fellow-parliamentarians:

> *Plants wither,*
> *Men die:*
> *To the Dietmen*
> *It is nothing —*
> *Faces of stone!*

All the papers had reported his speech and the subsequent exchanges in the Diet. But the government paid no heed to the Press, and for Shozo such publicity was worse than useless, for it merely lent credibility to charges that he was a self-seeking demagogue.

Another poem, appearing in his diary for 25 December, is called *Ch'ü Yüan*, after the Chinese poet-patriot of the 3rd century B.C. who drowned himself after being exiled as the result of his rivals' calumny, and left nothing but his suicide and his poems to keep his memory alive.

> *The waters closed*
> *Over Minister Ch'ü Yüan,*
> *Driven from office.*
> *Only so his name lives,*
> *For he achieved — nothing.*

Among other entries for the same date is a reference, barely more than the name, to another celebrated figure from early Chinese history, Chia I. When the great Ch'in dynasty collapsed at the end of the 3rd century B.C., the scholar Chia I recorded in an eloquent essay the reasons for the revolt that precipitated its downfall: '. . . [the King of Ch'in's] officers governed with the greatest severity. The rewards and penalties were unjust. The taxes and levies were unbearable. The empire was crushed under forced labour, the officials could not maintain order, the people were in the last extremity of misery, and the sovereign had no pity for them and gave them no help . . .' Yet Chia I could do no more than Ch'ü Yüan to influence directly the course of the events he deplored. For Ch'ü Yüan, his poems and final suicide: for Chia I, the measured rhetoric of his *Faults of the Ch'in*.

Such case-histories came only too readily to Shozo's mind — the lives of men like these had formed a substantial part of his education — and the thought that he too might be remembered only as a bystander, eloquent but ineffective, was all but unbearable:

Shozo [he often writes of himself in the third person] *has no learning. If anything he says resembles the sayings of the sages of the past, that will be a disaster. If anything he* does, *even by mistake, resembles their* actions, *that will be glorious.*

At the back of his mind was the pledge of action he had given the peasant marchers in the shrine compound at Fuchie, three months before. Nothing had been done since then to improve their lot. Twice in the early weeks of the New Year Shozo made use of questions on quite unrelated issues — the administration of Okinawa, and government borrowing abroad — to demand a reply to the charges he had made in his speech on 10 December. No reply came.

For many Dietmen, Shozo and his pollution were on the way to becoming something of a bore, when early in March 1899 the Prime Minister chose to consolidate his position by a stratagem which was to have the double effect of bringing Shozo back into prominence and of alienating him still further from the political institutions he had now served for nineteen years.

* * *

'Yamagata then formed his second ministry and silenced the opposition with bribes.'[1] Such is an American historian's bald summary of Yamagata's treatment of the party politicians from whose short-lived Cabinet he took over. The opposition was indeed silenced, but not without some difficulty, and Shozo was the focus of such parliamentary resistance as there was. Yamagata had a specific purpose — the forcing through the Diet of a steep increase in the land tax, which very many Dietmen representing provincial landowners would have done their best to block. In March 1899, in a crude move to buy them off, his government proposed an immediate increase in the ordinary Dietman's annual salary from ¥800 to ¥2,000. Predictably, there were cries of outrage, and the Speaker of the House of Representatives, a leading member of Shozo's party, hurriedly introduced an amendment to the rules governing Dietmen's conduct, giving them the right to refuse to accept the salary.

The Diet session was extended for ten days to allow 'discussion' on the government's proposal, with the obvious intention that Dietmen should return to their constituencies with the extra money already in their pockets. Shozo was chosen to present the case against the increase. In a speech on 6 March he fastened on the curious wording of the reason for it put forward by the government, that the present salary rate made it impossible for the recipients to maintain their position or 'character' as members of the Diet. This was not merely untrue, said Shozo, it was an insult. Entrusted as they were with the

1. Borton, op. cit., p. 237.

power of altering the financial arrangements of the entire country, members were bound to refrain as far as possible from accepting increases for themselves even when (as was certainly not the case now) they were clearly justifiable — only 'spiritual qualities' enabling a member to exercise this kind of self-control could establish the 'character' of his position; money was irrelevant.

Despite its uncompromising idealism, the speech evidently struck a responsive chord in men whose education had laid great stress on frugality and loyal service. The proposal was adopted, but by a majority of only ten.

Shozo was profoundly disappointed — not so much by the passage of the proposal as by the subsequent acceptance of the increase by those who had voted against it. As it happened, he himself was more dependent than many other Dietmen on his parliamentary salary. It was not only that he had no business connections or other source of income. The money he had set aside at the time of his vow of public service nearly twenty years before had been spent on his early election campaigns and his salary had been swallowed up in anti-pollution work, so that he depended for his livelihood on contributions from constituency supporters. One might have thought, therefore, that having made his protest he need not have felt over-scrupulous about accepting what had after all been passed by a 'democratic' majority. But for Shozo 'sincerity' precluded any such comfortable retreat from principle.

On 14 April, having given himself time to consider the consequences, he sent a note to the Speaker declining to accept, not merely the increase, but any salary at all. Newspapers throughout the country headlined this quixotic move. Nothing like it had been seen since the Diet began. However much they may grumble from time to time about the venality of their politicians, at heart the Japanese have never expected a lofty ethical standard from those who represent them — and least of all when it might compel a man to take a solitary stand. To such a way of thinking, Shozo's refusal to compromise was barely intelligible, his readiness to be the odd man out (of all the one hundred and twenty-three other Dietmen who voted with him against the increase, not one followed his lead in refusing to accept it) even less so.

Despite a good deal of praise for Shozo's action, therefore, there was much unfavourable comment on what many were only capable of seeing as yet another publicity stunt on the part of the picturesque but cranky Dietman from Shimotsuke. Similar criticism, prompted no doubt by guilty consciences, came even from party colleagues within the Diet, and back in Tochigi, some of his well-wishers resented his giving up his only source of regular income without consulting those who had been helping to support him. Amid the chorus of harsh voices Shozo remained unperturbed.

In a letter to his constituents on 21 March he thanked them for their support, acknowledged that he should have sought their views before taking his decision,[1] — and concluded very firmly that nothing could make him change his mind. An unfaltering conviction of the rightness of what he had done — that would be arrogant if it were not so quietly and simply stated — runs through a more personal letter, written two days later to his nephew:

Men call me a fool[2] for refusing a salary of ¥2,000. But they don't count the savings the whole country would have made if they'd listened to me, nor the power of the challenge there could have been to selfishness and corruption. It's the politicians that are the fools for not realising this truth; and the moralists and men of religion are as bad, for not living it . . .

Towards the end this letter takes on the meditative note which has already appeared in his diary, and which in this context surely reflects the struggle it must have cost even him to set himself once more against the less morally exacting majority:

There is no mystery in the world. The way of Man is nothing but the Way of God. To argue for the existence or non-existence of God is folly, it seems to me. Because Man is God. Whether one becomes Man or God is simply a measure of the shallowness or depth of his thought, of the weakness or strength of his power of endurance. Don't speak of 'God', as something 'other'. If I resolve to become God, I am God. To know what he is, a man must look within, and nowhere else.[3]

* * *

All this while the pollution crisis was smouldering on. Before the salaries issue came up, a petition from the pollution victims demanding relief had for the first time passed through both Houses of the Diet, which had then forwarded it to the government. It was ignored: a further illustration of the contempt in which the oligarchs held not merely provincial peasants but also parliament, in any issue where the government's survival was not at stake.

Conditions in Shimotsuke had not improved. 'Spies' sent up to

---

1. Here, perhaps, Shozo was for once being a little more wily than sincere. If he *had* consulted his constituents, they would almost certainly have forced him to moderate his stand.
2. The moral validity of his action was never widely recognised, but Shozo for his part never repented. Nearly three years later he wrote to another relative: 'There isn't one person in all Japan who understands why I refused the salary . . . When they *do* begin to understand, that'll be when Japan too will really be on the way to enlightenment. And so long as the majority *don't* understand, just so long will Japan be slipping back and back — to ruin, in the end.'

3 I have translated *kami* as 'God' rather than 'gods', although in itself the term can mean either, and it is impossible to say with any precision what meaning Shozo attached to it at this stage of his life. Probably it represented an amalgam of the Confucian 'Heaven', the Shinto *kami* or 'spirit(s)', and the Zen idea of the enlightened soul, released through discipline into freedom. It is hardly necessary, no doubt, to add that there is nothing of the *supermensch* attitude in Shozo's talk of man 'becoming God'. The nearest occidental equivalent might be the practical mysticism of some kinds of Quakerism.

Ashio once a month by the anti-pollution movement had found that contrary to statements in the national press, heavy rain was still causing many of the sediment basins to overflow. Detailed statistics collected by the victims showed the persistence of an abnormally high death-rate throughout the afflicted areas. Hoping to make a personal appeal to the government on the basis of these figures, Shozo called five times on Yamagata and three times on the Finance Minister; neither would grant him an interview.

With Saigo, the Home Minister, he was even more persistent, and with somewhat more success: after turning him away no fewer than fifteen times, Saigo at last agreed to see him. But the meeting brought no promise of amelioration. Driven into hospital by exhaustion and by eye-trouble, Shozo again came near to despair:

So far from there being any 'improvement' in politics nowadays, pollution has dragged politics down and down. The degradation of politics, the decay of education, the rottenness of religion — corruption's everywhere, worsening every day. Our struggle has failed — failed totally.

So he wrote to his nephew. Yet though he could admit defeat, lasting despair was an attitude of which he was no more capable now than when a false charge of murder had kept him incarcerated for three years a generation earlier. In the final sentence of this same letter, the old resilience returns:

But what do we say? — 'Undaunted by a hundred disasters'? These words too are just as much a part of life!

Along the banks of the Watarase the slow build-up of resentment since the failure of the demonstration of September 1897 was prodding the victims towards new forms of united action. In a remarkable outburst of energetic grass-roots organization, a 'pollution parliament' of 1,200 elected representatives met on 22 December, 1899, and voted to continue in being 'till all the waters of the Watarase had been cleansed'. A petition submitted to the government on 8 February, 1900 concluded:

'If you cannot cut off the poison at its source; if you cannot cleanse the waters of our river; if you cannot restore fertility to our land; if you cannot protect our lives; then murder us, your loyal subjects!'

Commending this petition in the Diet next day, Shozo, with the nominal backing of 128 other Dietmen, demanded to know why the government continued to ignore the earlier petition that had been adopted by both Houses. Why did they still do nothing, when the deaths of over 1,000 men, women and children had been shown to be directly or indirectly attributable to copper effluent poisoning? Shozo listed many other grievances — the ineffectiveness of the Pollution Prevention Order, the concealment by the authorities of the results of the medical examination of conscripts from the Shimotsuke area, the failure of successive Home Ministers to carry out flood-prevention work promised by the short-lived Okuma government, the injustice of the grudging tax remission granted — as if it were a special favour — to a limited number of victims, the total absence of compensation for losses now estimated at forty million yen.

Five days later he rose to speak again, asking the indulgence of members; he himself was tired of having to address them repeatedly on the same subject, but the government's silence left him no alternative. This time he confined himself to two points: a plea that they should send experts to evaluate for themselves the enormous losses of agricultural production caused by the pollution, and the question, wearily repeated, as to *how* they could dismiss a petition from fellow-citizens who were literally dying because of the government's indifference.

Even as he was speaking, the fifth — and as it turned out, the last and most dramatic, though also the most abortive — of the mass protest demonstrations was under way. It had been planned at a secret meeting two weeks before by the 'action committee' of the pollution parliament. Throughout the previous night, peasants from all over Shimotsuke had been assembling at Unryuji Temple, where they lit great bonfires to warm themselves till dawn. A detachment of 50 mounted police, arriving while it was still dark, ordered the crowds to disperse and tried to chase them away when they refused. Fighting broke out in the grounds and in the hall of the temple itself, from which the peasant leaders and the Zen priest of Unryuji had been encouraging defiance. But all the time new groups of peasants were arriving, till finally, in the face of overwhelming numbers, the police withdrew.

At nine o'clock on the morning of the 13th, after a do-or-die address from the priest, three thousand protesters set off in a ragged but determined column, singing their 'pollution song' as they went. To get round the probable police confiscation of boats at the River Tone crossing, they took two boats with them — mounted on carts, which were armed with sharpened bamboo stakes projecting from either side, to deter any police assault.[1]

At first they were hardly molested at all, for the main body of mounted police, consisting of nearly 400 men armed with sabres, had assembled to await them at the crossing, on the north bank of the River Tone. Here the marchers arrived in the early afternoon. Led by Noguchi Shunzo, riding on horseback and waving a maple-branch with a banner tied to it inscribed with the words NAMU AMIDA BUTSU — Hail to the Lord Buddha — the front of the column made straight for the police, in the hope of dragging the precious carts

---

1. The thorough preparations for this demonstration contrast with the spontaneity of the earlier marches. Soundings had been taken at the river crossing to ensure that the boats were of the right draught; and four doctors were hired to treat any marcher who should fall ill on the way.

straight through to the river bank. The police drew their sabres on the peasants, who had nothing to defend themselves with but bamboo sticks, and for a while there was fierce fighting on the road and in the fields.

The ferocity of the police onslaught was more than the marchers had bargained for. With their carts overturned and the boats captured in the first few minutes, resistance soon crumbled; the mass of the peasants melted into the surrounding countryside and the demonstration was killed before it had properly begun.

More than fifty peasants were injured, fifteen of them so seriously that they had to be carried home by their fellows. The police arrested sixty-eight of the 'leaders'. These were later charged with 'incitement to riot' and 'resisting the police'.[1] Many others who had taken part fled from the district to take refuge with relatives in Shikoku, Kyushu and Hokkaido, for it was rumoured that all able-bodied young men known to have connections with the anti-pollution movement would be jailed.

By mid-twentieth century standards the Kawamata Incident (as it came to be called, from the name of the ferry crossing where the fighting took place) may not seem very serious. No one, after all, was killed. Nevertheless the Japanese Press, to its credit, was almost unanimous in its condemnation of the government and police for their violent suppression of the demonstration, which they claimed would never have happened if the government had not failed in its duty.[2]

Once again, for a few days Shozo had the backing of the most influential organs of public opinion. Of this he took full advantage, in two of the most moving speeches he ever made. In the first, on the day after the break-up of the demonstration, the burden of his charge was that officialdom was 'killing innocent citizens, first with poison, then with police'.[3] But much of the speech was taken up with repeated

---

1. The trial of these men, with appeals by both sides, dragged on for 2½ years. In the end they were all acquitted, but not till most had already spent substantial periods in prison.

One of the most notable defendants was the young peasant Nagashima Yohachi, whose life was affected in more ways than one by the trial. To help while away the time in prison, he asked his father to send him a Bible, which he had never before found time to read; and as a result became an enthusiastic Christian. One of his jailers followed suit — and so did the judge presiding over the trial, as a result of having to read (in his capacity as censor of the prisoners' mail) the letters Nagashima wrote to his family extolling his new faith. The judge was baptised with Nagashima on the latter's eventual acquittal. Nagashima later became a Christian minister, serving most of his life in a town not far from Unryuji; and wrote a 600-page history of the whole Ashio affair, including eye-witness accounts of many of the most dramatic incidents.

2 One paper, the *Manchoho*, even suggested somewhat unrealistically that the only just solution at this late stage would be to hand the mine over to the pollution victims themselves to manage or close, as they thought fit.

3 As was pointed out earlier, no one was in fact killed in the battle with the police. The exaggeration here is partly an emotional heightening of language that is quite acceptable in Japanese. But it reflects too a mood of disillusion so acute as to border on hysteria, a mood still more in evidence in the second speech three days later. By those too blind to see the grounds of Shozo's outburst, it was indeed taken as hysteria and nothing else.

appeals to his hearers to believe in his sincerity — to accept that his pleas for help for the peasants were made for their sake and not for his own. The Home Minister, he said, had accused him at a private meeting of having personally instigated the demonstration of September 1898, simply in order that he could win headlines for himself by stopping it before it reached Tokyo. If the country's leaders had the slightest insight into the truth of the situation of the Shimotsuke plain, they would have known long since that the peasant communities were so parochial in their outlook, so resistant to *any* attempt to band them together in whatever cause, that no demagogue, however inspired or energetic, could hope to lead them if they had not first been goaded into action by misery. But to *prove* his disinterestedness, and thus, he hoped, to prevent any suspicion of his own motives from inhibiting sympathy in the Diet for the pollution victims, he announced his immediate resignation from the Constitutional Party. If after this he were still to be accused of using the pollution issue for his own ends, he would not hesitate, he said, to resign from the Diet itself.

Shozo may seem to have been exaggerating the probable effect of one man's resignation from a party which was not in government and had little influence on policy. But his action carried more weight than might at first appear. From a conventional point of view, it was a real sacrifice: much less than in most western parliaments could any politician on his own, apart from the power cliques of which the opposition consisted, hope for recognition or advancement. In terms of the lofty hopes which Shozo had invested in the development of the party system when he first entered politics, the sacrifice was far greater.

Yet it is also true — and the fact is evidence, if it is needed, that he was capable of acute political insight as well as crusading zeal — that he had long seen quite clearly the central weakness of political parties as they existed in Japan. In a letter dating as far back as 1882 he had noted that it was the 'adulation of personalities' that held parties together rather than any common set of principles. After witnessing party impotence at close quarters for so many years, it may not have been so difficult, therefore, for him to relinquish the party connection, particularly since he was now nearly sixty, and immune to the claims of political ambition or social dignity. Above all, he was so obsessed by the pollution tragedy, and more specifically by the need to fulfil in some meaningful way the promise he had made to the demonstrators in the shrine grounds at Fuchie sixteen months before, that every other issue receded into unimportance.

The journalist Kinoshita Naoe, who met Shozo for the first time this same month and later became one of his greatest admirers — and his posthumous biographer — recalls the alternation in him of this almost fanatical preoccupation with pollution with times of simple human warmth and a deep serenity. (It was Kinoshita's vivid reports from Shimotsuke, which began to appear soon after the abortive demonstration of 13 February, that gave the reading public their first comprehensive and systematic account of the extent of the pollution disaster.[1]):

'Our offices [Kinoshita worked for the *Yokohama Mainichi* newspaper] were in a red brick building of the early Meiji style, impressive enough outside, but startlingly primitive once you stepped through the door. A stairway, very narrow and almost vertical, with a ceiling halfway up so low you could hardly squeeze past: the crow's passage, we called it. People would clump up and down the wooden stairs in shoes, or even in clogs, on their way to the editorial office or the typesetting room. In wet or snowy weather they left a trail of mud.

Nomura told me Mr Tanaka wanted to see me. I went from the editorial office to the visitors' room, where he was waiting. It was a bare, cold room. A long gas pipe hung from the ceiling, providing the only light. Four or five wooden chairs, with a brazier for heating, were arranged round a big table of zelkova-wood. Dark patches on the cheap white paper that had been stuck over the ceiling showed where the rain came in.

There he was — an old countryman, elbows resting on the table, hands on his head; so deep in thought, he might have been asleep. I apologized for keeping him waiting. He looked up at once, as if out of a dream. A massive, round face, puffy and rather pale, with the muscles sagging.

When I said who I was, he bowed till his head touched the table, and introduced himself with extraordinary politeness. Then he took a bunch of newspaper cuttings out of his cloth wrapper. 'Afraid I've been so busy, I've hardly had time to look at them,' he murmured, as if to himself. How tired in mind and body he must have been, the depth of the lines on his forehead showed. He was so grateful, he said, for my articles on the ineffectiveness of the preventative works at Ashio, especially the smoke-purification chimneys, which looked so impressive but in practice were almost totally useless. In fact I had done little more than copy figures from tests made by the mine itself; but for Tanaka, who had gone on insisting that the mine should be closed even after the Pollution Prevention Order, when everybody — Government and Diet and public opinion alike — was assuming the problem had ceased to exist, even that must have provided precious ammunition for his cause.

Now and then, seemingly forgetting what he was saying, he would

---

1. Kinoshita also visited Ashio, where he was appalled by the complacency of the management. When he suggested that the sediment basins were obviously far too small for the function they were expected to fulfil, a senior official of the mine merely laughed, and said the terrain made any improvement impossible.

shut his eyes, and shake his head, saying with a frown, 'Something wrong with my head . . .' After we'd talked for a while he got up abruptly, tied up his cloth wrapper, and left, his feet unsteady beneath his heavy frame. I stood at the head of the stairs, watching him make his way slowly down through the crow's passage, his left hand gripping the rail, and the skirt of his coat flopping over each step.

After this first call, he often came to see me at home . . . at night mostly, after I'd come back from the office. Whenever we talked about pollution, he would get so extraordinarily tense and excitable, I hardly knew how to deal with him. But once off that subject, he seemed to move in a different world altogether, as if he had come up out of the dark depths of a valley on to a high plateau, bright with sunlight. The *breadth* of the man's mind and heart, the warmth of his affection, the living wisdom his spirit had culled from his long years of travelling in the borderlands of life and death, and the freshness of the words in which it found expression!

When he called, he would stay a long while. Time seemed to have no meaning for him. He would sit quite motionless, with eyes and mouth closed; tranquil, serene . . .'

Shozo's question to the Prime Minister on 17 February, the occasion for his next speech, was couched in unusual terms. It read as follows:

> *To kill the people is to kill the nation.*
> *To despise the law is to despise the nation.*
> *This is the end of the nation.*
> *If its resources are abused, its people killed, and its*
> *laws overturned, no country can survive.*
> *What will the government do about it?*

The speech itself was in part a passionate attempt to swim against the tide of Meiji progress and prosperity. Shozo was well aware of its apparent perversity. Knowing it would seem over-emotional if not unintelligible to many, he began by asking the Diet's pardon in advance — but begged Dietmen to keep their strictures till they had heard him out. A country whose government behaved as had the Japanese government over pollution, he declared, had no government: the administration had lost all authority to govern. If this was not realised, that was proof that 'ruin' had already arrived, that the country was already 'dead'. Nor were only Ministers to blame. But for the short-sightedness and lethargy of the people of Shimotsuke and of all the Kanto plain, the disaster would never have been allowed to develop on such a scale. An Osaka man (Furukawa) poisoned the soil; the bureaucrats of Satsuma and Choshu (the feudal clans that had dominated the government since the Meiji Restoration) pocketed their share of the mine's proceeds; the people of the plains, for the most part, suffered in silence..If the whole nation was not shocked by pollution, the reason could only be that by now

Unryuji Temple as it was at the time of the demonstrations.
(It now has a tiled roof.)

the whole nation was somehow polluted, blinded by infection to the truth.

As for the smashing of the demonstration at Kawamata, why did not the government arrest *him* for 'inciting to riot', if that was the charge they were bringing against the peasant leaders? He had spoken scores of times at meetings, urging the victims to claim their rights as citizens; and that, 'as was plain to any fool', was surely incitement . . . Let them arrest him at his Tokyo inn, or in the Diet building, if they chose; he would go quietly any time. Finally, in broken, emotional phrases, Shozo pleaded once more for *something* to be done even now, though he had little hope, since for nine years Prime Minister after Prime Minister, whatever his ability or authority, had lacked the courage to act decisively.

Naive and incoherent at times though the speech may have been, its message was clear. But Shozo's pessimism was well-grounded. On 21 February Yamagata gave a written reply, which must rank as a classic of lordly bureaucratic indifference.

The point of the question is not understood. No reply, therefore, is made.

Signed

Yamagata Aritomo, Marquis

Two days later Shozo submitted another question, under twenty-two headings. But since the Diet session was to end next day, he could make no speech this time, and confined himself to reminding Dietmen that if Ministers were incapable of seeing where the true interest of the nation lay, they were not the loftiest in the land: above them there was still the Emperor. How seriously he meant these words to be taken was not to appear till more than a year later. For the moment, no one paid him much attention, and his question remained unanswered.

Very soon afterwards, as if in deliberate challenge to Shozo's confidence in the Emperor as a final impartial court of appeal, Furukawa Ichibei, who had already been officially honoured during the Sino-Japanese War, was awarded a court rank for his services to the nation.

*   *   *

But Shozo's faith in the Emperor remained unimpaired. In his diary he notes that it was through no fault of its own that the monarchy was not fulfilling its proper function:

Our people's loyalty to their Emperor has no parallel throughout the world. But our rulers use this loyalty, as they use the whole polity of the nation — to serve their own power, and to hold down the ordinary folk . . . The Restoration was carried out in the Emperor's name; but now evil subjects block the Way, and that Name is misused.

Indeed, they use it now to destroy our nation, to kill our people . . .

He writes too of many other failings of Japanese society: subservience to officials, the weakness of the judiciary when the executive was so unresponsive to popular feeling, ignorance of the Constitution, a feverish preoccupation with money-making. But above all he was concerned with his own failure to influence events, when the only result of all his efforts seemed to be that sixty-eight innocent men had been dragged before a court of law:

By giving the evil ones the means to do their evil, I am guilty of a crime against society. Not only have I done nothing for the pollution victims, I've stirred up a nest of devils . . .

A poem, often repeated in later years with slight alterations, provides a wry self-portrait:

> *Beaten, buffeted*
> *By the rain and the wind,*
> *An ox drags his load*
> *Past, and is gone —*
> *Leaving only*
> *Wheeltracks in mud*
> *And the sadness of things.*[1]

At times he was tempted to give up:

> *So tired.*
> *What greater delight*
> *Than to lie down*
> *As if for a lunchtime nap*
> *And die.*

That he felt death might be near, either because of his recurring exhaustion or because of the 'direct action' he was probably already contemplating,[2] may be implied by a strange and beautiful letter to his wife dated 26 February, 1900. Since his first election to the Diet and subsequent absorption in the pollution struggle, they had been husband and wife only in name; even on the rare occasions he happened to pass through Konaka on business, he would as often as not merely pause at the entrance to the family house and shout a greeting to her before passing on. Once indeed, as he ruefully told a friend, when he had wanted to send her a postcard from Tokyo, he had even forgotten her name to put in the address. But now he was

---

1. If Shozo saw himself as the stubborn ox, heavy, unlovely, but with an infinite capacity for perseverance, he had another image for the modernizing intelligentsia of the capital. A poem headed 'My view of "civilisation"' reads:
> Leaping this way,
> Leaping that way,
> Needing only one jump
> To stand on their heads —
> They take lessons
> From the rabbits.

2. See below, Chapter X.

suddenly anxious to acknowledge the debt he owed her:

I am profoundly grateful for the way you took care of everything when my father died nine years ago and I myself could be of so little use. After serving him devotedly for so many years, you sat at his bedside and looked after him to the last; and arranged the funeral too, so perfectly. Indeed, you took my place in every way, and were a true daughter to him. Since then, I have been no more helpful than before. Thank you for managing the house in my absence, and for holding the proper services for my ancestors all these years. I humbly ask you to do the same in the future.

But whatever his health or long-term plans, for the moment the plight of the arrested demonstrators demanded his attention. Some of the sixty-eight had been arrested on the spot at Kawamata; others escaped, and were rounded up at their homes. A tiny poem in haiku-form records his compassionate sense of their helplessness before their captors, and also his own responsibility for their fate:

    In the deep mist
    Over the fields they go,
    The prisoners.[1]

And whatever the knocks, to remain despondent for any length of time was not in Shozo's temperament. Another poem shows him humbled but determined to go his own way still:

    All the world
    Consists of the clever
    And the fools.
    I alone grope forward,
    Blind, by the pale light
    Of my faint lantern.

By late March 1900, at all events, he was busy visiting the homes of those arrested, addressing huge meetings in Shimotsuke and going from lawyer to lawyer in Tokyo to beg help in defending the peasants when they should be brought to trial. In this last he was singularly successful. As the court case dragged on — it was two and a half years before it was finally settled — over a hundred lawyers participated in

---

1. By an ideographic pun, 'Over the fields' could also mean 'By way of (= because of) Tanaka'. Shozo had never led the demonstrators in person, as from a modern point of view one would doubtless expect him to have done. His sense of the dignity of a member of the Diet, and the persisting influence on him of the village-headman tradition, according to which the protector of the peasants fought on their behalf but not *with* them, still kept him from such direct participation. Conversely, his sense of responsibility for those whose cause he had undertaken to champion remained acute, particularly since the assurance he had given to the demonstrators in September 1898. As recently as September 1899, five months before the final demonstration, he had told a meeting at Unryuji Temple (according to a report made by a police officer who was present) that as far as pollution was concerned, Japan no longer possessed a government or a Constitution; to achieve relief, 'they had no choice but to act on their own, depending on no one but themselves'. They had so acted; and the result had been the fiasco at Kawamata. Once again, it must have seemed to Shozo, he had failed them.

the defence, many without a fee.[1]

Indeed, as often happens in such cases, the arrests seemed to have generated more sympathy for the pollution victims than had any of the earlier demonstrations and petitions to Ministers. This sympathy was deepened by Kinoshita Naoe's series of newspaper reports from Shimotsuke. It bore fruit in the setting up in September 1900, by a group of prominent Dietmen, journalists, lawyers and others, including one nobleman, of a new 'Pollution Group', calling for the purification of the Watarase, compensation for pollution victims, and the closing of the mine. The Group set to work at once to commission new analyses of water and soil, which confirmed the continued presence of large quantities of poison, including arsenic; a conclusion reaffirmed in other studies ordered by the court trying the Kawamata defendants.

Ripples from the Pollution Group's concern spread to many other parts of the country, culminating in the presentation to both Houses of the Diet in February, 1902 of a petition from 'Young Men's Pollution Groups' in Osaka, Kyoto, Gifu, and many other centres, for relief to Shimotsuke.

Shozo does not seem to have been greatly impressed, however, by these developments. No doubt they reminded him too closely of the short-lived outburst of public concern in 1897 that had led to the Pollution Prevention Order, and indirectly to its insidious sequel, the illusion that pollution had been banished. Near the end of 1900 his exasperation with the dismal years of official callousness found symbolic expression in an incident that in other circumstances would have been comic.

On 7 December, in court as usual for the trial of the Kawamata defendants, he stretched his arms ostentatiously and yawned aloud while the judge was speaking.[2] Instantly he was charged with 'behaviour insulting to an official'. This case too dragged, on through conviction, appeal, counter-appeal, to final re-conviction in June 1902.[3]

The fifteenth Diet met in January 1901. In the first week of February three Dietmen tabled a question to the government on

---

1. This is the first recorded case in which Japanese lawyers gave their services free to the defendants. It must have cost them a considerable amount of time and money, since they were all Tokyo-based, and the hearings were held in the provincial court at Maebashi, in Gunma Prefecture.
   The law itself came out of the affair well, in a curious way. The charge of riotous assembly (which carried penalties of 6-11 years of imprisonment) was thrown out. Two defendants were fined ¥5 for infringing the law on political meetings; one, a smaller sum for 'insulting a policeman'. An appeal by the prosecution was quashed on a technicality — the prosecutor had not signed the appeal document *in person*, as the regulations required.

2. Thus far an eyewitness, one of the accused. Another account, by one who may or may not have been present, says that he shouted to the judge, somewhat in the manner of a Western revolutionary of the 1970's, 'How *can* you, as a *man*, talk such nonsense!'

3 See below, p. 140

behalf of the Pollution Group, asking why no action had been taken on a vote of the previous Diet demanding an official survey of pollution damage with a view to setting up a relief programme. The government took no notice. Three weeks later, the same question was put by five other Dietmen, led by Shimada Saburo, editor of the *Yokohama Mainichi* newspaper, with a curt reminder to the government that for ten years, thanks to its indifference, the pollution of Shimotsuke had steadily worsened.

On 18 March the government finally offered its bland reply: relief (by which was meant, presumably, the minimal and grudging remission of tax on poisoned land) was already being given; the situation was under constant study, and the government saw no need to set up any further enquiry.

To these evasions Shozo reacted with something of his old fire. In a speech on 22 March he ridiculed the notion that when the facts had been known for nearly ten years any further 'study' was needed. That the whole tragedy could have been avoided if the government had had the will to stand up to Furukawa was proved by what had happened at a small copper mine in Shizuoka Prefecture, where local protest against a modest amount of pollution had prompted the government to use its powers and order the instant closure of the mine — the only difference between this case and that of Ashio being that the Shizuoka mine was small and its owner heavily in debt, while Furukawa was wealthy and had close connections with Ministers.

Furukawa, for his part, could have found other, if more expensive, ways of disposing of his waste: the enlightened management of a mine in West Japan were dumping theirs far out at sea, so as to avoid pollution not merely around the mine itself but in the offshore waters on which so many fishing villages depended for their livelihood. As it was, greed, contempt for the peasantry, and a false conception of the 'national interest' had led to injustice, hypocrisy, even to farce. Ministers claimed they were giving 'relief' by remitting taxes on land, the continued poisoning of which they still permitted; they accused of 'violence' peasants whom their own neglect and police harassment had goaded to desperation; and what could be more farcical than to sell off at a nominal price to Furukawa more mountain forests for him to fell as fuel and pit-props, as the government had recently been doing, while at the same time budgeting six million yen for dredging rivers in Tochigi and Gunma Prefectures whose silting up was directly due to Furukawa's mountain tree-felling?

Worst of all were the social consequences, to which the government still seemed blind, of both its support for the mine and its 'relief' measures — the virtual destruction of many formerly thriving and populous villages as viable, self-respecting communities. The collapse of incomes and land values in the polluted areas had led to the paralysis of all kinds of communally-supported activities, including education; remission of taxes had brought with it loss of voting rights, so that those worst affected had lost even the meagre representation in the Diet the electoral system adopted in 1889 had granted them. If the government continued to act — in effect — on Furukawa's behalf, Shozo declared, it was quite literally bestowing on the people the right to revolt. After this challenge, he concluded on a quieter note. Prince Ito, the Prime Minister, was getting on in years like himself; let such a distinguished statesman show the wisdom of age by refusing to endorse, even at this late stage, his predecessors' folly . . .

The plea fell on deaf ears. But this time, contrary to its practice hitherto, the government lost no time in reacting. A bizarre scene remained to be played, however, before its official reply was to be published.

On 23 March, the day following his speech, Shozo suddenly rose to his feet again. The House of Representatives was well used to harangues from the squat, almost grotesque figure with the black topknot and unkempt white beard, in the shabby black kimono he seemed to have worn all through his ten years in the Diet. Today, however, even before he began to speak he was crimson, all but speechless with anger — 'like a boiled octopus', wrote a reporter in the *Asahi* newspaper next day. Shozo claimed to have seen that morning, in the office of a secretary at the Ministry of Agriculture, a draft reply to his earlier speech, alleging among other things that contrary to all independent scientific reports, fish stocks in the Watarase river had *not* been depleted by pollution. Such a document, Shozo exploded, could only have been dictated by Furukawa agents. 'If the government was to be run by traitors who could decorate Furukawa while allowing him to ravage the fields that gave the nation its very life . . .' He was cut off in mid-sentence by a chorus of demands for his ejection from the Chamber, the word 'traitor' as a deliberate description of the Imperial Government being too much even for the otherwise far from submissive Diet.

When the Speaker put it to the House whether he should allow Shozo to speak, few raised their hands in his favour, and he was first ordered to resume his seat, and then, as he protested, escorted from the Chamber; but not before he had shouted that now he *knew* that traitors were indeed in charge, 'a decision would have to be taken' — words that seemed at the time merely a meaningless threat uttered in the heat of the moment, but which in the light of what was to take place ten months later suggest once again that he was already contemplating one final dramatic gesture on behalf of the peasants.

Later that day the government published its 'reply' to Shozo's speech of the 23rd. If it was very different from the draft Shozo had seen, it managed to outdo even Yamagata's laconic snub of a year earlier in its curt dismissal of all Shozo's pleading:

The question is not recognized as a question, so no answer is given.

Next day, the last full day of the Diet session — the Diet would not meet again for many months — Shozo was permitted to address the House again. His speech was short. In places it was scarcely coherent, and he apologised to MPs that an attack of his 'brain sickness' prevented him from deploying his arguments as clearly as he could have wished.

Ranging at first beyond pollution, he denounced the government's annual tax increases, which were only accepted because of the docility of the Japanese and which were anyway quite unnecessary. Huge resources could be released by applying a little commonsense to politics — by reducing the period of conscription, or by putting an end to the expensive plans for colonizing Hokkaido — or by abolishing the Ministry of Agriculture, which had become nothing but a 'club of criminals in the pay of Furukawa': and if that was strong language, he challenged members to stand up and prove that the substance of his case was wrong. Hardly able to continue — he felt he was on the verge of collapse, he told them — 'as no doubt you can see from my face' — there was yet one more thing he must say. For him the Constitution had always been an object of reverence. Yet when he had complained that rights enshrined in the Constitution were being trampled on, he had been told, 'Look, we have the Diet — that proves the Constitution is in full working order'. What was he to make of that, if a government could bring criminal charges against peasants who were only claiming their rights under that same Constitution?

The conclusion was inescapable: without a proper moral spirit in its guardians, and with 'a pack of hobgoblins' (in Shozo's country phrase) ensconced in the Home and Agriculture Ministries, even their beloved Constitution was worthless. All the governments he had witnessed had shown the same contempt for morality and for the people. 'All governments,' he ended, 'that for narrow selfish purposes ignore the Constitution must be resisted, so long as we have life in us . . . Gentlemen, if I have taken it on myself to address you, though many other matters claim your attention, it is because none of us knows what tomorrow will bring.'

These cryptic and apparently rather bathetic words, with which he had begun his speech as well as ended it (and which would come later to be seen as more than just the banal musings of a sick man) were the last that Shozo spoke in the nation's legislature. Next morning, just before the session ended, he tabled a final question, 'On the neglect of the Constitution', but it was not called. In October of the same year, 1901, he formally submitted his resignation from the Diet. But even then it was not till two months later that he took the last and boldest step of protest.

10

Appeal to the Highest

After a spell in hospital immediately following the end of the Diet session, Shozo resumed the task of coordinating the defence of the Kawamata demonstrators. The doctors at the Juntendo Hospital had been puzzled at his illness, as it seemed to have no obvious cause. An enigmatic letter of Shozo's, dated 11 May, may provide a clue, revealing as it does a depth of sensitivity that would have amazed those (and they were many) who still saw him as a pugnacious, loud-voiced demagogue. He links his 'sickness' with his feeling for his country's ills:

I've been running around on behalf of the Kawamata defendants, night and day, and on other pollution business and in trouble night and day, too, from my 'brain sickness' — a nameless, elusive thing, this sickness. It has nothing to do with physical wellbeing. Fortunately I am well, at the moment, in a physical sense, but my mind is worse than ever . . . the doctors can't make it out. In short, it saps my memory, patience, ability to think: terrible, the worst sickness you could think of. The spirit *isn't affected, though; sincerity, frankness, short temper, anger — I'm still capable of all these. Less pleasure, more pain. The pain isn't for myself, though. It's for the evil that has attacked our society. It's so hard to fight, and people don't* realise *how evil it is, either in the country or here in Tokyo. It's this that's eating my life away. I'm a sensitive fellow, you know; no hero. I feel the world's ills before the world feels them, that's all. Whatever you do, please don't think it's worry about being poor or anything of that sort that's made me ill . . . My sickness isn't an individual thing: it's the world's sickness. If society recovers, I'll live another ten years. If it can't save the Shimotsuke people from death, this year'll be my last . . . Remember this prophecy!*

In part, at least, the prophecy was fulfilled. Shozo was to live just twelve more years; and though society certainly did not 'recover' — indeed from his point of view the evil only deepened — a steady growth throughout the summer and autumn of 1901 in public understanding of the gravity of the pollution problem and in sympathy for its victims did result in the first serious attempts being made to relieve some at least of their distress.

The publicity given in the Tokyo Press to the trial of the Kawamata demonstrators was one reason for the increased interest. The judge in charge of the case ordered a technical investigation into the extent of copper poisoning of soil, crops and other plant life; three agricultural scientists, accompanied by numerous journalists, spent a week in Shimotsuke collecting and analysing samples, and the results thus obtained, which were widely reported, confirmed yet again the truth of the picture Shozo had painted so often in the Diet. The Christian leader and publicist of samurai origin, Uchimura Kanzo, toured the polluted areas and sent back reports expressing, in his own brand of the rhetoric typical of the day, his indignation at what he saw:[1]

'I have visited the homes of the sufferers, and seen 'despair' graven on their foreheads . . . My imagination ran straightway to the mansion of Furukawa Ichibei: I thought of his wealth, increasing day by day, of his intimacy with the nobles and merchant princes of our land, of his great power . . . Must tens of thousands starve, that one man may strut in glory? Is 'the survival of the strongest' really the 'Way of Man'? Is this what the new civilization means? Was it for this that Imperial Rule was restored? Thus I thought, and when I raised my head from these reflections, the Nikko mountains had hidden their peaks in mist, as if they shared my grief.

How can we help these people, sunk in such deep distress? Shall we urge their need upon the government? Plead their case before society with our pens? Or pray to Heaven on our knees? For seven long years the government has had no ear for the sufferers' cries for relief — what profit, therefore, in pressing their case in that quarter? Society, with no trace of sympathy for a part of itself that is withered and dying, hears but does not believe, or believes but fails to act. How then can we help these people? Is there no way but prayer? Are we only to show our sympathy in tears?

I say: men of religion! set aside a day, come and see for yourselves! You will find great profit to your faith. Novelists! ply your stick[2] upon the banks of the Watarase! You will find inspiration here, subject-matter for high tragedy. Poets! compare the poverty of our peasants with the wealth of our industrialists, and your verses will take on new life. Ashio pollution is a stain on the Japanese Empire. If we do not remove it, there is no glory or honour in all our Empire, for all its 13 infantry divisions and 260,000 tons of warships. Ashio concerns not just one province, but the whole nation, the whole human race. Indeed, it may destroy our nation . . . The eyes of the

---

1. Uchimura had taken an active part in earlier attempts to rouse public sympathy. That even he only now took the step of actually *visiting* the afflicted areas (which were only two hours by train from Tokyo) shows how remote the Tokyo intellectuals were from the problems of the rural areas.

2. The flaunting of a walking-stick being at this time a symbol of the 'progressive' intelligentsia.

Japanese are fixed now upon the west, upon the plains of Manchuria; our warships all head westwards. Do they not see that it is not in Manchuria but *here* that the enemy is to be found? Why not station the *Hatsuse* in Lake Chusenji, and send the *Asahi* up the River Watarase, to bombard the Ashio mine from both sides? That is what I would do, if I were made Prime Minister . . .'

Few if any novelists or poets heeded Uchimura's call. But the upsurge of public concern was unmistakable. Forty-two doctors submitted a petition to the House of Peers stressing the phenomenal increase in sickness in the polluted region; a group of over fifty lawyers followed suit.

It was left to Uchimura's 'men of religion', however, to organize material relief — though in fact it was women, not men, who took the initiative in what was to be the first manifestation on any scale of social conscience in modern Japan.

In November 1901 some Christian women formed the Association of Women for Pollution Relief, to collect clothes, money and medicines. One of their first meetings, held in a hall in the Kanda section of Tokyo on 29 November, had a strange sequel. Two days later, workmen laying an underground cable found in the Kanda River a body, which proved to be that of Furukawa Ichibei's wife. From evidence that emerged later it appeared that, worried about the press reports of Ashio pollution, she had sent a maid to the meeting on the 29th, and had been so overcome with shock on hearing from this girl her account of the speakers' descriptions of the sufferings for which her husband was ultimately responsible, that she had walked out of the house that night and thrown herself into the river from Kanda Bridge.[1]

A number of Japan's early socialists (of whom there were as yet very few — the first Japanese 'Social Democratic Party' was founded by a handful of intellectuals on 21 November, 1901) joined the women in

---

1. Another source suggests a slightly different but no less dramatic explanation. According to this account, Mrs. Furukawa's suicide was precipitated by hearing a company of elderly peasant women from a polluted village chanting outside her gate for several hours the *nenbutsu* (Namu Amida Butsu — Hail to the Lord Buddha), an invocation commonly repeated in times of distress or disaster. In any case the peculiar circumstances of her death make it highly probable that it was the revelations of what the mine had done to the peasants of Shimotsuke that led her to take her life — though she also had plenty to complain of in her husband's private life, which was the subject of adverse comment in some Buddhist journals at the time.

A pleasanter incident illustrates the immediacy of the response in other quarters to the Association's campaign. When a speaker appealed for gifts of clothing, a student named Kawakami Hajime (who later became a noted economist) instantly took off his coat and handed it in. On returning to his lodgings he packed all the clothing he possessed — mostly student uniform — apart from what he was wearing, and sent it by rickshaw to the Association's address. The idea of such charity being quite new, the ladies were worried — how could a poor student afford to part with so many precious clothes, and at the beginning of winter, of all times? The gift was anonymous; but fortunately a visiting-card of Kawakami's was found in one of the pockets, and the President of the Association hurried round to his lodgings to find out 'whether he was really mad', as all the good ladies thought, and to return the clothes if necessary. The landlady was able to reassure her, however, that Kawakami was 'sane, if a little impetuous'; and his clothes were duly sent on their way to the pollution victims.

the work of relief. Buddhists formed their own relief association some weeks later. Christianity remained the dominant force in the relief movement, however, even among the socialists, whose inspiration was visionary and religious as much as political. Six ladies from the Association who toured Shimotsuke to assess the kind of relief needed were amazed to find how ignorant they had been of the devastating effects of pollution on individual, family and community life.

For eight years Shozo had been repeating the story; but in a country traditionally 'compartmentalized', where inhabitants of one district took little interest in what went on beyond their local boundaries, in a real sense only seeing for oneself could engender belief. The six ladies' many detailed reports (they were written up by one of their number, an experienced journalist, for the *Yokohama Mainichi* newspaper) including interviews with individual peasants, admirably complemented Uchimura Kanzo's moving but more generalised articles. Published very soon afterwards in book form, with sketches of deformed crops and of the distressed conditions in which many of the victims were now living, they were distributed to all members of the Diet, and were widely read. A typical extract:

'We then interviewed Moro Sakuzo (aged 58) and his wife Saki (50), who live at 37 Takayama with their daughters Saku (24) and Kiyo (10).

"We used to be quite comfortable, as farming folk go," said Mrs. Moro, "but since the poison came we've had no harvest, no money coming in, and what with the poison and all the worry, my eyes have gone. I can see a little with one — not enough to make out the stripes on my own kimono, though. I was born in this house. Sakuzo, my husband, was adopted into my family when we married. We had lots of land then, and buildings too, but we've had to sell everything. Ever since the bad floods started, ten years back, eye-sickness has spread in these parts, till now there's hardly a soul in the village has the proper use of his eyes . . . If only I could see — but as it is, there's nothing I can do, nothing. I can just see enough to cook the rice, but no sewing: I can't touch my needle any more. My husband grumbles all the time. I'm no use, he says, now I can't see, so he has to go out to find bits of work, or we can't eat, though as he says, he's past the age for it . . ."

Tears gathered in her unseeing eyes. We had nothing to give her, only a bit of cloth and an apron. With hands that trembled she raised them to her forehead, and bowed to us again and again, murmuring that she didn't deserve such generosity . . .'

Largely as a result of the activities of the ladies of the Association, words like 'social justice', 'atonement' and 'humanism', hitherto little used by speakers or writers on pollution, began to gain currency. Gradually, but with increasing effectiveness, the relief movement got under way.

In this movement the government took no part.

* * *

During the summer and autumn of 1901, apart from continuing to help with the defence of the Kawamata demonstrators, Shozo busied himself with showing Tokyo journalists round the polluted areas and with campaigning as usual for the closure of the Ashio mine, though in some districts the severity of the police at Kawamata had cowed the peasants into refusing him their support. November, after his resignation from the Diet, saw him involved in the work of the women's Association, addressing their meetings and helping them to set up operations in the field. Then there followed, with apparent suddenness, the single-handed protest that put him once more — for a brief moment — at the centre of the national stage, and that was to accelerate, by its unforeseen outcome, the radical development of thought and action which would make his last decade the most original and least understood of his whole life.

On the morning of 10 December, 1901, the Emperor formally opened the sixteenth session of the Diet. Shortly after eleven o'clock his carriage, escorted by a posse of mounted police, left the Diet building to return to the palace. As the procession was passing the offices of the Speaker of the House of Representatives, near the Sakurada Gate, a squat figure in a black kimono, shoeless but wearing white-soled Japanese socks, detached itself from the crowd and rushed across the road in the direction of the imperial carriage, holding up a scroll and shouting 'Petition to the Emperor! Petition to the Emperor!' A policeman jerked his horse violently round, so that he could block Shozo's path with his lance; swerving to avoid him, Shozo stumbled and fell, causing both horse and rider to lose their balance and fall beside him. Other policemen surrounded them instantly; the imperial carriage proceeded on its way unimpeded. There was no indication that the Emperor had even noticed the brief disturbance.

A trivial non-incident, perhaps, viewed across the gulf of three-quarters of a century. Even in Meiji Japan, the *jikiso* or 'direct appeal' to the ruler was an anachronism, a curiosity of the vanished 'feudal' age. Yet that age had not receded far enough for the word *jikiso* to have lost all its aura of the daring, the spectacular, the revolutionary.

Every Japanese knew, and had once been thrilled by, the story of Sakura Sogoro, the village headman who in 1653 had thrust a petition into the Shogun's palanquin as a formal protest against the maladministration of some hundreds of villages by their feudal chieftain. The Shogun, to his credit, did order an investigation of the complaints, though under feudal law such a 'direct appeal' to the country's supreme authority was automatically punishable by death; but Sogoro's own lord was so furious at his subject's action that he had him decapitated together with his wife and all his children, of whom the youngest was only three. The martyrdom bore fruit, however. Thanks to Sogoro's sacrifice the injustices were put right, and Sogoro himself was deified in his native village.

It was not surprising, therefore, that by early afternoon newsboys in the streets of Tokyo were advertising a special Extra on 'Tanaka's Petition to the Emperor', and selling to eager buyers every copy they were given. And not in Tokyo alone. Two such 'Special Extras', reaching a village 400 miles away in the island of Shikoku that same day, and a handwritten account of Shozo's *jikiso* posted with an ink drawing of the incident on the village notice-board, made such an impression on an eleven-year-old schoolboy in the village that fifty years later he could still recall his feelings of frustration at not knowing enough ideographs to be able to read the full account.

Bathos followed. After being questioned at a nearby police-station, Shozo was released the following morning without any charge being preferred against him. The rumour spread, probably with official inspiration, that he was mad — a view which would conveniently defuse his action of any inflammatory potential and which was adopted in an editorial by one of the leading dailies. Once again officialdom had followed its old tactic of simply ignoring him. 'The question is not recognized as a question, and so no answer is given.'

Understandably, Shozo was angry and frustrated at his prompt release and the rumour of his madness. His action might have been misjudged — ironically, public discussion focussed on the question of the *propriety* of a 'direct appeal' to the semi-divine Emperor rather than on what Shozo was appealing *about*, the sufferings of a hundred thousand of the Emperor's subjects — but mad he certainly was not. The appeal had been meticulously planned. With good reason, in a period when *any* conduct that could be interpreted as 'disrespect' for the Emperor was regarded as close to treason, Shozo had fully expected the death penalty. Two days earlier he had posted to his wife Katsu a 'note of divorcement', for her to act upon if she wished, so that she need not be involved in the consequences of his action.[1]

Over the text of his appeal he took extreme care. Lacking confidence in his own ability to present the case about which he felt so passionately in the special reverential language that was required for any address to the Sovereign, for he wished not to give the smallest ground for offence, he needed help with its composition. Yet the plan depended entirely upon the greatest possible secrecy. A first draft, written by some unknown friend, Shozo apparently rejected.

---

1. Katsu must have been astonished to receive this document out of the blue, for as usual she knew nothing of her husband's plans. But she was not kept in ignorance long, since a few hours later on the same day the newspapers arrived with the report of Shozo's 'direct appeal'. Uncomplaining, as always, she took no steps to renounce her absentee husband.

Late on the evening of 9 December he called on the radical journalist Kotoku Shushui, who was well known for his prose style, told him what he wanted to say and asked him to draw it up in appropriate language. The task took Kotoku all night. Early next morning he delivered his final draft to the tiny down-at-heel inn where Shozo was staying and soon afterwards Shozo left to take up his position on the Emperor's route from the Diet to the palace.

Arriving too early, he found an empty waiting-room in the offices of the Speaker of the House of Representatives where he could read over Kotoku's text at leisure. Within the limits of the formal style, this was a model of clarity and concision, setting out very briefly the history of Shozo's campaign and humbly requesting the Emperor to ensure the rehabilitation of his poisoned lands, so that his subjects could once more enjoy the benefits of the Constitution he had so graciously bestowed upon them.

Surprisingly, however, Shozo made several corrections in his own hand. Trivial though most of them are in themselves, they nonetheless provide evidence of a quality that his detractors were fond of claiming he signally lacked — a scrupulous concern for truth of fact. Where Kotoku had written, for example, 'many thousands of Your subjects have lost the produce of their land, have had to abandon their occupations, and for lack of food and medicines have succumbed to starvation and disease', Shozo, heedless of the rhythm and rhetorical balance[1] over which Kotoku had taken such pains, carefully inserted in every clause after the first '*some* people' and 'in *some* districts'. Another alteration was even smaller, but of no less interest. In the closing sentence of the preamble, 'Your subject humbly begs that in Your Majesty's profound benevolence and compassion You will deign to look with pity upon the mad foolishness of your subject, the compiler of this petition', Shozo substituted 'exceeding' for 'mad'. At one level, perhaps, he was rebutting in advance the assumption that in modern Japan only a madman would go to such lengths as to petition the Sovereign in this sensational way — while readily accepting the charge of 'foolishness'. But in retrospect the tiny correction has other overtones, of which Shozo may at the time have been only dimly aware.

In a sense his career during the previous decade had been that of a 'madman' indeed, an archetypal Outsider battering the Establishment from within its own walls in language that to the

---

1. Which cannot, unfortunately, be reproduced in translation.

majority of his hearers was all but unintelligible.[1] But now he had left the Diet, and while his resignation was in itself a negative move, an implicit declaration of loss of faith in representative institutions, it also opened the way for new forms of action on behalf of those whose cause he championed.

The 'direct appeal' marked the beginning of Shozo's shift from 'madness' to 'foolishness', from 'agitation' in the established political world on behalf of the powerless and the have-nots to the much more demanding 'folly' of an attempt to identify his life totally with theirs. The change links him to a Japanese tradition represented by such figures as Shinran, the great saint and self-styled 'bald-pate fool' of the medieval period, or Ryokan, the 'democratic' priest, poet and philosopher of the late eighteenth and early nineteenth centuries.[2] A Western mind may perhaps see in him something of the Shakespearean Wise Fool [3] — though in outward appearance, at least, he looked to the end of his days more like a real-life Japanese Lear.

There remains the question of why he should have chosen to make his ultimate protest at this particular moment, when his efforts were already bearing some fruit in the growing volume and seriousness of public sympathy for the pollution victims. His critics dismissed his action as a stunt to squeeze the last ounce of publicity out of his colourful reputation as a dissident Dietman before it faded into limbo. In doing so they misunderstood him utterly.

What had driven him to take this step was that stubborn sense of responsibility that had marked him out as a boy — responsibility in this case to the pollution victims, and in particular to the peasant

---

1. There were, it should be said, many issues quite apart from pollution on which Shozo demonstrated his non-conformity. One such was when Hara Kei, the Deputy Foreign Minister of the day, in reply to a question in the Diet on the recent sinking of a Japanese merchant ship, remarked laconically that '20 or so seamen had died'. Satisfied, the questioner made no attempt to pursue the subject. Instantly there was a roar of 'Mr Speaker! Mr Speaker!' from Shozo, who angrily accused the Minister of revealing, by his vagueness as to the precise number of deaths, his contempt for the lives of his fellow-citizens — only to be ordered out of the Chamber for 'unruly conduct'. In such vehemence in such a cause, most of his Diet colleagues at the time could see only hypocritical demagoguery.

2 This 'placing' of Shozo in a specific and honoured Japanese tradition I owe to a specialist in Japanese literature, Professor Amano of Hiroshima; and I at least find it persuasive. The point has not been followed up, however, by other Japanese students of Shozo's life. The reason for this may be that in Shozo's case the 'traditional' aspect is obscured by the fact that Shozo based his life during these last years on no easily identifiable body of doctrine (e.g. Buddhism), only on a concept of integrity he had developed out of his own experience and found confirmed in what he knew of the classical statements of several religions; which made his ideas difficult to assess within the framework of customary Japanese thinking. This would explain why much less attention has been given in Japan (until very recently) to Shozo's post-Diet years than to the earlier period, when he 'fitted in' the political scene as an elected representative, albeit a recalcitrant one, and could therefore be more easily classified in terms of ordinary political orthodoxies.

It is interesting that the most distinguished of contemporary authorities on Shozo, Professor Hayashi Takeji of Sendai, is a lifelong student of Socrates, another 'outsider' to whom Shozo bears certain resemblances, despite the much more obvious differences.

3 The remaining chapters of this book will, I hope, provide some justification for this suggestion.

demonstrators to whom he had solemnly promised, in his speech at Fuchie in September 1898, that if the government paid no heed to their protest, he himself would 'march at their head to the capital, and die with them, if need be'. To Shozo, such an undertaking meant precisely what it said; and on this occasion, contrary to his usual habit, he is known to have kept a written record of his words.

Since then pollution had continued unchecked, a fifth demonstration had led only to police violence and arrests, and the government had taken no more notice of Shozo in the Diet than it had ever done. An appeal to the Emperor presented itself to Shozo as the only honourable way remaining of fulfilling his pledge. That it would cost him his life, he was all but certain, but his still untarnished reverence for the Emperor and absolute belief in the justice of his cause[1] prompted a hope that by his action the government might somehow be shamed into changing its attitude.

In the event, as we have seen, not merely did he not die, but he was not even charged, let alone punished in any way: though the Emperor was said to have been moved, remarking that Tanaka's only error was to have 'chosen the wrong place', most newspaper comment dilated predictably on his 'disrespect' for the Sovereign, with the final ironic result that all he achieved was what his detractors had accused him of seeking — publicity. On 18 December he wrote to his wife:

You will have heard, I suppose, of what took place on the 10th . . . Since then I have been keeping quiet — because I feel I must, not because anyone has told me to act so.

Shozo is no longer of this world. He should have died on the 10th. It was a mistake, an unavoidable mistake, that he survived . . .

But he was incapable of dwelling on the 'mistake' for long. A few lines later he is once again full of concern and counsel for others: the villagers must be urged to respond with sincerity to the generosity of the Tokyo ladies' Relief Association, Katsu herself must not walk too far if she is not feeling very well, but must do her best to pave the way for the relief work, and pray, as he did, that the peasants might live 'in peace and without jealousy, but mindful of their rights'; he himself was well enough, in better health than of late, though a constant

---

1. Time had not dulled the intensity of his feeling for the suffering of the peasants. One of his friends was present with him at a meeting with a number of lawyers working on the Kawamata case, two days before his 'direct appeal'. As a student was giving a report of the latest figures for the still rising death-rate in Shimotsuke, his friend noticed that Shozo was weeping. He was now sixty years of age.

throng of visitors[1] sometimes brought on his 'brain-sickness so she was not to worry. . . .'

If for a while he was 'no longer of this world', his return to it was not to be long delayed. Kinoshita Naoe recalls a day in February 1902 when Shozo acted as guide to him and two ladies of the Relief Association. After years as a Dietman, and therefore, inescapably, as one of the 'upper ones' in the eyes of the peasants, Shozo now moved among them for almost the first time as just a countryman like them, with no status and no automatic entitlement to their respect.

'We — Mrs Ushioda, who was 60, her secretary, Tanaka, and I —walked through one of the worst-polluted districts distributing food and clothing from a rickshaw. The sun was warm enough, but there had been a severe snowstorm the day before, and the snow came halfway up our legs as we plodded along the country tracks in our straw sandals. Tanaka, in his usual old black cotton kimono and divided skirt, was our guide — though even for him it was a new experience to talk to the peasants so intimately in their homes. . . .'

During the day they heard many stories of appalling hardship. Sometimes Mrs. Ushioda would stop in her tracks, close her eyes, and pray; as often, Shozo would explode with anger at the 'enemy' who was responsible for the misery they saw.[2]

'We stopped for the night at a little inn. Mrs. Ushioda and Miss Matsumoto went to bed at once, exhausted by the day's labours. In our tiny room, dimly-lit by a paper-covered lantern, Tanaka sat in meditation, upright and perfectly still. Such stillness; as of the Void itself, in the midst of this clamorous world. How long he sat thus I do not know. Suddenly he spoke, not to me but to himself: "While I played politics, the people died". The words rose calmly from his lips, like a thread of smoke on a windless day. The silence continued. Then he looked up, as if in surprise. "Still up, are you?" — glancing at me. And with that he rolled his great bulk over on to the bedding, pulled

---

1. One such visitor was Kurosawa Torizo, a sixteen-year-old schoolboy whose home was in Shimotsuke, who was so moved by the account of the 'direct appeal' he had read in a newspaper Extra on 10 December that he went to call on Shozo soon after he had been set free by the police. To his surprise, he found Shozo not at all the 'heroic rebel' he had imagined, but a 'pale, kindly old gentleman, amazingly polite to a sixteen-year old'. A few days later, on another visit, Kurosawa listened to a furious argument between Shozo, who was still adamant that the Ashio mine be closed, and the newspaper editor Shimada Saburo, who despite the steady sympathy for Shozo he had shown over the years maintained that compromise was inevitable if the country's industrialization was to continue. At the time Kurosawa thought that Shozo was in the wrong; but such was the magnetism of Shozo's personality that Kurosawa gave up his studies to work as his helper for four years. Later, as founder and president of Japan's leading dairy company in Hokkaido, he became a well-known public figure. In a lecture in Tokyo in 1968, he remarked that 50 years of experience in farming had taught him that it was Shozo, after all, who had got his priorities right in the argument with Shimada Saburo in 1902. The health of its natural environment was the basis of a nation's *whole* life, and if that truth were ignored the long-term price would be heavy indeed — a truth which polluted Japan is experiencing in the 1970s.

2 The suffering was not only physical. Worry, and no doubt the (to the peasant mind) inexplicable nature of the poisoning of their land and lives had driven numbers of Shimotsuke peasants, especially among the old, out of their minds.

the coverlet up to his chin, and fell asleep. I got into my own bed, but couldn't sleep; my mind was as clear as water.

'Whenever I think of Tanaka I remember that scene. The 'new life' of his last decade had its beginning, I can't help thinking, in that single sentence he spoke then.'

* * *

Public concern for the plight of the Shimotsuke peasants was still mounting as the year 1901 drew to a close. One of its most remarkable manifestations was a mass 'visit of sympathy' to the banks of the River Watarase by nearly 1,000 students from over thirty Tokyo schools and universities, who left Ueno Station in a special train at dawn on 27 December and returned late at night after seeing some of the worst-hit villages.[1] Though the idea for the visit had originated with the ladies of the Relief Association, it was organised by the students themselves; some Buddhist priests and a few journalists accompanied them, but hardly a single teacher.

Many were so appalled by what they saw that on returning to Tokyo they formed themselves into small groups to hold street meetings, reporting on the effects of pollution and appealing for money for the relief fund. These meetings continued day after day with remarkable dedication, in different parts of the capital, despite constant harassment by the police.

On 7 January notices were posted in schools to the effect that all visits to the Watarase region and all street speaking on behalf of the relief fund had been forbidden by the Governor of Tokyo as 'political and disruptive activities'. Undeterred, students of Tokyo Imperial University planned a further visit of their own for 27 January — with the open encouragement of the University's President, who told them he hoped that on their return they would call on government Ministers, to bring home to them the extent of the misery they had witnessed. But the Ministers themselves were less well disposed.

The evening before the projected trip, the Minister of Education sent for President Yamakawa, and ordered him to cancel it, issuing for good measure a ban on all group visits or campaigns whatsoever. When news of the ban was conveyed at six o'clock the next morning to the 250 students who had assembled at Ueno Station, they got round it with true student ingenuity by the simple device of paying the full instead of the student-rate group fare, which enabled them to declare

---

1. There had already been a few visits by smaller parties of students. Among the first to demonstrate their concern in this way were the members of a literary group at the Peers' High School. One of the group's leading members, Shiga Naoya (who later achieved fame as a novelist) was forbidden to go by his father. This father-son clash was an early stage in a bitter estrangement that lasted several years, and is now remembered as one of the classic incidents in the struggle by modern intellectuals for independence from the traditional authority of the family.

that they were travelling not as students but as 'private persons'.

But the Minister meant business, and since the students, however idealistic, had never seriously contemplated defying the authority of the government, their part in the relief movement came to an early end.[1] The Christian and Buddhist groups continued their efforts, which reached a peak in the spring of 1902; much food and clothing was distributed, and hundreds of patients treated in emergency clinics set up in villages where the need was greatest.[2]

At the same time, Shozo's attempted appeal to the Emperor injected new life into the peasant campaign against government indifference and against the mine. Shozo was now dividing his time between speaking at meetings in Tokyo in aid of the relief fund and touring the villages, exhorting them to continue the struggle in unity, but a number of factors combined to sap the strength of peasant protest.

Under Prime Minister Katsura, government horror of 'socialism' (in spite of the fact that the new doctrine was held only by a handful of journalists and other intellectuals, and then only in the vaguest form) led easily to the labelling of *any* protesters as socialists, and therefore almost by definition as 'traitors', by the police and other local officials; facing this charge, few peasants had the courage to follow Shozo's call to renewed resistance, particularly now that Shozo himself no longer carried the authority and prestige of a Dietman. Funds and energy were both lacking; only too easily local jealousies reasserted themselves. And then, abruptly, the government *did* something: on 17 March it set up an 'Ashio Mine Pollution

---

1. But not before it had cost one of them his life. Nakanishi Kensuke was a student of classical Chinese, who had already shown his independence by running away from home rather than go in for a business career as his father insisted. A young man of poor physique and health, he nevertheless took a leading part in the students' street meetings, speaking at all hours and in all weathers almost every day for eight weeks, till illness forced him to take to his bed at the end of February. A month later he was dead.

A diary, interspersed with poems in Chinese, that he kept of the student campaign reads curiously like an account of some of the similarly motivated activities of Western students of the 1960s. It tells of arguments with the police, an encounter with drunken hecklers and a protest from a downtown shopkeeper who feared that speechifying outside his shop would lose him business — and of much sympathy from the public. His account of the Imperial University students' visit to the Watarase includes a description of a meeting with a wealthy landlord in a polluted area who was widely believed to have been bribed by agents of Furukawa to help suppress agitation against the mine. Calling at his mansion, the students challenged him either to give part of his fortune to the relief fund or to go and share the life of the peasants; at which he 'turned pale, and made no reply'. The students offered him no violence, however, confining their protest to burning his visiting-card while one of their number shouted, with more passion than clarity, 'Thus we punish him, the vile animal with the human face. The red of this flame is the people's blood; the blue of this flame, the people's anger!'

1. Not surprisingly, since this was the first example of relief work undertaken by a voluntary body in Japan, the work was sometimes marred by the naivete of the well-to-do and the excessive religious zeal of some of the ladies of the Relief Association. The handing out of silk bedding to peasants in desperate need was greeted with resentment as well as gratitude; several of a number of children who were taken from Ebise, one of the worst-off villages, to be educated in a Christian charitable institution in Tokyo found the hymn-singing too much and made their own way home, preferring destitution in familiar surroundings to the alien atmosphere of the orphanage. But the contribution of the Tokyo well-wishers was substantial, particularly in the medical field. Nearly 5,000 patients were treated by volunteer doctors and nurses.

Investigation Committee' — exactly what its predecessor had done five pollution-filled years before. Ineptitude could hardly go further, one might think. But at least officialdom had shown interest, and the Shimotsuke villagers were still too prone to take the words of authority at their face value: so general support for Shozo's stand weakened still further.

In due course the recommendations of this Committee were to involve Shozo, now in his sixties, in the bitterest and most hopeless — yet in retrospect, perhaps the most significant — fight of his whole career. For the moment, however, his days followed a familiar pattern. Ill in hospital at the beginning of April, he left his bed to speak in honour of the dead student, Nakanishi Kensuke,[1] at a memorial meeting held by Nakanishi's friends and teachers; then back and forth between Shimotsuke and Tokyo, where his friend Shimada Saburo was forming an Association for the Solution of the Mine Pollution Problem, with commendable, if rather vague, objectives. Then came an interruption — 41 days in a Tokyo jail, the sentence for his 'behaviour insulting to an official',[2] all his appeals against which had finally been disallowed.

To Shozo the unsought rest was a godsend. His critics, however, were busy. Some, perhaps Furukawa-inspired, began to say that Tanaka was at last discredited, that he had only got what he deserved, for he had been 'living off' the peasant movement. Uchimura Kanzo stood up for him, writing in his newspaper column that Tanaka's imprisonment was 'the greatest tragedy of recent years'. Such voices were few, however. Another man might never have recovered from this latest in a long series of defeats. But Shozo was very far from finished yet.

---

1. See above, p. 139 n. 1.
2. See above, p. 124

11
New directions

As sympathetic citizens of Tokyo tried to alleviate some of the worst hardships, the central government's second Pollution Investigation Committee turned its attention belatedly to long-term remedial measures.

Very soon, however, nature intervened. In August and September of 1902 exceptionally heavy floods swept down the Watarase, covering much of the polluted area with up to five feet of water. Damage to buildings was heavy, but astonishingly these floods, unlike those of the previous decade, proved to be life-giving;[1] when they receded, they left behind a thin layer of rich new soil spread over the poisoned fields, recalling the pre-pollution inundations to which the region had owed so much of its traditional fertility. The water itself, miraculously, was poison-free. Slowly, plant and wild life began to recover, and with it, the agriculture of this once rich region. Autumn-planted crops bore a modest harvest next year, and by 1904 many fields had regained something approaching normal productivity.

The reversal was dramatic enough. But there could be no guarantee that it was final. The severity of the 1902 floods was the result of Furukawa's unrestricted felling of trees in mountain forests which the government had continued to sell him cheaply, and though the sediment basins constructed as a result of the Pollution Prevention Order of 1897 may have had some effect in limiting dangerous effluent, experience over the five years since the Order was not reassuring in that respect.

Early in December 1902 a group of intellectuals, led as already mentioned by Shimada Saburo, proposed a 'Solution to the Pollution Problem', the closest that 'reasonable men' ever came to Shozo's

---

1. The most likely explanation of this dramatic change is twofold. First, Furukawa's continued heavy tree-felling in the mountains had caused severe landslides (of unpolluted soil) near the source of the Watarase, and paradoxically the floods must have spread some of this new soil over parts of the Shimotsuke plain. Secondly, the record-breaking floods of 1902 swept out to sea a substantial part of the deposits of contaminated rock that had accumulated since the 1880s on the bed of the Watarase. Now the river itself was relatively clean, the anti-pollution measures imposed on Ashio by the government in 1897 must have had a much better chance of taking effect.

The River Watarase in flood

insistence on closure of the mine. They suggested the strictest prohibition of all tree-felling in the Ashio district, all necessary timber to be brought in from elsewhere; a huge replanting programme; decontamination of all water used in mine processes; and other measures to prevent the break-up in rain of the poisoned slag that had so frequently tumbled into the Watarase and cascaded downriver with the floodwater — the mine to be closed at once, and kept out of operation until all these measures had been carried out.

If the government had adopted these proposals, a long train of tragic events involving Shozo and many others might have been avoided, and in the end it would have saved itself huge sums of money. But as always, its links with the mine were too close for it to be able to contemplate such action. And as it happened, another 'solution', more tempting in that it would not involve bringing any pressure to bear on the mine, had already suggested itself to the Pollution Investigation Committee.[1]

This alternative was a grandiose plan to create a vast catch-basin or artificial lake at the south-eastern tip of the polluted area, which would supposedly drain off all floodwater from the Watarase. The plan was presented purely as a flood-prevention measure, with no mention of pollution — which was odd, to say the least, since it was with pollution that the Committee was by definition concerned. For this curious evasiveness there appear to have been two reasons: first, the official concern, dating back to feudal times, to prevent the Watarase floods reaching Tokyo via the connecting rivers Tone and Edo;[2] and second, a belief that (given the apparent beginnings of a return to normality after the floods of 1902) the pollution issue could be dealt with once and for all by ensuring that in the future any poisonous effluent would find its way to the projected lake instead of to the peasants' fields.

There was one snag in this otherwise neat scheme: it involved the submersion of the greater part of three large villages bordering the Watarase, Kawabe and Toshima in Saitama Prefecture and Yanaka in Tochigi Prefecture. In effect these communities, 50 miles downstream from Ashio, were to be sacrificed in order to create an enormous

1. The full story of the events the Committee set in motion is extremely complex, involving the central government, the mine, prefectural officials, and some unscrupulous Shimotsuke landowners in a complex network of negotiation and intrigue. The details are of little interest to the Western reader: I have included only what is necessary to set the scene for the next phase of Shozo's life.

2. Some floodwater — heavily polluted into the bargain — had in fact reached Tokyo in the floods of 1896. Unostentatiously the government had at once taken steps to complete certain flood control works begun by the feudal Tokugawa government. The effect of these works was to narrow the River Tone, below its junction with the Watarase, at a place called Sekiyado. This accentuated the 'backflow' of the Watarase floodwaters, and inflicted worse damage than ever before (while keeping the floods away from the capital) on the three villages of Kawabe, Toshima, and Yanaka — which in turn enabled the government to suggest, in the Committee's scheme for an artificial lake, that if *any* villages were to be sacrificed, these were the obvious choice, since they had been so severely ravaged by floods already . . .

sediment basin that would make up for the inadequacy of the small basins Furukawa had built in the vicinity of the mine.

The scheme was given little publicity at first. But already in the autumn of 1902 Kawabe and Toshima got wind of that part of it which would affect them. The two villages banded together from the first to resist the compulsory purchase and destruction of their ancestral lands, announcing that they would withhold military service and refuse to pay all taxes if the plan were carried any further. After 1000 villagers had mobbed the Saitama prefectural office, the Governor agreed, not merely to have nothing to do with the lake scheme, but to make a substantial prefectural contribution to the repair of flood damage in Kawabe and Toshima.

The result was that over the next few years both villages made a steady recovery, regaining most of their former prosperity. Yanaka fared otherwise. At first, indeed, there seemed a good chance that it too might escape. On 16 January, 1903, scarcely a week after the government's Pollution Committee had published its revised recommendation that since the flood damage in Yanaka was 'too severe to be repaired', this village alone should be the site of the new lake, the Governor of Tochigi tabled in the Prefectural Assembly a proposal for the necessary purchase of Yanaka Village: it was immediately thrown out.

Eleven months later, in December, a new Governor put it forward once again; once again a small group of determined opponents were able to secure its defeat. Still the plan was not abandoned. During 1904 pressure was brought to bear on individual Assemblymen, Furukawa influence being stronger in Tochigi than in the neighbouring prefectures. When the plan finally reared its head again, on 10 December, 1904, its real purpose was carefully disguised: the proposal spoke only of 'moneys required for emergency repair work in the face of natural disasters'. Government aid would be forthcoming if the motion was passed. But not one of the thirty Assemblymen present can have been deceived by this camouflage. No explanation of the proposal was given. Three vigorous speeches were made against it, none in favour. Before the vote was taken, the Governor declared that the rest of the sitting should be in secret; the public were excluded, more than fifty policemen summoned to the chamber, and it was only in the face of this open intimidation that at last, after midnight, the Assembly in which Shozo had served his apprenticeship as a 'people's rights' politician twenty years before meekly accepted the plan on which the Tokyo experts had determined.

Such was the inception of the long drawn-out tragedy of Yanaka Village, a once prosperous rural community with four centuries of peaceful and productive history behind it, and a population, when its destruction was decreed, of nearly 3,000. With the fate of Yanaka

Shozo's last years were to be inextricably linked.

His imprisonment in the summer of 1902 had provided more than a much-needed rest. A Bible sent in to him, probably by Uchimura Kanzo, gave him his first chance to make the acquaintance of the Western scriptures. At the age of sixty he read the life of Christ with a mixture of childlike wonder and of excitement at finding so much that seemed not merely to confirm the lessons of his own experience, but to point beyond them to modes of truth of which he was only just beginning to be aware. Soon after his release he acquired a cheap copy of the gospel of Matthew, which he carried with him to the end of his life, refusing the offer of a complete New Testament from a Tokyo Christian on the ground that 'there was more than enough to live out in Matthew alone'.

In the highly individual religion[1] Shozo distilled for himself, Christ became as revered a source of wisdom ('my work-teacher', as he describes him in his diary) as the mentors of his youth and upbringing — Confucius, Mencius and the Buddha. But the written word was not his only introduction to Christian ideas. Earlier in the year he had met the little-known but remarkable Arai Osui, an Oriental sage in the traditional mould whose spiritual apprenticeship had been served in one of the less likely by-ways of Western religion.

Arai's interest in Christianity had been kindled when, as a rather serious-minded young samurai in 1867, caught up in the upheavals preceding the Meiji Restoration, he had made the acquaintance of a Russian Orthodox missionary. Four years later Mori Arinori, on his appointment as Japan's first Minister in Washington, included Arai in a party of promising young men and women he took with him to America as pioneer students of Western learning.

On their arrival, Arai was the only one of the party who did not proceed to an orthodox educational institution; instead he joined a small religious community based on the sharing of all possessions, manual labour and absolute loyalty to the leader, T. L. Harris, a Swedenborgian Christian who had founded the community in the conviction that all the churches without exception had forgotten the

---

1. Though indeed it is hardly appropriate to use this word of Shozo, for whom 'religion' had nothing to do with any body of dogma, but consisted in a series of expanding (and sometimes contracting) insights arising from reflection on every aspect of daily experience. A readiness to respond to new truth from any source, provided only it spoke to his condition, kept him from the prejudice against the 'foreign religion' that manifested itself (often for excellent reasons) among more conventional Japanese.

meaning of the truly religious life.¹

Here Arai remained for no less than 28 years. On his eventual return to Japan in 1899 — with nothing but the clothes on his back, and with not a single relative surviving to welcome him home — he lived for five years in rooms provided by friends, belonging to no church or sect and never preaching or imposing himself on anyone, but quietly befriending all with whom he came into contact, helping them in any way he could, and writing in a severely classical style a series of mystical essays for any who might care to read. In 1904 an admirer provided him with a sizeable house in the Sugamo district of Tokyo, which he shared with a score of students, naming it 'House of Humility and Harmony', till his death in 1922.

Men of diverse conditions felt his power — a Western-style painter, workers of all kinds, educationalists, lawyers, a dairy-farmer, the first Japanese translator of Dante. What attracted them to him was the integrity and serenity of a life in which 'belief' and 'practice' were indivisible and from which everything superfluous was quietly but firmly excluded.² 'Religion', he wrote, 'cannot be understood except through work. It cannot be experienced through academic study or reading the Bible over and over, as church members do; it must arise from one's everyday tasks ... We should avoid above all the temptation to clothe our half-understood notions in fine phrases and impose them on others.'

Such 'sincerity' makes a man more open to the same quality in others; Arai saw at once the true motive of Shozo's attempted appeal to the Emperor, and wrote a moving article defending Shozo from his critics.

Shozo met him soon after. No doubt the two men, one pugnacious and restlessly active in the public world, the other a contemplative by nature, living a hermit-like life in the centre of a great city, felt the attraction of opposites; but Shozo's need of Arai was greater than Arai's of him, and soon he was calling the younger man (Arai was now 56 to Shozo's 60) 'my teacher'. At first the attraction was mixed on his side with less positive feelings. Arai told him to his face that he was obviously on the verge of mental illness because of 'sheer excess of

---

1. Arai seems to have joined the community at Mori's suggestion; Mori himself (who was only 24 at the time of his appointment as Minister), while living for some months as a member of the community on a previous visit to the West, had been immensely impressed with Harris's teaching that to be truly free men must be made new, 'reborn' through disciplined, selfless work in a common cause. Mori later became Minister of Education — a highly reactionary one, according to the common view; but Professor Hayashi Takeji has recently shown that some of Harris's ideas, which were exceedingly progressive for their day, were a persistent and important influence on Mori, though in the end they could not survive the many very different pressures on a leading Japanese politician of the period.

2 Arai maintained his testimony to simplicity in death as in life. When he died, he left strict instructions that the ground in the Buddhist temple cemetery where his ashes were to be interred should not be commemorated by any kind of tombstone, however small, nor dignified in any other way. His instructions were followed: only a circular dwarf hedge marks the spot.

activity', and ought to go into hospital at once — advice which Shozo did not take at all kindly, in spite of (or perhaps because of) the fact that Arai offered to raise the money needed for a doctor and medicines.

Eleven years later, musing on this incident in his diary shortly before his death, Shozo speaks of how long it took him to realise that Arai was right, and of his great debt to his 'teacher' for the measure of inner peace he has attained . . . 'There were so many things in those days that I did not understand.'

His view of God and Christ at that time was of a childlike simplicity. The beneficial floods of 1902 were a divine miracle, 'Christ come alive on the banks of the Watarase, for all to see who could spare half a day and 40 sen for the fare from Tokyo.' Nor did his irascible, all-or-nothing temperament yield easily to the teachings of Arai or of the New Testament, as his treatment of Nagashima Yohachi, one of the young peasant leaders who had been arrested at Kawamata, showed.[1]

On being released from prison, Nagashima was astonished at the extent of public sympathy for the pollution victims. As he saw it, this new situation called for less shouting of 'Fire! Fire!' and more actual fire-fighting: the moment was ripe for a quieter campaign, co-operating with relief workers and scientific experts, to replace the demonstrations and 'agitation' of previous years. Many of his fellow-peasants, incapable of such objective reasoning, thereupon suspected him of treachery, regardless of the fact that he was one of the tiny handful of peasant leaders who had paid for their forthrightness with a prison sentence; they assumed that he must have taken Furukawa bribes.

So — to his shame, for it was his example that had inspired Nagashima to join the anti-pollution struggle — did Shozo. Nagashima was profoundly hurt. Even his old father, who had so far backed him throughout, now urged him to give up the whole business and stay quietly at home. 'This I would have done,' wrote Nagashima afterwards, 'but for my Christianity.' He fasted for three days, till his father relented and told him to go to Tokyo and ask Shozo's friend Shimada Saburo to intercede on his behalf. Shimada readily agreed, knowing that Shozo only too easily mistook any deviation from his own uncompromising view, however honest, as betrayal. Eventually Shozo repented — but not for nearly two years.

The reconciliation, when it did come, was complete. As always when finally convinced that he had been wholly in the wrong, Shozo apologised with the ready openness that was as characteristic of him as the initial suspicion of any who could not see things quite in his black and white terms. Thereafter the old fighter and the young were closer than they had ever been.

1. For Nagashima Yohachi's subsequent career, See above, p. 116 n. 1.

As the scope of his outward life narrowed, from the Diet to the confines of a prison cell in June 1902, by way of the blaze of publicity and taunts of madness that followed the attempted appeal to the Emperor — as the obstreperous non-conforming politician was reduced to a 'rat-in-a-bag', in the words of his first biographer — so his inner horizons expanded.

Not long after his release from prison he was making speeches in provincial centres calling for total, worldwide disarmament and the switching of all military expenditure to a fund for financing the exchange of diplomats and students. His pacifism, apparently based on his reading of the New Testament, ran right against the trend of feeling in the country since Japan's victory in the Sino-Japanese conflict. It was no transient enthusiasm, but remained with him for the rest of his life; even during the Russo-Japanese war, when public support of the military was almost hysterical, he wrote in his poems of the 'crime of war, the delusion from which the world must awake', and in a remarkable anticipation of the neutralist fervour of post-World War II Japanese youth, urged his fellow-countrymen to 'learn from the Swiss, who have achieved dignity and pride in their country without fighting'.

Friendship with the small group of socialists, most of them Christians as well, who were helping in the relief work, prompted a sympathetic interest in the new political creed too. But he was too familiar with the recalcitrant realities of peasant life to have much faith in a system of ideas as such. More truly indicative of the bent of his thinking is the increasingly frequent appearance in his diary of the word *seijin* — saint, sage, or holy one, in the sense of an ego-less man whose sainthood is effortless, *natural*, because of his 'closeness to God'.

In his eyes, no doubt, Arai Osui was such a saint; and a dozen years' experience of politics and pollution had brought home to him Japan's need of such men. Interspersed among poems, notes of his speeches and of conversations with friends, comments on pollution, politics, students, and many other things, appear fragmentary meditations on similar and contrasting aspects of the teachings of Confucius, the Buddha and Christ. But Shozo was not a philosopher nor a theologian, nor even a 'man of religion', a type of whom in his diary he is mildly contemptuous. For him, the truths he was now glimpsing could only be apprehended as they were lived out situationally, against the grain of the pressures of convention and arbitrary authority that he had resisted all his life. A new opportunity for such experimental living was soon to come.

From late in 1902, and for most of the following year, he devoted much of his time to helping the villages of Kawabe and Toshima to maintain their resistance to the government plan to submerge them in the projected lake. The defence of the threatened peasants evoked all his old pugnacity and stubbornness. A poem scribbled in his diary in December 1902 (and repeated eight times during the following few months) reads:

> *You — endlessly falling, piling-up snow:*
> *If you won't stop —*
> *All right, keep falling!*
> *Treading you down,*
> *Kicking you aside,*
> *I go forward.*

As we have seen, the opposition from these two villages was so strong that eventually they were quietly dropped from the plan. It was Yanaka that was to draw Shozo into his last and most testing — and in terms of his own development, most fruitful — struggle.

12

Murder of a village

For as long as any of its inhabitants could remember, Yanaka had been one of the most fortunate villages of the Shimotsuke region. Protected from the nearby Watarase by a long dyke designed two hundred years earlier by the famous seventeenth-century reformer and practical economist, Kumazawa Banzan, its value was recognised by the small daimyo to whose fief it belonged; his samurai retainers would regularly join the peasants in repairing any serious breaches of the dyke. Moderate floods about once in three years provided the fields with rich manure from the mountain forests surrounding the upper reaches of the Watarase.

After the Meiji Restoration productivity, population and land values had all shown a steady increase. That prosperity had instilled a mild distaste for the obligations imposed by the new central government is suggested by the custom that had grown up of the relatives of any young man liable to military service offering prayers for his exemption at every Shinto shrine and Buddhist temple in the Yanaka area, with readings from the *Hannya Shingyo* or Heart Sutra and solemn invocations on the *taiko* drum.

Prayer, however, was the limit to which the villagers were prepared to go in their defiance of authority. No opposition met the government scheme for submerging Yanaka in a man-made lake, as had happened at Kawabe and Toshima. This was due in part to the severity of the impact of pollution on the village. With the Watarase encircling half the village land, the catastrophic floods of the 1890s, in addition to poisoning most of the fields, had breached the dyke beyond the ability of the villagers to repair it.

There were other reasons, too, for Yanaka's lack of spirit. For several years the village had been dominated by a wealthy landowner named Anjo, who was related by marriage to a government minister and had also had close connections with Furukawa Ichibei and Count Mutsu Munemitsu.[1] In collusion with the corrupt headman of Yanaka, Anjo (who later became President of the Tochigi Prefectural

---

1. See above, p. 73 ff.

Assembly) had insisted on alterations to Kumazawa Banzan's dyke, designed to reclaim more land for his private use. The alterations were completed in 1894, but proved disastrous, the polluting floods breaking through in greatest force at precisely the altered sections — to remedy which, Anjo installed at his own expense some secondhand but expensive pumping equipment, having first got the unsophisticated villagers to agree to pay him back over five years the entire sum he had spent, irrespective of whether or not the equipment functioned successfully. In fact the pump proved useless.

Not content with saddling the village with a heavy debt at a time when it could least afford to pay, the cynical Anjo even offered the peasants 'relief loans', at a rate of interest highly profitable to himself. Some genuine relief funds donated by sympathisers in Tokyo were embezzled by the headman (himself a substantial landowner, in whose family the office, though supposedly elective, had by custom become hereditary), who then promptly resigned, to be replaced by a prefectural nominee. When the plan to submerge Yanaka became known, therefore, the village was not merely debilitated as a result of pollution, but thoroughly demoralised by Anjo's machinations, all but bankrupt, and with no elected headman to serve as the traditional buffer against the depredations of authority.

The beneficial effects of the 'miraculous' floods of 1902 had encouraged the peasants to make such repairs as they could to the dyke thereafter, but further violent floods in May 1904 reopened the breaches, devastated most of the village and all the young crops. A prefectural order forbade neighbouring villages to send any assistance, despite the fact that Yanaka's human resources were more than usually depleted by the absence on military service of nearly 50 of its young men. Before long many of Yanaka's four hundred and fifty households were near to starvation.

Into this disintegrating community Shozo, with two young helpers, moved in July 1904. He was now 62. His motives, which seemed incomprehensible even to his well-wishers at the time and have only recently been clearly established from a study of his diary and correspondence, were twofold. On the one hand he saw the plan to sink Yanaka in a vast lake as another step in the pollution war — a government attempt, the more likely to convince because it seemed so daring and spectacular, to bury the whole issue of pollution for good. As such it had to be fought, on two grounds: because it did nothing to restrict pollution at its source, and because of itself it would not (so Shozo, with the intimate knowledge of the habits of the Watarase River he had gained over the years, insisted) prevent dangerous floods in the future.

There was another reason, or set of reasons, why for him the defence of Yanaka should seem so crucial. Having been brought up in a traditional, largely self-governing rural community, with which in normal times — and provided taxes were duly paid — the feudal authorities interfered very little, and having experienced also the harsh consequences of arbitrary rule in many forms during the period immediately before and after the Restoration, Shozo had enthusiastically welcomed the granting of a Constitution and the setting up of a Diet as large extensions of freedom, guarantees that the injustices he and his constituents had suffered from would not be repeated. Ten years in the Diet, fighting for a rural population against the combined forces of industry and the new government, had shattered these hopes. A 'modern', though not democratic, system of provincial government had been established; in practice, its appointed officials had proved entirely subservient to the central government, prefectural governors and district chiefs showing in general no disposition to stand up for the interests of the old semi-autonomous villages when they conflicted with those of their superiors.

To make matters worse, farmers were being taxed ever more heavily to help pay for industrial expansion, and even the time-honoured teaching that the rice-producing peasants were the class society should honour most, after the samurai, had been forgotten.[1] Yanaka drew together all these discontents. Here was a village the central government had decided — without consulting its inhabitants, and after tacitly allowing industrial pollution to deprive them of their livelihood — to destroy. To its defence, as to that of his own community in the struggle against the Rokkaku forty years before, Shozo was irresistibly drawn.

Staying alternately with two peasant families who gave him a warm welcome,[2] he set to work at once, organizing a young men's group to repair breaches in the dyke, preparing petitions, and urging on all who would listen to him the need to join forces to save their community, which was protected by the Constitution, if only the government could be brought to act constitutionally. The task was a daunting one.

Cowed by disaster and sullen at Anjo's machinations, the villagers were for the most part unresponsive, even hostile. To them Shozo was after all an outsider, an ex-politician from the remote world of the metropolis who, if the rumours fostered by Furukawa agents were to be believed, had even appropriated to his own use money contributed for pollution relief. He himself, invigorated by the new challenge to

---

1. As was symbolized by the contemptuous shouts of *'don-byakusho!'* (dirty peasants!) with which the police, representatives of the 'new order', had charged the demonstrators at Kawamata in February, 1900. In his Diet speeches on Kawamata, Shozo spoke with particular bitterness of this attitude.

2. Later he adopted the practice of moving to a new household every few days. In a letter of August, 1906 he says that apart from his first two months in Yanaka, and except for short periods of exhaustion or illness, he had not stayed in the same house twice.

his combative spirit, was unperturbed by his reception. A letter written soon after his move to Yanaka shows the paternalistic attitude he still retained — an attitude which was later to change — together with a typical combination of eager humility and sense of mission:

The people are victims of all kinds of rumour and false talk, so that they don't believe half of what I tell them. . . . [The government and Furukawa] have their agents everywhere, and the poor folk have no means of telling who is honest from who isn't. But we have no need to worry about the ignorant villagers. It is our job simply to work as 'messengers' of the gods of heaven. The villagers are fear-ridden, and can think of nothing but where their next meal is coming from. . . . Show them a one-yen piece, and you'll be risking your life; a bowl of rice is enough to start them quarrelling! . . . I want to seize this new chance to study and to learn. I'm starting this new life at 62, and am so grateful for the opportunity, in spite of all the misery that's involved. There's such a thing as the 'study of society', but it's not often anyone can have had a chance to put truth into practice in this kind of way. . . . It's not that I've had to steel myself to face the misery of Yanaka; it's been inevitable that I should come here, the natural thing. Buddha had to take the decision to seclude himself on Mount Dantaloka. A common mortal like me comes to Yanaka because it's here, that's all. But maybe, allowing for the difference between us of the great and the insignificant, what he was after and what I'm after are not so different; only he knew the truth, while I have only the realities of everyday for guide. He found the Way with ease: for me, it will be hard. . . .

Lacking the extraordinary, compulsive sense of justice that made it seem to Shozo simply 'natural' for him to take up the cause of an obscure village against the whole weight of government and public opinion, even his admirers could see only the width of the gap between him and the villagers. Kinoshita Naoe, his first biographer, records *his* feeling eloquently:

'Shozo's constant theme and slogan was "defence of the Constitution" against a government which in its dealings with Yanaka was acting unconstitutionally and contrary to simple humanity. He saw the people of Yanaka as soldiers in a campaign to protect the Constitution and the unwritten laws of human behaviour. But in this respect he and the villagers were at odds. For all his angry speeches, their passions were not roused; he piped, but they would not dance. . . . He saw them only through the veil of his own imaginings. *They* had never set eyes on this "Constitution" of which he spoke so much. All that was in their minds was that for generations they had lived on and by their land. They had seen the Shoguns come and go — the Ashikaga, the Tokugawa, and the rest; and now it was the era of Meiji. . . . But with all these changes in the outside world they had nothing to do. At heart they were as subservient to their latest rulers as to the Shoguns of an earlier age.'

Kinoshita's account is not altogether fair to the people of Yanaka. A townsman himself by birth and upbringing, he was far less capable of divining the peasants' true feelings than Shozo; and the contemplative life into which he had withdrawn after some years of literary and political work tended to blind him to some of the significance of a life such as Shozo's. For all his immense admiration for Shozo, the gulf was as much between himself and Shozo as between Shozo and the villagers. But gulf there was, though it was to narrow strikingly.[1] Shimada Sozo, a Yanaka boy who joined Shozo in his teens, became his most devoted disciple and assistant, and has spent much of the sixty years since Shozo's death in collecting and preserving the records of his work, was clearly aware of it:

'Shozo would tramp in straw sandals and sedge hat round the various hamlets that made up the village, tirelessly scolding and exhorting any who showed signs of breaking and giving in to the miserable financial inducements the government agents were offering if they would leave.[2] But the promise of cash was too tempting, and they thought him only a nuisance.... Walking along behind him and listening to the talk he had with them, I couldn't help feeling sorry for him; here he was, working so hard for a village not his own, yet few showed any sign of gratitude. One day I asked him — I was only a boy then — if he thought the people really understood what he talked to them about. He wasn't the least put out. The way I roar at them, it's bound to sink in a bit, he said, laughing. But even so, as I walked behind him and looked at his shoulder-bones pushing out from under the ageing flesh, I had an impression of a terrible loneliness, of almost total isolation....'

Shozo's championing of Yanaka, quixotic at best and seeming almost lunatic in that it was undertaken when the public interest had been captured by the war with Russia, in which Japan had already won notable victories, did isolate him gradually from the sympathy of all but a handful of friends.[3] A few attempts were made to get him to withdraw into dignified retirement. Some money collected and sent to him for this purpose was promptly appropriated for his work in

1. See below, p. 166 n. 2
2. See below, p. 175 ff.
3. There were, of course some, apart from Shozo's personal friends, whose support for the war did not blind them to the tragedy of Yanaka. One such was the headmaster of a Middle School in Utsunomiya (the principal town of Tochigi Prefecture), who wrote after visiting Yanaka: 'Everywhere in the world outside there are torchlight processions to celebrate our great victories. Here, the whole village is in darkness, save for a few poor lamps gleaming dully over the floodwaters. Who would not weep at such desolation?' But as a rule such sympathy did not lead to action.

Shozo's own indifference to the general war fever is thrown into relief by the profound sadness with which he heard of 'Bloody Sunday' (January 22, 1905) in St. Petersburg, when 1,000 unarmed workers were killed by troops dispersing a demonstration. Comparing it with the 'murder' of Yanaka, he wrote of his fears that such tragedies as the Russian massacre would be repeated in Japan, and of his longing to 'appeal with tears to all men of principle for a better way, on behalf of all the poor of both Russia and Japan.'

Yanaka. He commented in a letter:

Old age will not make me retire. I must go forward till I drop, or until age simply withers me away. The old saying is true: 'Having heard the Way in the morning, one may die content in the evening'. . . .[1]

A village that invited him to settle there 'to teach religion to our young men' met with a similar response. His commitment to Yanaka was total, and lasted till the day of his death nine years later.

* * *

The final crisis for Yanaka was slow in coming, but the wheels that had been set in motion by the government decision of 1902 continued to turn inexorably. A visit by Shozo to the Governor of Tochigi Prefecture in November, 1904 to plead for abandonment or postponement of the lake plan was ineffective; less than a month later the Governor railroaded the plan through the Assembly in the manner already described.

On 16 January, 1905, the same day that Toshima and Kawabe generously despatched petitions to the Speakers of both Houses of the Diet for the reprieve of their neighbour community, the District Chief went from house to house informing the villagers that their land would be purchased and they themselves moved elsewhere in the Prefecture — to be followed next day by Shozo, insisting that no one, no matter what his authority, had the right to drive them from their ancestral lands.

On the 18th the District Chief reappeared, with a police escort. Meeting him face to face this time, Shozo vehemently denounced his activities as unconstitutional. This confrontation was the first of many during the next eighteen months: more often than not they ended with the bizarre spectacle of the elderly ex-parliamentarian, in dirty black kimono and straw sandals, and with the hair he never had time to cut tied behind his head with string or straw, chasing the representatives of authority — officials, surveyors, police — from the village with his stick, shouting in the thunderous voice that had commanded such attention in the Diet, 'Robbers! Bandits!' The accusation of unconstitutionality[1] was unanswerable; all the officials

---

1. The 'saying' is from the Confucian Analects (IV, 8). As so often with Shozo's quotations, he uses it in his own way. Increasingly for him, 'hearing the Way' came to signify acting out such of the Way as he already knew, and learning as he went along from all and sundry, both processes to continue while there was breath in his body. Another of his favourite Confucian sayings in his last years: 'The Master said, When I walk in a party of three, my teachers are always present. I can select the good qualities of the one and copy them, and the unsatisfactory qualities of the other and correct them in myself.' (Analects VII, 21, tr. Soothill.)

1. As in his first Diet speech on pollution in December, 1891 (See above, p. 63), Shozo based his assertion primarily on Article XXVII of the Meiji Constitution, dealing with the inviolability of the rights of property.

could say was that 'higher authority had decided. . . .'

Despite the open challenge to its position, officialdom saw no need to make a martyr of Shozo: it was not in a hurry, and there were other methods of bringing pressure to bear on the Yanaka population. On this first occasion, soon after the District Chief's undignified retreat, four police posts were set up within the village bounds, manned by nine policemen. Another policeman was assigned to keep track of Shozo's movements. Astonishingly, this 'shadow' followed Shozo wherever he went — in Yanaka, up and down the Prefecture, or in Tokyo — for eight years. This proof of how 'dangerous' authority thought him Shozo regarded as a huge joke, and the two became good friends,[1] with Shozo making sure that his shadow was kindly treated, in spite of his invidious position.

Shozo's defiance of the District Chief rallied some at least of the villagers. With some financial help from Kawabe and Toshima, the vital task of repairing the dyke was restarted in the hope of guaranteeing some kind of harvest, and was just completed, by desperate efforts, by the end of June, 1905. A public meeting in Tokyo organised by Shozo aroused some temporary interest: volunteers distributed leaflets on the government's 'inhumanity and violation of the Constitution' in regard to Yanaka. But other events were discouraging. A request to the Prefecture for funds for permanent rebuilding of the Yanaka dyke was rejected out of hand; an appeal to Tokyoites to come and see the situation in Yanaka for themselves, sent to all Tokyo papers, was printed by only one of them.[1]

Taking ten villagers with him, Shozo made two trips to Tokyo in the hope of seeing the Home Minister. The first time, the party were arrested by the police on their arrival at Ueno Station, and spent the night at a police-station before being put on a train back to the country. On their second attempt, they managed to reach the Tokyo home of a former Yanaka villager, but the following morning their host was arrested by local police and they themselves ordered to leave that section of the city. The same thing happened when they made their way to the only other friend they knew would receive them, and finally, without money or food to stay longer, they were forced to return empty-handed to Yanaka.

In March the Governor of Tochigi issued an order — which was not, however, immediately put into effect — directing the villagers to comply with the arrangements for the compulsory purchase of their

---

1. More than once the shadow helped him out of a difficult situation. When a Furukawa agent tried to break up a meeting Shozo was holding to draft a petition to the Home Minister, and called in the police after Shozo had chased him out, the shadow testified at the police-station that Shozo had only acted under great provocation, which led to his immediate release.

The shadow is said to have become such an admirer of Shozo that when he was at last released from his charge, he at once resigned from the police, at the cost of considerable personal hardship.

1. Local papers in Tochigi Prefecture, when they chose to refer to Yanaka, dismissed Shozo as 'mad'.

Murder of a village

land. The harvest was safely gathered in, though it amounted to less than a fifth of the normal average; but almost immediately afterwards renewed floods breached the dyke once again, undoing the patient work of six months. Then in November the process of compulsory purchase began in earnest. The prices offered to the peasants were derisory — which was not surprising, since only ¥480,000 had been set aside for the entire operation, whereas on the basis of the current land prices and the average value of the harvest, Shozo had estimated that a fair figure would be ¥5,000,000.

Particularly resented was the compensation proposed for the 'cemetery land', in which the villagers' ancestors were buried, and to which they clung almost more tenaciously than to the fields on which their livelihood depended: the sum offered for each four-yard-square plot was 'no more than would buy a couple of postcards'.

Promises of a resettlement grant were not kept, the money being either not paid at all or cynically deducted from the purchase price of the land. Some resettlement *land* was provided in the north-east corner of the Prefecture, but in this respect as in others the authorities were guilty of cruel deceit. The land was of the poorest quality, and those who moved were not told in advance that it was not public land (the owners of most of it were Prince Konoe and Marquis Saigo), so that when they arrived they suddenly found themselves no longer owners but tenants of their fields, and were thus degraded, through no fault of their own and without redress, into one of the most insecure of all social groups in Meiji Japan. As if that were not enough, the local villagers attempted to drive out the first Yanaka 'refugees' by force.

At first the number of villagers submitting to compulsory purchase was small. Throughout the spring and summer of 1906 the pressure on them was increased to such an extent that Shozo could say with no very great exaggeration, at a meeting in Tokyo, 'What was the point of the nation having fought a war, when at Yanaka the government was at war with its own people?'

First there was the use of middlemen to coerce individuals, by tricks so crude and obvious one would hardly believe them, were they not so well documented. (One must constantly remind oneself, in following the Yanaka story, of the naivety and traditionally submissive attitude of the villagers, the wretched prospect for their crops, and the desperate financial straits — most of them were already in debt — which made them clutch at any straw. Given all these factors, it is extraordinary that so many of them held out so long.)

Prefectural officials began confiscating chattels for 'non-payment' of taxes and village debts. Scores of second-hand dealers suddenly descended upon the villagers, claiming 'inside information' that their houses were going to be demolished anyway, so that it was in their obvious interest to sell to the dealers, even at the nominal prices offered, their farming tools, their boats, their furniture — even, in

The destruction of Yanaka

advance of demolition, the timber from which their houses were built. Moneylenders' agents posing as lawyers threatened debtors with prosecution if they did not find money from somewhere.

Sometimes the methods were more roundabout. One young man of some substance whose opposition to compulsory purchase had made him prominent was befriended by an official, who first persuaded him to take up gambling, then introduced him to a geisha in Koga, the nearest town. Very soon, having duly infatuated the country boy, this geisha was demanding that he buy her out of her contract with her employer. He complied, and was before long in debt to such an extent that he was forced to accept compulsory purchase — earlier he had made over half his property to his sister, but meanwhile the official had quietly found a husband who (her property having become his) was conveniently ready to give way to the authorities' offer.

Less subtly, a villager who for twenty years had been practising one of the traditional forms of Japanese massage, treating his fellow-peasants, was suddenly told he was contravening the Medical Practice Law and would face either a heavy fine or a sentence of prison with hard labour. Shozo got two Tokyo lawyers to prepare a defence, though in fact the case was never called before the final destruction of the village. As soon as any family left Yanaka after having signed the purchase agreement, its house was destroyed by workmen from the Prefecture.

Ironically, in one such case, a soldier whose parents had not had the courage to tell him they had sold out came home, 'from the defence of his village and fatherland against the Russian enemy', to find his own home a heap of planks and rubble. Tension in the village increased. One peasant woman, driven out of her senses by uncertainty and fear of the future, was murdered by her brother.[1]

Meanwhile the attack on the community as a whole was intensified. In March the village primary school, Yanaka's pride and the most obvious symbol of its former confidence in its future, was demolished, without reference to the village council. Shortly afterwards, when the new crops were just beginning to sprout, the Governor of Tochigi

---

1. Perhaps the most curious — and in its effect, most cruel — example of bureaucratic manipulation was the case of a peasant named Sayama Umekichi. On 17 April, 1906, the Governor of Tochigi directed Sayama to 'remove' his house by the 25th, on the ground that it stood on public land and he had not obtained proper permission, under current legislation, to reside there. In fact Sayama had applied for such permission fifteen months before; two weeks before the Governor's directive, his application (stamped with the date of its receipt, March, 1905) had been returned, marked simply 'rejected'. The inference is unavoidable that the application had been suddenly returned in order to prevent the onus of Sayama's eviction being placed on the authorities. In the event he and two others were forced to pay for the demolition of their own houses.

Not a few of the Yanaka refugees, finding themselves unable to make a living on the land allocated to them, made their way eventually to Hokkaido. Nor did the story end there: during the Second World War, thirty-five years after the last house in their ancestral village had been destroyed, some refugee families applied for and were given permission to resettle yet again on land a dozen miles from Yanaka, which they still could not forget.

ordered the villagers to destroy within ten days the dyke repairs on which they had been working under Shozo's leadership, since the floods of the preceding summer: if the order was not complied with, the work would be carried out by the Prefecture, at the villagers' expense.

The order was ignored. On the day it expired, a score of students came from Tokyo to help Shozo and the villagers in the event of a confrontation with the Prefectural workmen, but the latter did not appear, and the students went home.[1] Two days later the workmen did turn up — at night, and in sufficient strength to undo the repairs and retreat before dawn. In another move, just before his order on the dyke, the Governor had sent to Yanaka a brief document ironically termed a *shimon* or 'consultation paper', proposing that the village should cease to exist (on the ground that 'it was no longer able to fulfil its obligations under the law'), its territory to be incorporated in that of the neighbouring community of Fujioka, and requiring an 'answer' from Yanaka Village Council within two days.[2]

The prefectural official who had been appointed village head at once summoned *two* council meetings for the following morning and afternoon. His object in so doing was to stay within the council rule which provided that if at the first meeting there should be no quorum, at a second meeting called to consider the same business decisions might be taken without a quorum. In the morning, as the official had correctly anticipated, the quorum was not forthcoming; but the stratagem still failed, since the second meeting refused to be browbeaten and flatly rejected the Governor's proposal to decree their community out of existence.

For Shozo, 1906 was a bitter year from the beginning. Of the New Year's Day poems in his diary, one is a variant of a favourite already quoted:[3]

> *Though all night long*
> *The snow never ceases,*
> *I kick it aside*
> *And trudge forward*
> *On this way of mine.*

The second is more hopeful.

---

1. They had come in response to a hurried trip to Tokyo by Shozo a week before, when he had asked for help for the villagers at a meeting of the Shinkigen (New Era) group of Christian Socialists. According to his own account, Shozo had been so exhausted at the time that he literally did not know what he was saying at the meeting.

2 This was clearly in breach of the spirit if not the letter of the Municipal and Local Government Regulations, which provided that a minimum of three days notice of the summoning of a village council must be given, 'except in cases of extreme executive urgency'.

3. See above, p. 149.

*From heaven
The light of a new sun
Shines alike
Over heaven and earth
This New Year's Day.*

But the sombre mood must have been uppermost, as may be judged from a letter he wrote at the end of February to Takahashi Hideomi, a Tokyo lawyer who had been active in the earlier anti-pollution campaign, asking him — unsuccessfully, as it turned out — to come to Yanaka as village head, and help Shozo lead the struggle. Already about one third of the families had succumbed to the pressures being concentrated upon them, despite all Shozo's efforts:

Since coming eighteen months ago to this village-under-sentence-of-death, I've had so much to do trying to help them, there hasn't been time for a single day of rest, not half a day, even. So busy, I've had no energy left to write to friends in Tokyo, no time to go up to the city myself and try to work on the Diet or the Ministries. I can do nothing — nothing but go from house to house here, hearing their troubles and sharing their tears. . . . No one comes to us from outside now. No one hears the cry from the sinking ship.

Satori, one of the two young helpers who had come with him from Tokyo to Yanaka, had deserted him, and was now on the Prefectural payroll, urging the villagers to reject Shozo's leadership.[1] In Tokyo, the composition of the new government under Prince Saionji made it even less likely that any Ministry doors would admit Shozo even if he did find time to visit the capital more often. Hara Kei, Saionji's Home Minister, within whose province the Yanaka affair fell, had started his political career as a protégé of Count Mutsu, whose secretary he had been when the latter, as Minister of Agriculture and Commerce, had done his best to block Shozo's first protests against Ashio pollution in the early 1890s. A firm believer in industrialisation, Hara had always had close ties with Ashio, and in 1905 these were cemented when he accepted the vice-presidency of the re-organised Furukawa Industries.[1]

With his appointment as Home Minister the slow drift towards a final collision between the authority and policies he represented and the single dissident village led by the mad old man (as he must have seemed to Hara and most Tokyoites) whose eccentricities he had first helped to frustrate fourteen years before in the Diet, acquired a tragic inevitability.

Three days before the Governor of Tochigi invited Yanaka to

---

1. This was a particularly bitter blow; from his student days at Waseda University Satori had been one of Shozo's most devoted helpers in the later years of the anti-pollution struggle.
1. The post was far from nominal, owing to the poor health of the president, Furukawa Junkichi — the son of Count Mutsu who had been adopted by Furukawa Ichibei.

approve its own death-warrant, Hara attended a banquet to celebrate the first anniversary of the founding of the new firm, as he noted with some complacency in his diary. With him thus firmly ensconced in positions of both political and industrial power, the fate of Yanaka could only be a matter of time.

Early in June the Governor had Shozo served with an order forbidding him to 'incite' the villagers to defy official directives. In a personal visit to Yanaka, accompanied quite needlessly by a substantial bodyguard, the prefectural chief of police tried in vain to persuade him to abandon his activities. On 1 July, Yanaka was officially declared non-existent. Two days later Shozo was arrested, on a charge of 'insulting an official': the prefecture-appointed village head had declared an auction of some common land, above flood level, apparently as a further device to intimidate the remaining villagers, for which Shozo had repeatedly denounced him as a 'robber of the people'. After being held in prison for two weeks he was released on bail,[1] partly because he was ill with severe eye-trouble. When the case was heard in August, he was sentenced to 40 days hard labour — at the age of 64 — and a fine of ¥7; but he appealed immediately, and ten months later the conviction was quashed.

While he was still in prison the floods struck again, earlier than usual. Pouring through the breached dyke into the village, they had at least the effect of proving that siphoning off flood-water into Yanaka not only did *not* lessen the flooding of other villages by more than an inch or two, but even worsened the effects elsewhere by allowing the water to lie up to ten days longer than hitherto, and thus to rot crops that had previously survived the summer inundations. Even the Governor of Tochigi seems to have had doubts: on a visit to Yanaka to see for himself, he remarked to an Assemblyman that it was clear now that turning Yanaka into a lake would solve nothing. But in what looks like one of the behind-the-scenes moves that recur constantly in the Ashio pollution story, within a month he was transferred — to an innocuous post in the Ministry of Education.[1]

---

1. This was Shozo's fifth spell in prison, and his last, though he evidently expected otherwise. When Kinoshita Naoe and another Tokyo friend visited him in the jail, he told them cheerfully 'not to worry, it was bound to happen many more times yet.' Detention gave him time to rest, and to write at least one poem:
    Prison windows
    Let in so little light.
    Groping my way
    To freedom, I long to see
    The morning-glory.

1. Despite his admission of the futility of submerging Yanaka, Shozo's poor opinion of this Governor did not change. On hearing of his transfer, Shozo got his youthful Yanaka assistant to write on his behalf over 100 postcards announcing the departure of the 'robber Governor' for his Ministry post, and adding that 'this could only mean disaster for Japanese education.' Such was one of the more colourful examples of his unceasing output of letters and postcards, most of which consisted of straightforward accounts of events at Yanaka, or, as time went on, of religious insights derived from them.

Murder of a village

Surprisingly, his successor was openly sympathetic when Shozo took him round Yanaka and told him he was confident that if only governmental interference ceased, money could be found from wealthy men of goodwill for the permanent rebuilding of the dyke; but in a matter of weeks he too was transferred, after less than four months in office, and the new Governor, the third in five months, showed no such disposition to question the central government's policy.

That the odds were weighted so heavily against any reprieve for Yanaka does not seem to have weakened in the slightest Shozo's determination to continue the fight. One of the very rare occasions when he came near to admitting that defeat was inevitable was in his reply to a Buddhist priest who asked him in 1905 whether he thought there was really any prospect of the community surviving. 'That I can't tell,' said Shozo, 'but can one abandon someone who's dying of TB, just because you don't think he'll recover?' (In Japan at that time tuberculosis was still a common, and more often than not a fatal, disease.) For him the struggle had now acquired a religious dimension. As he wrote in January, 1906 to Shimada Saburo:

The physical destruction of Yanaka may not be far off now. I'm doing what little I can — it's the truth of religion — for the others: reborn themselves, they're trying to carve out a new Way of humanity for the world.

By the 'reborn' ones, he meant those peasants who still held out: but in reality the words could have been applied more accurately to himself.

Earlier, his growing interest in religion (and in the Bible in particular) had prompted him to write to the same correspondent of his eagerness to 'study religion really seriously, after the Yanaka business is settled.' But gradually, under the impact of life in Yanaka, with no possessions of his own, sharing the hardships of the villagers and experiencing at first hand the threat that hung over them, this attitude changed. In November, 1905 he wrote:

There have been both victories and defeats since I joined this battle for the Way of humanity, and after a year and a half the outcome still isn't settled. As far as Truth goes, the final victory will surely be ours, though outwardly we may be defeated. There is so much I am learning! Looking back over the last thirty years, I know I have learnt more in the past one year than in the previous twenty-nine. Shozo is a different man from what he was twelve months ago; and because of it, I shan't have the faintest regret if I die tomorrow.

And then, as if in an afterthought:

I should be sorry I haven't studied the Bible enough, though.

In modern terms, his religion was becoming secular, an existential wresting of meaning from day-to-day experience, though with religious writings still valued as a point of reference and a source of confirmation of his own discoveries. In prison in July, 1906, the only writings he asked Kinoshita Naoe to bring were a Bible and 'any writings of the sages'.

Later that year, by which time 340 of the original 400 families had given up the struggle and left Yanaka, he writes of himself as a 'wandering priest, a beggar-landowner whose property is wherever he spends the night. . . . We shall strive for resurrection. Yanaka is the central point of the whole pollution fight, the fight itself in a different form. . . .'

The resurrection of which he speaks obscurely here (and later with greater frequency) is not that of Yanaka as a physical entity, but the recovery, in Shozo's own life and in that of society at large, of a 'Way of humanity', based on a new openness and humility, that would make pollution, oppression and injustice impossible. His ideas are often obscurely put, representing as they do a 'spin-off' from action rather than the results of reflection. Nor, at this stage, did he himself understand all their implications. Yet already the state of mind they imply can give his writing on occasion a buoyant, almost lyrical note; as for example in a letter written on November 26 to Harada Kanshichiro, a relative who helped to support him from time to time with gifts of money.

Like most of Shozo's letters from now on, it moves back and forth with entire naturalness between the mundane and the spiritual. He begins by thanking Harada for his recent gift of ¥50, and tells him not to worry about the sentence just passed on him,[1] because several sympathetic lawyers would be helping with his appeal. In any case he himself has resolved to follow the 'divine teaching' to ignore all outward forms, of which house and family and political party are typical, for they are nothing but stumbling-blocks; to take the whole world as one's family — that is a form of the divine Way which is not of the outward, enslaving kind. Then he speaks of his regret that contrary to his vow of twenty-seven years before he has now to accept support from others, and reiterates his determination to reduce his own needs to the lowest possible limit, so that he can give most of what he receives to Yanaka. He goes on:

For myself I don't need more than two or three yen a month. I wear the same kimono day and night, and rarely have a pillow to lay my head on: I sleep nearly every night in a different house. A bit of rice with the boiled barley is a treat! We can get a bath sometimes, but we're proud of our filthy clothes. But then there's the police, with their insults and the brutal way they treat us — it's utterly inhuman: but the people outside know nothing of all this, because the papers ignore it. Such a den of devils is this Japan of ours, and here am I in the middle of it. . . . The floods have been continuous for five years,

---

1. See above, p. 162

the dyke keeps breaking, we have to row our way from house to house. All in all, it's no place for human beings to be, and it's not nature but evil men that have made it so. If I can help just one of these people in their misery, I shall be happy to die here, for the sake of the Way. For to die in the Way is not to die but to live. Again and again through all my life heaven has taught me its lessons. The times I spent in prison when I was young were all stages on the divine Way. ... Every misfortune, every hardship is a chance to train the spirit. Inwardly, now, I feel more alive, have more energy than when I was twenty-three or four. Only my body is old and tired. After this appeal hearing is over, I must do more public speaking. The Japanese are so smallminded! Such a nation of fools, they judge only by externals, and can see nothing else. They are so excited at getting a grip on Manchuria.[1] How absurd! My love may be tiny, but it reaches to the whole world. 'The stars in heaven, the sands of the earth, all are mine.' Of what do these words speak but of the reach of universal love? If one man helps another, his love can touch the entire world. They gloat over getting control of territory abroad. How pitiful the smallness of such minds, the meanness of the actions they praise!

That Shozo's religious interpretation of his Yanaka experience was neither the otherworldliness of old age nor a self-indulgent escapism, compensating for years of defeat, is warranted by the fact that a nucleus of peasant villagers — who would have been the first to see through any such weakness — continued to hold out with him as their constant adviser and spokesman, against all the intimidation of which the authorities were capable; so magnetic was the force of his conviction and of his personality. If at heart he even now felt himself the *nanushi*, the paternal guardian of those too ignorant to protect themselves, his 'love' for the peasants as people, not simply as victims of an injustice to which he happened to be opposed, was obvious.

Apart from Shimada Sozo,[2] who was little more than a boy at the time, the villagers were not articulate, least of all in writing, so there are few first-hand records of what they thought of the elderly rebel who had come at his own invitation to share their misfortunes. The occasional visitor from Tokyo, however, was invariably struck by the relationship he had succeeded in establishing with them. One of the more frequent visitors was Arahata Kanson,[3] who recalls Shozo's eccentricities as a travelling companion:

---

1. Perhaps a slip for 'Korea', over which Japan began from 1905 onwards to exercise increasing hegemony.

2. See above, p. 154: His recollections, written down over the years with the most painstaking attention to detail, and eventually published in two large volumes in 1972, are the primary (though far from the only) source of information on Shozo's life in Yanaka, particularly from 1907 onwards. Everything he says corroborates the impressions quoted below from Ishikawa and Arahata.

3. A journalist, later a well-known socialist. He was elected to the Diet after the Second World War.

'In the summer of 1906 I went to Yanaka three times with Shozo, after he had been up to Tokyo on Yanaka business. Once, I remember, we bought some milk from a platform milk-boy at some station on the way. Shozo asked him to make it cheaper; the boy said he couldn't. All right then, said Shozo, we'll drink it now and give you back the bottles, so let us off the cost of the bottles, anyway! What with the boy losing his temper and the other passengers smiling at the way my companion was carrying on, I didn't know where to look.

'It was evening when we reached Yanaka. The place looked desolate enough, with the orioles chirping among the reeds; but I noticed a few wisps of smoke from cottages where there was still food to be cooked and someone to eat it. Just then we came across a pedlar. Taking a little bottle of spices from his cart, he gave it to Shozo with a bow. "He's a Yanaka man," Shozo told me afterwards, "but he's moved to Sano. Just managing to keep himself alive." I can't forget the look of reverence on the pedlar's face when he offered Shozo his gift, nor the delight on Shozo's as he accepted it.'

Ishikawa Sanshiro[1] was no less moved when he accompanied Shozo as the latter went from house to house one night, with encouragement for any who were losing hope, and an ungrudging welcome for those (of whom there were several) who having abandoned Yanaka in defiance of all Shozo's urging had now shamefacedly made their way back, unable to survive elsewhere.

'He spoke from outside one tiny cottage (the shutters were all up) to someone who was lying ill inside. Suddenly his voice trembled a little. I looked round: his eyes were filled with tears, like so many jewels. I can see them still. It's nearly fifty years ago now, and who it was he was talking to I can't remember; but it was then above all that I saw the marvellous light his personality shed on the darkness. Everything else about him I may forget, but that light shines still, and will, so long as the memory of that moment survives.'

If Shozo succeeded in retaining a commanding influence over a section at least of the villagers, the secret clearly lay in the impression he gave of complete integrity, deriving from a deeply religious sense of significance in everything he did, that gave him the strength to ride over the shocks and hardships while sharing them to the full; of complete 'sincerity', to use the customary Japanese term, or of 'naturalness', as Ishikawa puts it:

'From the start Tanaka Shozo was utterly indifferent to any hardship or danger. In his mind there wasn't the slightest room for anything but his lifelong struggle for human justice. Self-sacrifice such as his (to use the ordinary term) was for him nothing out of the ordinary, but the natural way to live. To 'ordinary' people, of course,

---

1. A Christian Socialist; later a prominent anarchist and writer. The lines quoted are from an interview he gave in 1954, 48 years after the incident they describe.

he seemed in every respect extraordinary. But in his own eyes what characterised everything he said or did was merely its naturalness. People have called him a martyr, an off-beat hero, and all kinds of other things, but the grand titles don't fit. It was this air of naturalness that made him unique.'

Thanks to the 'naturalness' of an undivided personality, on the rare occasions when he could withdraw from the tensions of Yanaka, Shozo could be wholly at peace — gentle, and boyishly cheerful, even: an aspect of his character that excited as much admiration as the heroic.

A description by Kinoshita Naoe of one such 'day off' a few weeks after Shozo had been released from prison on bail is perhaps worth quoting at some length.

'On the evening of 9 September there was a meeting in Sano on the Yanaka affair. Ishikawa and I went along. Shozo had managed to come from Yanaka, though it was difficult for him to get away, he was so desperately busy there. After the meeting, which was in a theatre called the Manza, we walked back late at night to the inn, took down the screen doors between our two rooms and hung up two mosquito-nets, one for Shozo and one for Ishikawa and me.

'I was irritable and easily angered in those days. That night I hadn't been able to restrain my fury at the idiotic applause with which the audience — the theatre was packed — greeted Shozo's speech. It was my turn to speak after him. "What d'you think you've come for?" I shouted at them. "Tanaka Shozo isn't an entertainer! What kind of insincerity is it that can clap its hands but ignore the fight he still carries on despite his age, this great man, who is no stranger either but was born not many miles from here? I have come here from Tokyo this evening, but I shall not demean myself by speaking any longer to such an audience!" In such a rage I hardly knew what I was saying, I came down off the platform. The audience were flabbergasted. I heard afterwards, though, that they had gone home assuring one another that I must have been drunk. . . .

'I went to bed, but somehow couldn't get to sleep. I called out to Shozo, who was lying under the adjoining mosquito-net.

' "Sensei, I've often wanted to see the village where you were born, and we're so close to it now. Could you take us there tomorrow?"

' "It's a poor sort of a place," came the reply from Shozo's bed.

' "Poor or not, I'd like to see it."

'Ishikawa was keen to go too, and eventually Shozo agreed. So next morning we set off in three rickshaws: Shozo in front, in his ancient black kimono, hatless, and with his white beard blowing in the wind; then Ishikawa in Western dress and straw hat, constantly turning his head to admire the country landscape; then myself. Suddenly I heard the grating of wheels behind me. It was the policeman, Shozo's shadow, in a fourth rickshaw. . . .'

On the way they passed the little shrine where forty years before Shozo had lived and taught local children after being expelled from the Rokkaku fief.

'"Tanaka-sama, surely!" An old woman with a little girl, evidently her granddaughter, came out to greet us from the cottage nearby.

'"Still looking after the place as faithfully as ever, are you?" said Shozo, smiling, as he introduced her to us. "She helped take care of me when I lived here. We went to the village temple-school together. I was a year younger — how she used to bully me!" — with delighted laughter. The old woman's worn face softened as she too smiled. There were only two or three teeth left in her mouth, I noticed, sticking up like tiny stakes. She told us of the day Shozo had first arrived at the shrine. Knowing he was coming, her mother had been on the look-out for him, but when at evening there was still no sign of him, she wondered whether he might not have gone straight to the shrine, and went to look. Sure enough, there he was, sitting quietly inside in the dark, but with the door wide open. "But you haven't even got a light!" she exclaimed, at which he smiled and pointed through the door. "There's my lantern!" he said. Far away, beyond the furthest edge of the plain, a full moon had just begun to show itself.

'. . . Crossing a little stream, we came into Konaka, Shozo's birthplace. The clatter of the four rickshaws in the still autumn air drew the villagers out of their cottages, to stare and whisper among themselves when they saw who it was. A gate on the right marked "Dr. Nakamura" proved to be the entrance to Shozo's house. A small two-storey building, looking like some kind of shop, stood next to the gate; this was where Shozo's father had spent his last years before he died, and the old woman who had helped to look after him was still living here. . . . She came out now, and greeted us very politely. Taking a little rice-cake from his pocket, Shozo gave it to her. "A present for you!"

'Down a path from the gate was the main house. A tiny cottage originally, it had been enlarged two or three times since Shozo's grandfather's time. Dr. Nakamura took us into the living-room; we went out on to the veranda, where Shozo sat quietly talking of old times. He was so calm and quiet, like a different being. . . . Suddenly he got up and went out. "A most extraordinary man," murmured Dr. Nakamura, looking after him. [Dr. Nakamura was the third of the doctors Shozo had brought to live in his house rent-free, first as a precaution in case his father fell ill, and later to provide the village with medical care.]

'Shozo came back with a dusty box, some old scrolls and a queer-shaped stone. This last he put in the place of honour in the alcove; then sat upright a few feet away to admire it.

'"There's a fine shape for you — the Lao Tse, the Chuang Tzu of stones!" It was a dripstone[1] from the Prefectural office building he had picked up and brought home when he was President of the Prefectural Assembly. Collecting stones was his only hobby.

'... Opposite the gate is a little shrine with a statue of Amida Buddha. Shozo's family had always kept the key, but the statue was passed round from house to house, so that except for a brief return to the shrine on the 23rd of each month it was almost never at home. "Just like me," said Shozo with a smile.'

Among the few who regularly saw him in Tokyo were Henmi Onokichi, an idealistic socialist who ran a business on 'worker participation' lines in Tokyo, and his wife. In their admiration for his work the Henmis not only provided him with a room for his use whenever he needed to come to the capital, but gave considerable sums of money for his use in Yanaka, in particular to help in the repeated rebuilding of the dyke on which the dwindling community's livelihood depended. They too testify to his gentleness and courtesy, Onokichi speaking of Shozo as

'... a perfect second father to replace the father I had lost a few years before; it was a true delight to welcome him whenever he came to us. To us and to everyone in our household he was always kind and courteous, which was perhaps not surprising when he treated rickshawmen and the like with such natural politeness. He would listen quietly to the conversation, unwilling to impose himself: but when he did speak, there was such weight and depth behind his words....'

Mrs. Henmi remembered him with equal affection.

'It was only for the last seven years of his life that we knew him, but during that time we were very close. Sometimes the rickshawman bringing him to our house in the evening would imagine he must be the senior member of our household, and would shout "The master's back!" as he set him down. I recall so vividly his talk of Christianity, of Tolstoy, of Nishida Tenko;[2] his hatred of any kind of bullying, that made him flare up when the policeman, his shadow, spoke roughly to our maid; the care with which he would treat *things* — anything, no matter how small or cheap, that came into his hands; the stones he would pick up on his journeyings and carry in his sleeve.... Above all, he was a man of action. There was some lesson for us in everything he did.'

*   *   *

1. In pre-gutter days, dripstones were placed on the ground under the eaves of a building to take the force of rainwater dripping from the roof.

2 Founder of the syncretic religious community near Kyoto, Garden of the One Light (Ittoen). For his life and writings, see Ohashi and Byles, *A New Road to Ancient Truth* (London: Allen & Unwin, 1969).

In Yanaka, the tension was steadily increasing. Attempts to repair the dyke after the summer floods had been hampered by mockery and intimidation from those villagers, now rapidly growing in number, who had decided to sell out. Among the latter was the man who had been paid a small sum to guard a simple drainage system the village had improvised to draw off some of the floodwater; no sooner had he left them than the sluice-gates were found to have been locked at night, and the key stolen. Stakes planted as an aid to fishing in areas most liable to flooding were removed.

Undaunted, the small group of Shozo's most faithful adherents drew up and signed a 'pledge of joint action' committing them all to fight on. The pledge was broken almost immediately, ironically by the villager who had been the first to welcome Shozo to his home when Shozo first went to live in Yanaka.[1] But the rest held firm. In the first week of January, 1907 they restarted work on the dyke.

Eye trouble, made worse by exhaustion and constant exposure to winter weather, forced Shozo to leave Yanaka for some days, to rest and to consult a doctor in Tokyo. He took the opportunity to promote an ingenious scheme intended to hinder final action by the authorities against Yanaka. This was to invite a number of prominent Tokyo personalities, including for example Shimada Saburo, the Dietman and newspaper editor, and Miyake Setsurei, a well-known writer, to associate themselves with Yanaka by accepting the title to plots of Yanaka land. Twenty-eight of those he approached agreed. Most of them were discouraged from going through with the plan, however, when on 26 January a Cabinet announcement put the government's intentions beyond doubt by authorising the compulsory requisition of the remaining land without any resettlement allowance.[2]

When their protests addressed to the Governor of the Prefecture were rejected, Shozo went to Tokyo with a deputation of villagers, one from each remaining household, with the unlikely hope of interviewing members of the Cabinet. No one would see them though they spent four days knocking on Ministry doors; being almost penniless, they were hard put to it to find a place to stay at night, ending up at a Salvation Army Hostel called 'The Ark'.

Late in March, Shozo did succeed in getting Shimada Saburo to introduce in the House of Representatives a motion of protest at the

---

1. This 'defector' disappeared suddenly at the end of November, 1906, taking with him a quantity of documents dealing with Ashio and Yanaka that Shozo had left with him for safe keeping. Totally mystified at first, the others eventually discovered that he had been persuaded to desert them by his son, who some weeks earlier had secretly joined the Prefectural department responsible for the harassment of the village.

2 Four of them did become 'owners' of Yanaka land, and stood by the peasants to the end. They were Henmi Onokichi, Abe Isoo (a Christian Socialist), Fukuda Hideko (a leading educator and campaigner for women's rights) and Ishikawa Yukiko (the wife of Shozo's friend Ishikawa Sanshiro).

government's treatment of Yanaka, which attracted 31 signatures, and was given added point when three days later the Board of Audit pronounced that it was 'improper' to apply to the destruction of Yanaka public money which had been voted for disaster prevention. But to these strictures the government, aided by the unfortunate timing — the Diet session was due to end that same week — and the indifference to the Yanaka issue of the majority of Dietmen, did not deign to reply.

Also in the last week of March, the Governor of Tochigi served notice on the villagers that he would now seek authority from the Requisition Committee (set up under the government's January ordinance) to confiscate their houses and land. While appearing to invest whatever further action he might take with legality, the move was disingenuous, to say the least: the Governor himself was Chairman of the Requisition Committee, nor did any of its members visit Yanaka before deciding on its fate.

On the villagers' side, work was still going ahead on the dyke. Resources were running pathetically low. Only nineteen families, or just over a hundred men, women and children, still remained; paradoxically, these were among the poorest of the original Yanaka community, those to whom their land was their only imaginable source of life-support, to which they therefore clung more tenaciously than the better-off. The unexpected success of a plea for funds that Shozo had persuaded Shimada Saburo to carry in his newspaper provided much-needed encouragement.[1] But only for a few days. In the middle of May the River Watarase, flooding a month before the rainy season because of snow melting on the denuded mountains round Ashio, burst once again through the dyke, destroying about half the crops but fortunately not reaching the remainder, which were on higher ground.

More petitions to the Governor, to the Home Minister, and to the Diet, drafted by Shozo and claiming that the Requisition Ordinance was unconstitutional and should be withdrawn until it could be

---

1. In fact it produced more than Shozo reckoned was required for the immediate repairs, whereupon he at once wrote to Shimada telling him to return any further contributions to their donors. Some of the villagers, not surprisingly, jibbed at what seemed to them (and will no doubt seem to others) this excessive moral fastidiousness on Shozo's part. Another target of criticism was his trip to Tokyo on 22 April to attend one of the meetings held for the 78-year-old General William Booth of the Salvation Army. The publicity the latter's visit to Japan attracted, inexplicable perhaps to anyone unfamiliar with Meiji Japan, was enormous, the municipality of Tokyo sponsoring a 'welcome' which was attended by senior statesmen, industrialists, and at least one Field-Marshal. Ambassadors and university professors were among those who could not get in because of the crowds. But Shozo's purpose was not simply to hear what a famous religious leader from the West (of whose work for the under-privileged he already knew something from the nights he had spent in Salvation Army hostels in Tokyo) had to say. He went to great pains to obtain a private interview with the General, at which he handed over a two-page plea he had prepared urging him to give public support for the cause of world disarmament. One sympathizes with the villagers who could not see why he should leave them at such a moment on such an apparently irrelevant mission. But in spite of his total commitment to their cause, Shozo's horizons were not bounded by Yanaka.

publicly demonstrated beyond all doubt that the 'public interest' demanded the sacrifice of so much rich agricultural land, were all returned.

One 12 June, when Shozo was in Tokyo attending the final hearing of his appeal against his conviction for 'insulting an official',[1] the heads of the remaining households were summoned to Fujioka, the small municipality into which Yanaka had been officially incorporated the previous year, to be confronted by four senior officials of the Prefecture, including the chief of police, and thirty policemen. Uematsu, the police chief, told them that 'the law' having decided that Yanaka was to be replaced by a lake, the authorities could no longer tolerate local 'interference'. Each man was handed a document ordering him to remove all his property, including even trees on his land, by 22 June: otherwise such property would be destroyed by the Prefecture at the owner's expense, and the owners themselves 'thrown out'[2] together with their families.

The peasants refused to give any answer. (Their silence was the result of a similar meeting to which they had been called five months earlier. On that occasion some of them, still naively patriotic, had said that if they could be convinced the country really needed the Yanaka lake scheme, they would not merely be willing to sell their land, they would gladly *give* it to the government. The absence of any response to this overture would have been enough to destroy the last vestiges of any belief in official 'sincerity'. To render the peasants' disillusion even more complete, it had come to light that the one among them who had most enthusiastically supported the conditional offer to give their land free to the authorities — and who happened to be illiterate — had been recorded in the police record of the meeting simply as having 'agreed to compulsory purchase'.) Returning immediately to Yanaka, they busied themselves feverishly with the task of getting in what harvest they could before the ultimatum expired.

A week later the chief of police, with the usual posse of policemen,

---

1. Though the appeal was in the end successful, it nearly foundered at one of the earlier hearings when Shozo once more spoke out against what he considered the insensitivity of those in power. The presiding judge had been indiscreet enough to smile when some of the witnesses (Dietmen and lawyers who had volunteered to help with the defence) testified to the sincerity of Shozo's passion for justice. Springing to his feet, Shozo denounced such levity as unworthy in one whose profession it was to judge cases as the Emperor's representative — the more so when the case under review concerned the fight for a village where, 'thanks to the callous violence of officials, the Emperor's writ no longer ran, the nation was being destroyed. . . .'

2. The phrase here translated as 'thrown out' was a strong one, implying physical violence. One of the peasants, Mamyoda Senya, remembered Uematsu's words carefully. Three weeks later, when his own house was being smashed under Uematsu's direction, he refused to leave. 'The law has decided it, the law, the law — that's what you've always said when we've asked you why the government must rob us of our village and our land,' he protested to Uematsu. 'Three weeks ago you threatened you would throw us out by force. By what law will you use such violence? Show me that law! If there is such a law, I will submit to it.' Even Uematsu was embarrassed by such unexpected defiance, but only momentarily, and as he had promised, Mamyoda was brutally dragged out of his ruined home.

Eleven years to the day after his threat to the Yanaka peasants, Uematsu's connection with the Yanaka affair was renewed in a brief but significant incident. See below, p. 225.

came to Yanaka to make a last attempt to persuade Shozo to surrender. Adamant, Shozo merely lectured him on the unconstitutionality of all his actions. Do you still plan to resist the Requisition Order, asked Uematsu: to which Shozo replied that the peasants were like virgins, without the power to resist, and any violence practised on them would be like striking a girl who wouldn't consent to her own rape. Uematsu could only answer that while what Shozo had said was true, he himself was only 'carrying out the law'.

The Governor gave much the same answer when Shozo called on him at the prefectural capital of Utsunomiya the next afternoon. Outwardly he was sympathetic; but insisted he could not right wrongs that had been set in motion long before his arrival on the scene (he had been appointed to Tochigi five months before). Whether this sympathy was genuine or not is hard to tell, for the crude attempts by his subordinates to compel the villagers to submit, or at least to break their unity, were continuing.

When he returned to Yanaka, well past midnight, Shozo found his young helper and secretary, Shimada Sozo, waiting up to tell him how in Shozo's absence he and his father, and the heads of three other families, had been summoned again to Fujioka by the police, and offered twice the amount of the compensation originally proposed, if they would agree to leave Yanaka at once. Shimada Sozo had demanded written confirmation of the offer before any of them would consider it. The official wrote down the sum he had mentioned on a scrap of paper, but when asked to stamp it with the personal seal that alone gives validity to Japanese documents, he could only reply that 'in this case no seal was necessary'. Their suspicions confirmed, the villagers refused to discuss the offer any further, and after promising to send a reply the next day went straight home. Shozo was delighted to hear of their firmness. Despite extreme exhaustion, he stayed up with Shimada Sozo till cockcrow, drafting a letter of rejection.

On the evening of the 22nd, after working in the fields all day as usual, the villagers held a party to commemorate what they believed would be the last night they would have roofs over their heads. Shozo was away again, making yet another appeal to the Governor to agree to a stay of execution. The guest of honour was his friend and admirer, Kinoshita Naoe. Kinoshita had come down from his mountain retreat to witness the destruction of Yanaka, expecting arrest or even death for himself, but too worried about what might happen to Shozo to be able to keep away.

In a short but emotional speech to the little group, he praised them for their determination to submit without violence to the destruction of their homes and livelihood rather than abandon their ancestral lands — 'a living example of the precept "Resist not evil".'[1]

There was a communal meal of noodles, rice-cakes and saké; songs were sung and old times recalled. At midnight, after renewing their pledge to stand by each other, they were about to disperse when a party of policemen arrived with a message from the Governor. The demolition of their homes was to be postponed for five days, till 28 June; they themselves were to appear before the Governor at Fujioka next day.

Any breathing-space, however short, was welcome. But agreement was unanimous that the Governor's summons should be ignored. They had been deceived too often to be in the mood for any further attempt on the part of authority to cow or trick them into submission. As the policemen were leaving, Shozo returned — by boat, for much of the low ground was still flooded.

The Governor's decision to postpone demolition must have been due in part, he thought, to his own plea that the peasants should be spared the misery of seeing their houses razed at what was for them the busiest time of the year; a few more days, and they would be able to finish harvesting such grain as had survived the floods, which would at least save them from starvation for a while. But there was another reason. The Mayor of Koga, the nearest town of any size, from which the Prefecture had begun to recruit labourers for the demolition squad, had let it be known that any citizen of Koga who offered his labour for this purpose would be expelled from the town and forbidden to return. The threat was apparently successful, and the Prefecture had to look elsewhere.

Next day, the 23rd, in a sudden display of interest by the outside world, a number of journalists arrived from Tokyo to check that the village had been reprieved and to interview Shozo. (Reporters were in fact the only visitors allowed by the police guard that had been posted at every entrance to Yanaka. Even relatives of the remaining families, some of whom came to help with the harvest, found it difficult to gain admission.)

All the villagers gathered that night for a second 'party'. This time Shozo was with them. In a short speech of encouragement, contrasting with Kinoshita's rhetoric of the night before, he compared their lot and his with that of a family of mud-snails playing in a paddy-field who suddenly hear the footsteps of the human snail-catcher. The baby snails run to their mother in terror, pleading for her to lock them up in their houses: but the mother cannot help, for she

---

1. Kinoshita's remarks were rather confused: he compared the villagers' stand with the decision of the last Shogun's Minister, Katsu Kaishu, in 1868 to hand over Edo (Tokyo) Castle without bloodshed to the forces of the new Meiji Government. Nor was his praise of their non-violent refusal to surrender altogether consistent with his later assessment of their attitude (See above, p. 153); but perhaps he was more aware of the truth when, as on this occasion, he was actually sharing their lives, however briefly. In any case his sincerity at the time was not in doubt, and it was this, rather than anything specific that he said, that moved his hearers.

knows the pitiless snail-catcher will pick them up and boil them, houses and all. . . . 'You are like the snails; but you are more than animals or insects. As human beings you have the right and the duty to live out your lives where you belong, to watch over the graves of your ancestors; as Japanese citizens, your freedom of residence is guaranteed in our Constitution.[1] The snails die with their shells, but we can still defend ourselves even after our homes have gone.'

He himself was ready to face beggary or death rather than give up the fight for the recognition of their constitutional and human rights, since without such recognition 'the nation itself was dead', and for themselves, to continue the struggle for truth and justice was the only way to retain their self-respect. If they could face the odds together, perhaps Yanaka might yet be reborn.[2] Shozo had no word now of anger or hatred for the Governor or any of those responsible for Yanaka's years of suffering. In place of the old fury, according to Kinoshita's account, the words 'they are not evil, only ignorant' were often on his lips.

Before the villagers separated for the night, one produced a sheet of paper and asked Shozo to write something for them to remember the occasion by. Under the heading *Disaster, gateway to joy* he wrote:

  Steeped in joy —
  What need then of bedding
  Or mosquito-net?
  Offer your body
  To the fleas, to the mosquitoes!

Smiling, he explained that the words were not to be mistaken for a love-poem. If faced in this spirit, any kind of pain or grief could be borne with ease.[3]

Five more days passed. With the harvest all but finished, relatives from other communities carried out some of the villagers' belongings by boat and on carts. On the 28th, the day of the Governor's final deadline, nothing happened, though the four Tokyo sympathizers

---

1. Art. XXII of the Meiji Constitution reads: 'Subject to the limitations imposed by law, Japanese subjects shall enjoy full liberty in regard to residence and change of abode.' It had been Shozo's contention all along that the plan for the destruction of Yanaka had been arbitrary and contrary to the spirit of the law, so that the 'limitations' proviso in this Article could not fairly be invoked.

2. The bond between Shozo and the villagers was closer now than it had ever been. In Shimada Sozo's words: 'Though we had never heard of Tolstoy or Gandhi, we were resolved to offer no violence. Nor did we have any thought of escaping, or even of removing any of our belongings to safety. The time was past for any such thoughts of our own advantage or interest. What united us was something like religious faith, a conviction that we must stay with Shozo and follow his lead whatever happened.'

3 Often in later years when he wrote this poem down for people who asked him, as is the Japanese custom, for some specimen of his calligraphy as a souvenir, it *would* be taken as the rather crude love-poem it appears at first sight to be, the recipient finding it difficult to conceal his disappointment. The state of mind at which Shozo was hinting was beyond the understanding even of most of his admirers.

who now 'owned' land in Yanaka came to give their moral support.[1] Then at last, on the morning of 29 June, a force of over 200 police, officials and labourers descended upon the village, and the work of demolition began. As each house was pulled down, the timber was carted or ferried beyond the village limits to a dump, over which a police guard was mounted to prevent the owner trying to recover his property.

Inevitably there were scenes both pathetic and bizarre. The head of a family that had been settled in the village for over 400 years sitting on the grass outside his house as it was being destroyed, clutching the memorial tablets of his ancestors and apologising to them hysterically for having to abandon his inheritance; the screams of a girl, the sister of one of the peasants, already mentally ill, and now bereft altogether of her reason by the shock of seeing the walls of her home fall; the quiet resistance of Mamyoda Senya and his wife to police orders they insisted were illegal,[2] till they were dragged out by hands and feet, though both were ill; Shozo thundering alternately at the wreckers for their 'illegal violence', persuading the stubborn ones to submit quietly and with dignity, and comforting those for whom the blow, when it fell, was almost unbearable. He himself succumbed now and then to exhaustion, as when he fell asleep like a child under a persimmon-tree one afternoon, after arguing all the morning with the police that they should spare an old shrine in the Shimadas' garden.

Some distinguished visitors from the capital, among them Miyake Setsurei and Viscount Matsudaira, courageously denounced the police and officials for what they were doing,[3] but without effect: day after day the operation went forward with brutal efficiency. Those whose homes had been razed had to spend the nights in the open, since the building of lean-tos was expressly forbidden. In the Japanese summer this in itself was no great hardship as long as the rains held off; when they did come, the distress was extreme. Shimada Sozo gives a hint of it in his brief account of the second night after he and his family had seen their own house pulled down:

'We hung up our mosquito-nets from bamboo sticks cut from bushes in the garden, and went to bed under the open sky. About one o'clock it began to thunder. Heavy rain followed immediately.

---

1. For the identity of these four, see above, p. 308. The only one of them who was not a journalist, Shozo's friend Henmi Onokichi, wore a journalist's badge, in order to get past the police guard at the entrance to the village.

2 See above, p. 164 n. 2

3 It is thanks to Miyake that some pictorial record of the destruction has been preserved. The police forbade him to take photographs, but refusing to be cowed, he demanded to know what right they had to stop him photographing actions which they insisted were merely 'carrying out the law'. Finally they gave way, on condition the photographs were not published. This condition he observed for nineteen years: the pictures were shown in public for the first time in October, 1926, at a commemorative exhibition of Shozo's calligraphy.

Huddling together under a single broken umbrella, the eight of us (including my grandmother, who was 70, and a baby of eight months) sat waiting for it to end. Suddenly we heard voices in the distance. We listened intently — whether because we were instinctively on our guard against the police or just because of the general tension, I don't know.... A lantern shone out of the tall grasses, and a greeting rang out, "So there you are — how are you doing?" It was Tanaka Shozo, with Kinoshita and two other friends from Tokyo, all drenched to the skin. They had been staying for the night at Mamyoda's house, which was still standing, but had got up the moment the thunder and lightning started, anxious about the people who no longer had a roof over their heads. They had been going round through the driving rain from family to family, now rowing, now plodding through the mud, now pushing their way through the head-high summer grasses. After comforting us as best they could, they moved off through the darkness to see how Shoemon and his family were faring.

'Shozo was sixty-five then. I shall never forget how deeply I was moved that night by his warmth, his sincerity, that was more precious then than anything in the world.'

Next day Hara Kei, Home Minister in the Tokyo government, wrote in his diary:

'3 July. Had an audience of the Emperor. I conveyed our gratitude for the Crown Prince's recent journey through the western provinces. ... Took the opportunity to report on the destruction of the remaining houses in Yanaka Village, Tochigi Prefecture. There was no special reason to trouble His Majesty with a matter such as this; I only did so because accounts have been appearing in the press for the last few days. Most of the villagers left some time ago, but a small number, instigated by Tanaka Shozo, have been refusing to go, in defiance of the law. So their houses are being destroyed.[1]

Two days later, on 5 July, the operation was completed. That afternoon the Governor of Tochigi came on a visit of inspection. To signify the importance of the occasion, he was photographed standing in front of the ruins of the last house to be destroyed.

Other more welcome visitors came in the next few days, bringing sympathy and a few small comforts; among them the women leaders of the Pollution Relief Association, and some of the lawyers who had

---

1. Ironically, Hara had had to cope with trouble at Ashio itself five months earlier. Despite the ruthless methods he had used to develop the mine at such phenomenal speed, Furukawa Ichibei had kept very close to his workers, and was rewarded by intense loyalty on their part. After his death in 1903, resentment gradually built up against the impersonal administration of Minami, the ex-bureaucrat he had put in charge (See above, p. 94). In February, 1907 it erupted into violent rioting, in which hundreds of houses were set on fire; the police failed to restore order, and Hara had to send in troops from the Takasaki garrison. 1,700 miners were dismissed, though most were subsequently reinstated after signing a written apology.

given their services defending in the Kawamata case.[1] Cheered by this evidence that they were not altogether forgotten — and urged on by Shozo, who was afraid that if they continued camping in the open the authorities would make it an excuse to arrest them as vagrants — the villagers busied themselves in erecting lean-tos (which were still illegal) from any timber the labourers had omitted to cart away.

On 11 July a notice was delivered from Uematsu, the police chief. In ponderous officialese this remarkable document reminded them that they were forbidden to remain in their new shacks, 'which in any case were dangerously unhygienic'. If they applied for permission 'in the proper manner', they would be allowed to re-erect dwellings on the site at Fujioka where the timber of their homes had been dumped, or on certain other sites; but the policeman who had been guarding the dump would now be withdrawn, and the Prefecture would take no more responsibility for the safe keeping of the timber.

The message aroused the resentment it deserved. The site at Fujioka was far too small to accommodate them all, and the suggestion that they should rebuild from the material of their former homes was hypocritical in the extreme. The houses had been literally smashed, not dismantled, Uematsu having specifically refused a request from Shozo that the timbers should be taken down with care and numbered so as to ease re-erection. Too weary to answer Uematsu's directive, the villagers ignored it.[2]

Torrential rain returned the next day, and continued intermittently for several weeks. Conditions were appalling: many of the lean-tos collapsed and could scarcely be repaired before the next monsoon downpour.

The culmination came in the last week of August, when not only the Watarase but the Rivers Tone and Arakawa rose in massive flood. Water poured over the dyke into Yanaka, sweeping away the shacks and the last traces of the original houses and gardens, and leaving only a few patches of high ground unsubmerged.

The planned 'lake' became a reality overnight. Not, however, with the beneficial effects that the Tokyo sponsors of the plan had claimed would follow. The rivers still burst their banks at many points across the Shimotsuke plain, and on this occasion, as if to press home the futility of the scheme, the inundations even reached Asakusa and Fukagawa, in Tokyo itself. But Yanaka was beyond reprieve. Officially declared non-existent a year before, and physically wrecked

---

1. Kinoshita ends his description of the lawyers' visit with these words: 'We saw them off to Koga by boat. On the way, one of them asked Shozo to write something on his fan. Shozo took out his brush and inkstone from his sash. After a moment's thought he wrote in bold, clear characters
                    Disaster, gateway to joy
Returning the fan, he laughed aloud.
   Not one of us in the boat but was too moved to raise his eyes.'

2. Uematsu was to make another appearance in the Yanaka saga 12 years later — in a very different capacity. See below, p. 215, n. 1

when its inhabitants obstinately refused to disperse, it had quite literally sunk without trace.

But the history of Yanaka did not end there.

Gathering for Shozo's funeral

13

'The care of rivers is the Way of Heaven'

Now that the physical destruction of the village had been accomplished, the interest of the outside world in the Yanaka affair declined sharply.

In defeat, it seemed, Shozo himself was not newsworthy; occasional references tended to dismiss him contemptuously as a socialist — an ironic consequence of the fact that a few idealistic Christian Socialists had been the only Tokyoites to lend him consistent moral support.[1]

But some of the lawyers who had been brought face to face with the realities of pollution and its effects in the Kawamata case were still sympathetic. In the midst of the struggle for survival that followed the demolitions, Shozo had managed to contact them, and within three weeks proceedings had been initiated on behalf of the Yanaka villagers against the Tochigi Prefectural government. Perhaps inevitably, the villagers and the Tokyo lawyers who wanted to help them did not entirely see eye to eye. The lawyers, who had formed themselves into an 'Aid Yanaka Association', took a realistic view: clearly there was no hope whatever of recreating the now broken and scattered community, but court action might conceivably pressurise the government into offering something approaching reasonable compensation, both in money and in resettlement land.

Shozo and the villagers objected. For them to haggle over

---

1. An earlier factor in Shozo's growing isolation had been the demise, in the face of increasing government repression of all 'left-wing' or liberal political thought, of the newspaper *People's Daily* (Heimin Shinbun) and the journal *New Era* (Shinkigen), which had done much to publicise his work.

compensation implied acceptance of the illegal act of destruction.[1] But they soon had to give in; to retain the goodwill of the lawyers was essential, since their interest in the case was voluntary and they would be giving their services free. The first hearings were held at Tochigi in September 1907. Unbelievably, they were to drag on for nearly 13 years.[2]

Meanwhile, in Yanaka itself the struggle for existence continued. New shacks were erected to replace the lean-tos that had been swept away in the floods of August 1907, and work was resumed in the sodden fields to prepare them for the next year. Morale among the sixteen remaining families was sometimes low. Shozo described their moods without illusion:

Yanaka folk have little idea of their rights. They belong to an age long past. They are slow to anger when their dykes are smashed, and even then they soon forget . . . I have to remind them sometimes!

They think only of receiving, and grudge the lateness of any help that comes . . . They forget how it has all happened.[3]

Peasants are earth. The earth is their 'property', their food; they are like worms. But they are human too; a kind of special human type on their own, as different from merchants and businessmen as the earth from the sky. They do not need money.[4]

But none of them left. Gradually regaining some of its fighting spirit, despite terrible hardship and frequent sickness, and with some financial help from the Henmis in Tokyo, the tiny community kept itself alive by survival farming, eked out with the fish that were now beginning to reappear in the Watarase River.

In the spring of 1908, in defiance of the prefectural ban on any settlement in Yanaka, a few of the families that had earlier sold out and moved elsewhere actually returned. At the centre of the recovery — after a bout of fever, the result of prolonged exposure during the rains — was Shozo, 'caring for us all like a father for his children', in

---

1. Until recently, many accounts implied a clash between Shozo and the villagers at this point, the latter being ready to settle for the hope of cash and the former holding out, as always, on the *principle* of opposition to arbitrary authority. Shimada Sozo's recently published memoirs, which are certainly to be trusted, make it clear that there was no such split. (Shimada says that Shozo had expected to leave Yanaka after the destruction of the houses, at least temporarily, but changed his mind when the villagers refused absolutely to go.) It is true, however, that (as he says) the Tokyo lawyers, unable to believe that the peasants would take a stand on principle if left to themselves, insisted that when they and Shozo met with the lawyers to discuss what kind of legal action should be taken, Shozo should keep his mouth shut. This incident does not reflect any discredit on the lawyers, who were to prove their sincerity by the time and energy they were to spend on the case, mostly without monetary reward. But it does reveal their inability to comprehend the possibility of a real understanding between the peasants on the one hand and the elderly ex-parliamentarian on the other. Such an understanding did exist, even though it was rooted in different motives on either side: in Shozo's case, unyielding opposition to unconstitutional action, and in that of the villagers, half-instinctive attachment to their ancestral lands.

2. For the final outcome of the case in 1919, See below, p. 225 (The first stage ended in 1912; see p. 195-196

3 From letters written to Henmi Onokichi in September 1907.

4 From Shozo's diary, October 1907.

'The care of rivers is the Way of Heaven'   183

Shimada Sozo's words.

Any time he could spare from Yanaka he devoted to touring villages roundabout, badgering their inhabitants into sending petitions to the Prefecture and the Diet for the reconstruction of Yanaka and the widening of the Watarase in its lower reaches.

The Prefecture seems to have been embarrassed by the refusal of the peasants to leave their non-existent village. For a whole year the flouting of its authority was allowed to continue unquestioned. It must have seemed to Shozo that there was a real chance that the past might be quietly forgotten, now that the lake scheme had been shown to be largely ineffective in preventing flooding elsewhere. If so, Yanaka might yet be resurrected. But the officials had neither forgotten nor forgiven.

In July 1908 the Prefecture announced the designation of Yanaka as a 'river area', to which the Rivers Law was therefore applicable; anybody attempting to reside or work there 'without permission' was ordered to leave by 10 September or face arrest. The order was not sent to Yanaka till halfway through August. With backing from the Tokyo lawyers, Shozo immediately arranged for an appeal to the Home Minister for the revocation of the order.[1] An application he and the peasants submitted for the 'permission to reside and work' specified in the order was rejected out of hand by the Governor, without any reasons being given. Shozo was furious; the more so when it came to light that the Prefecture was secretly negotiating to sell some of the Yanaka land to a brick company. To him the devious means adopted over the years to drive the peasants from their land were tantamount to murder. 'They kill their fellow-countrymen as a peasant kills the pests in his fields,' he wrote to Kinoshita. But there is another dimension now to his attack. Neither the officials nor the Tokyo lawyers can comprehend, he goes on, that to make rich land unproductive is blasphemy:

If, in their disgust with the people of Yanaka, the bureaucrats do not want them to cultivate its land, all right — let somebody else till its fields: Japanese, American, Chinese, anyone. That the soil should be tilled is the law of Heaven. It doesn't matter if the Yanaka folk don't eat what's grown there. Let the birds eat the crops — the deer, the wild boar: Heaven's laws would still be observed. Let thieves come, even, and steal the rice! That men and animals should eat the fruits of the earth is Heaven's law. God would have none of them starve.

Respect for the land and its productive power appears here as a categorical imperative. The passage is an outburst of anger at a specific action, but it reflects also a process of expansion in Shozo's thought. Hitherto his central concern had been the plight of

---

1. The appeal was rejected, but not until March 1909.

inarticulate peasants, conditioned by history to bear injustice as a form of natural disaster, and prevented by ignorance and narrowness of vision from combining in defence of their 'rights', which indeed they hardly knew they possessed. Now, after four years in Yanaka, the natural environment — soil, river, and mountains — from which they drew their sustenance began to loom as large in his diary and letters. Ultimately he was to see the problem of human attitudes towards the 'environment' (an abstract term he himself never used and would certainly have disliked) as above all a moral one. For the moment, however, his interest in conservation (to use the modern term once again) was part and parcel of the fight to save Yanaka.

For a while there seemed to be a gleam of hope. A group of unusually independent-minded officials in the prefectural office of Ibaragi, a prefecture bordering Tochigi and likewise affected by flooding and pollution, drew up a document proposing that instead of the ineffective Yanaka lake and the huge consequent expenditure which the prefecture was still having to devote to building embankments at various points along the River Watarase, the simplest way to reduce flooding would be to provide the floodwaters with easier outlet to the sea by widening the 'gap' at Sekiyado.[1]

Delighted at this unexpected support for what he had been saying for years, Shozo travelled all over Ibaragi to raise support for the proposals. At about the same time Usui Yosaku, an old friend and admirer of Shozo and a member of the Tochigi Assembly, reopened the whole question of the scandalous way in which the plans for the 'purchase' of Yanaka had been forced through the Assembly four years earlier. Seeing in Usui a possible successor to himself, Shozo gave him all the backing he could, having his speeches printed and distributing copies to Tochigi notables and to Dietmen in Tokyo. As many as 33 Tochigi Assemblymen signed Usui's protest to the Home Minister. But neither in Ibaragi nor in Tochigi were these moves successful. Though the proposals put forward by the non-conforming officials in Ibaragi were adopted by the Prefectural Assembly, collusion between senior officials and the contractors building the embankments ensured that they were not acted upon; while in the Tochigi Assembly, Usui's strictures were ignored.

Undaunted still, Shozo turned his energies once more to bringing pressure on the Diet, as he did every year during the three months it was in session. First he and the villagers sent petitions to both Houses, demanding the protection of the Constitution. Then he moved to Tokyo, to canvass individual Dietmen. Few of them would receive the unkempt, tramp-like figure, which was not very surprising, since one temple, even, refused him a night's lodging on account of his appearance: but Shozo was contemptuous of what he called such a

---

1. See above, p. 143.

'frivolous' attitude. Some would advise him kindly to give up such an obviously hopeless cause. Such advice only convinced him the more of their need to be 'educated'. There were other difficulties, including periodic bouts of eye-trouble, besides the hostile reception he often met with; but he would not give up:

It's fifty-seven days I've been in Tokyo now. They're tired of me here, just as they are in Utsunomiya [the prefectural 'capital' of Tochigi]. *There's a lot to cope with — illness, having to borrow money for medicine, for train-fares, for postage; listening to the arguments they put up to keep the truth at arm's length . . . There isn't a soul in the world, I suppose, who wouldn't hate this kind of thing. I shall go on with it, though. Imagine the perseverance it needs, if you can*[1] . . .

Near the end of the Diet session, in March 1909, he did succeed in getting a question about Yanaka, 'On the violation of the Constitution and of the Way', put to the Home Minister in the names of four Diet members — though the wording was unmistakeably his. Milder and more philosophical in tone than many of the questions he had spoken to in his own parliamentary days, it ended with a sentence that applies with prophetic accuracy to the perpetrators of pollution — and of botched attempts to evade its consequences — in contemporary Japan and other industrial societies:

Is it not true that, as we think, these men [the leaders of government and industry] *become prisoners within their organisations and are in fact poisoned by them, so that they are led to commit in ignorance crimes of which they have not even dreamed? Is not this the true nature of this problem?*

The sponsoring Dietmen, however, did not speak to the question, which was tabled only in writing — and the Minister's self-justificatory reply followed their example, so that there was no debate.[2] In fact the government, having tacitly recognised that the Yanaka lake had not fulfilled its ostensible object of making the Watarase area flood-free, was preparing plans for further large-scale dredging and strengthening of dykes up and down the whole length

---

1. From a letter to Usui.
2 The Minister himself, one Hirata Tosuke, seems to have been sympathetic. He was a member of the *Hotoku* or 'Indebtedness' movement (so-called because it emphasized the indebtedness of men to nature and to each other), originated by Ninomiya Sontoku (1787-1856), the so-called Peasant Sage. Shozo later got to know him well, visiting him frequently at his house in Tokyo. A diary entry briefly records their first meeting: 'Had meeting with Hirata. Reminded him how many times we have been deceived. It's not enough to feel *for* the people, I said — you must *become* the people. That pleased him.' But Hirata did nothing for Yanaka. Evidently a 'prisoner of his organisation,' he was also a protégé of Marquis Yamagata, who as Prime Minister had displayed such studied indifference to Shozo's final Diet speeches.

Hirata's predecessor as Home Minister, General (and Count) Kodama Gentaro, had actually sent for Shozo so that he could hear his views, and had persisted in the invitation, even though Shozo had at first refused. When the interview did take place, the Minister was so impressed with the written account of the Ashio affair and its Yanaka sequel which Shozo brought with him that he had it printed and distributed in government circles. But very shortly afterwards the Minister was moved to another department.

of the river. These plans, almost all of which Shozo insisted to the end were unnecessary, were announced in the spring of 1909, railroaded through the elected Assemblies of the four prefectures involved, and put into action from 1910. The work took seventeen years to complete, and cost a total of eleven and a half million yen.[1]

Unknown to Shozo, some relatives and friends had acquired in his name over 1,500 acres of land, and towards the end of 1910 he suddenly learned, to his great astonishment, that he was not penniless. Within a few days he had made the land over to a young relative who had helped him in the past, with the hope that the income from it might be used for educational purposes in his native village of Konaka. For by now, as his inner life had grown more real, possessions held no meaning for him.[2]

A series of reflections scribbled in a little note-book one evening in July of that year while he was resting for an hour or two in a little inn not far from Yanaka give some clues as to the nature of his inner preoccupations. Though he headed it *Seijinron* (Essay on the Sage)[3] before sending the note-book off to his friends Kinoshita and Henmi in Tokyo, it is not in fact an essay, but a shapeless collection — like most of his voluminous diary entries in these last years — of thoughts without any very coherent theme; written, however, as he told Kinoshita they were, under a strong sense that he had not long to live, the sayings have an immediacy that makes up for the lack of connectedness. A few extracts:

If a man wishes with all his being to see God, he will see him there and then. If you truly wish to see God, look into yourself first.

---

1. The massive expenditure did bring considerable benefits. But neither floods nor pollution were halted for good. See Epilogue, pp. 216-9

Shozo's attempts to organise opposition to the government's plans were emasculated by divisions among the peasants living along the Watarase. Those from the upper reaches, who were most likely to benefit from them, gave the plans their enthusiastic support — which was mobilised, ironically, by a man who had been one of the most determined leaders of the peasant anti-pollution demonstrations of the late 1890s. Those from the lower reaches, on the other hand, feared that the end result would be an extension of the futile Yanaka lake. With the narrowness Shozo had so often deplored, neither side made any attempt to see the other's point of view.

2 All his life he had aimed at simplicity in living. But whereas in his earlier years the simplicity had been rather forced, too deliberately aimed at showing up by contrast the extravagance of others, it was now 'natural', the outward sign of a personality that had discarded as superfluous most of what other men regard as the basic needs, not of a comfortable, but of a barely tolerable, way of life. A friend who interviewed Shozo for a Kyoto Buddhist newspaper at about this time wrote: 'Looking back over his earlier years with a moving humility, he told me how when he had been President of the Tochigi Assembly he would always spend the nights in Tochigi in a 25 sen inn, while the other Assemblymen chose to spend 80 sen or a whole yen; and when he was a member of the Diet in Tokyo he would make a point of eating cheap barley-and-rice out of a peasant's lunch-box in front of the other Dietmen. Then he said, in a low voice but with all the power his words habitually carried, "It wasn't genuine. I was showing off then." ' Shozo's diary jottings on the importance of 'uncluttered' living often invoke Christ's teaching not to possess two coats (to which he was literally obedient) and the example of Confucius, who according to Shozo was not above finding work as a shepherd. (Cf. Mencius (tr. D. C. Lau), p. 155: 'He [Confucius] was once a minor official in charge of sheep and cattle'.)

3 'Sage' is a common translation of *seijin*. In Shozo's usage it is closer to 'saint', or more precisely 'the profoundly religious man, whose inner and outer lives are in perfect accord'.

'*The care of rivers is the Way of Heaven*' 187

Looking up to heaven will not help you. Look within you with all your strength, with all the strength of your being: and if there is no dark cloud within you, however small, if your words and acts are clear, if you truly desire to see, you shall see. They say, 'God is invisible'. What pitiful folly!

The sin is in you. You have no right to blame anyone else. This is my truth, my sincerity; my secret, my secret way to God ... The scholars, the clever ones of the world, run too fast after mere knowledge, they play so skilfully with arguments big and small, yet this power of theirs is only power of display, it is not real power, not their power: *they can speak of God but not see him — and because they cannot see, they have no faith. This God they do not believe in, they tell the young to accept. So it is that the Way is neglected ... Japan is dying — of madness, of luxury, of victory, of superiority, of aggression, deceit and banditry; of the lack of religion ... A man may become God or a beast. Both are easy: but men do not see this. How sad it is ...*

Arai Osui, by his friendship and example, had introduced Shozo to a type of spirituality which, though recognisably oriental in its mystical, intuitive aspects, was nonetheless based on a form, if an unorthodox one, of Christianity. Now, at the age of seventy, Shozo found another 'teacher', who was even more eclectic in the sources of his inspiration. While a successful farmer in Aichi Prefecture, Okada Torajiro had undergone Zen training, but not content with this austere discipline he had studied the lives and work of an astonishing range of Western and Oriental 'sages' — the list includes Christ, Buddha, Plato, Shakespeare, Pestalozzi, Longfellow, Emerson, Rousseau, Luther, Montesquieu, Confucius, Mencius, Lao-Tse, Chuang Tzu, Chu Hsi, Su Shih, Shinran, and Kumazawa Banzan. After three years in America, an experience of mystical illumination during a solitary retreat in the mountains of Yamanashi Prefecture impelled him to devote the rest of his life to the propagation of *seiza*, 'silent sitting'.[1]

In *seiza*, a kind of 'poor man's Zen', the emphasis is not on meditation so much as on correct posture and a certain form of deep breathing which is said to improve physical and mental health. It is associated with no one religion, and the *seiza* groups, some seventy of which sprang up all over Japan as a result of Okada's teaching, would

---

1. The years in America were spent in 'studying'. What Okada studied is not known, for in his mature years he spoke little of himself, and refused to leave any written record of his life, apparently with the intention of forestalling the emergence of any new cult centred on himself. A partly Western origin for *seiza* is hinted at in the following intriguing passage: 'I have been told that Okada began his *seiza* when he was in America and heard how some priests and suchlike folk' (Quakers?) 'meditated in silence, sitting on chairs; and that his *seiza* was an adaptation of this practice to suit the Japanese.' (Ishii Tsunezo, quoted by Karasawa Ryuzo in the privately published journal *Yanagi*, October 1965.) But Okada probably owed a much larger debt to the great Zen Master, Hakuin (1675-1768).

meet to 'sit together in silence' in each other's homes or in any temple or other meeting-place that offered itself. Shozo's Tokyo friends Kinoshita Naoe and Henmi Onokichi were among Okada's earliest and most fervent disciples. When they urged Shozo to join them in their *seiza* sessions whenever he was in Tokyo, he at first refused; partly out of the instinctive reluctance of an active man to believe that 'sitting in silence' could be anything but a waste of precious time, and partly because Okada, unlike Arai Osui, lacked the dignity that age lends — he was thirty-eight years younger than Shozo.

The decision to 'sit in silence' himself was the result, not of any urging from his friends, but of the wordless example of two country girls who were living in the Henmi household as maids. Getting up very early one morning after spending the night at the Henmis', Shozo went to the kitchen, to find the two girls 'sitting' there, and their demeanour and posture, 'like that of Kannon, the Bodhisattva of Mercy', so impressed him that from then on he began to practise *seiza* himself and attend Okada's meetings whenever he could.

The physical effect was almost immediate. Not only did the rheumatism he had had to endure for most of his life cease to trouble him; *seiza* released in him new energy, of which after the privations of six years in Yanaka he was badly in need. Even more striking was the spiritual effect. It was as if the discipline of silence and the quiet discourses with which Okada would conclude a *seiza* session pared away still further what little dross still clung to his personality, leaving him with a new clarity of vision and an even profounder, yet more tranquil, conviction of the rightness of the seemingly hopeless cause in which he was engaged. Very soon, though because of Shozo's multifarious activities it was not often that the two could meet, he became an ardent disciple of the younger man.[1]

Often in his diary there are references to what *seiza* has taught him, whether in mystical terms — 'By *seiza* I have come to know the great Way of Heaven', or by linking these periods of stillness with strictly practical issues, in this case the government's long-term plans for controlling the River Watarase — '*Seiza* has shown me the *natural* way to control rivers and flooding. Our country is ignorant of the

---

1. One of Shozo's most pleasant characteristics was his readiness, especially in these later years, to acknowledge with a childlike humility how much he owed to others. 'From Mr Okada and from "sitting in silence" I have come close to the power that animates all things. Thanks to Mr Arai's Bible-teaching I have not lost the mental habit of reflection, three times a day, upon what I am doing. My friend Henmi has taught me the idea of progress; from Kinoshita, I have learnt to throw away old, conventional ideas like worn-out shoes.' (From a letter of February 1913.) In reality, of course, Okada and Shozo were giants of equal stature. Kinoshita Naoe put it in his usual picturesque way in letters he wrote nearly thirty years later, recalling his impressions of the two men: 'Okada was a dragon, whose flight no man could follow; Shozo a great elephant, and the rest of us but puny mice that could do no more than trace his footprints. . . .' 'The years have brought me to a clearer realisation of the loftiness, the depth, the *greatness*, of Shozo. I had intended [in his biography of Shozo] to describe the first meeting between him and Okada, but there was such a grandeur about them both — the grandeur of the sun and the moon — as defeats both my tongue and my pen.'

natural way, and it is because it does not sit in quietness that it is ignorant. The country is everywhere injured and diseased, and the great works they prescribe can no more heal it than a quack's medicines can patch up a broken body.'

Most moving, perhaps, is the new light in which Shozo now began to see the peasants among whom he was living in the ruins of Yanaka. The instinct, inherited and so deeply ingrained that he is hardly conscious of it, that he is a leader whose constant duty it is to guide and teach, irrespective of how eagerly or otherwise his pupils may respond, recedes — only at times, for the total loss of that instinct would have undermined the whole basis of his personality — and the effect is powerful and liberating. Writing of himself in the third person, he records his new attitude to one of the humblest of the villagers, who was illiterate:

Thanks to Takada Senjiro, Shozo has woken out of his long dream of forty years and more. Always Shozo was watching others and not himself; and because he did not look into himself, he had no true understanding of others. Only when a man sees clearly into himself can he begin to see into others. . . . To watch and judge others without first watching and judging oneself is like climbing a tree to catch fish. . . . Takada pays no attention to others, but studies only how he should live. As a child he learnt no letters, he is ignorant of quite ordinary customs and ceremonies, he knows nothing of the tools and the arts of civilisation. But other things he does know — the true Way of Man, the meaning of 'country', of law, of the mystery of things; he works with zest, keeps his household orderly and his family happy; quarrels with no man, performs all that is required of him. He does not bend the Way; he neither fears the rich nor despises the beggar; flatters none, but speaks plainly and kindly to all. Being without desire, there is nothing he craves for, nothing he regrets. He is never angry, never arrogant. In all that he says or does, there is no fault.

The passage has the exalted tone of a revelation. But the new insight is not only into moral qualities; there are moments too of the quiet, limpid delight in 'naturalness' and spontaneity in small things that comes easily only to those who are inwardly at peace. Another diary extract, relating to another member of the Takada family, records such a moment:

Senjiro's daughter had got out of bed early to go to the toilet outside the house. There is a fence round the toilet, its bamboo struts entwined with leaves of morning glory. She blew her nose with her fingers, then picked a leaf from the fence to wipe it. I saw the flowers of the morning glory smile. . . . The girl is innocent, her mind and spirit unclouded, uncluttered. How wonderful, how blessed!

It is not the least of Shozo's claims to uniqueness that his deepening inner life entailed not the slightest diminution of outward activity, despite the physical limitations of his age and the naturalness, accentuated by Oriental tradition, of withdrawal in a man's final years to a life of leisured contemplation. He was still fully occupied in helping the tiny community to stay in being — so fully occupied, indeed, that we find him estimating in his diary that he needs three more years to be able to read right through the New Testament, and hoping he will live that long.[1]

The villagers' struggle to survive had lost none of its severity. The spring of 1910 was a particularly bitter time, with the village lands flooded but few or no fish to be found in the rampaging waters, fields drowned, and a regional depression in economic activity making it impossible for the womenfolk to find any outlets for their sewing and weaving. There was a plague of fleas, which so tormented Shozo at night that he made himself an enormous cloth sleeping-bag in an attempt to keep them at bay. Just at this time he writes to Kinoshita:

Of what use would it be to retire to a philosopher's life in the mountains? What good would it do? If a man can only stay on in the world, polish and sharpen himself and turn himself into a philosopher while standing firm in the thick of the fight — that's my faith at this moment, ignorant though I am.

Thanks to him, the villagers held together, even managing a little party at the end of June to celebrate the continued existence of Yanaka three years after its destruction. Then, little over a month later, the tragic story of so many earlier summers was repeated yet again when the Rivers Watarase and Tone rose in one of the worst floods ever, spreading disaster as far as the inner suburbs of Tokyo, and proving once more the uselessness of the Yanaka lake. Most of the villagers' shacks were swept away. For once Shozo himself was forced to leave Yanaka, there being quite literally nowhere for him to lay his head, and stay with a friend in neighbouring Fujioka.

After surveying the flooded areas by boat (and nearly being drowned in the process, the currents were so violent), he set about getting in emergency supplies of rice.[2] This done, he bombarded prominent men in Tochigi and Tokyo with printed leaflets charging that the floods were not natural but man-made disasters, and journeyed to Tokyo to argue the case in person. In the capital the shabby figure in the ancient black kimono, bespattered with mud, a stick slung over his shoulder with the peasant's straw cape which Kinoshita had given him wrapped round it, his hair tied with string, was not a little conspicuous.

Once as he walked down a residential street to call on a

---

1. In fact he died three years and two months after writing these words.
2 The prefectural sub-office at Fujioka provided the villagers with two days supply of rice; but when the official in charge demanded that they sign a formal application for any further relief, the villagers indignantly refused, on the ground that to suggest they go cap in hand to those whose negligence had caused the flood was an insult. Hence the need for Shozo to organise his own relief programme.

parliamentarian, having come straight from two days in the mud and slime of Yanaka, a policeman on patrol rebuked him for his dress, which was 'too outlandish altogether for Tokyo'. 'Fool!' Shozo roared back, 'don't you see that those who wear Western clothes and shoes and cream their hair at a time of national disaster and distress are the real outlandish ones?'

Shozo's reaction to the floods of 1910 went beyond protest and efforts at material relief for they were the immediate cause of his decision to devote the rest of his life, or as much of it as he could spare from the day-to-day problems of Yanaka, to *chisan chisui*, 'the care of mountains and rivers', or mountain and river conservation. (Mountain, in this context, means in effect 'forests', since it is in thickly-forested mountain ravines that most Japanese rivers have their source.)

Partly, perhaps, this change of direction was due to the knowledge (which he was never willing to admit to in so many words) that the long fight to resurrect Yanaka was doomed to failure, which for a man of his temperament meant that even at the start of his seventies he had to find another cause to which he could commit himself.

But there were stronger motives impelling him to this new concern and shaping the form it took. A lifetime's experience had taught him that decisions on water resources, flood control and pollution taken by officials in Tokyo would always be designed to serve industry or to protect the metropolis, never to benefit the rural communities through which the rivers ran, nor to promote the 'natural well-being' (to use his term) of the mountains and rivers from which so much of the historic fertility of the Shimotsuke plain was derived. The officials, relying for the most part on the most general surveys, did not *know* enough about the rivers for the 'control' of which they produced such vast and expensive civil engineering schemes; thorough, intimate study of the waterways from their sources downwards would show, he was convinced, that such schemes were ineffective and unnecessary. Detailed knowledge of the behaviour of rivers, gathered over several years and in all conditions, and throughout their length, was the first priority; and this knowledge being nowhere available, he determined to gather it himself. But knowledge by itself would solve nothing. Rivers and mountains must be *respected*, as men respect one another, and interfered with only so much as may help them to fulfil their function in the natural cycle.

This moral attitude to nature Shozo did not define with any precision, but hinted at, merely, in characteristically Oriental terms: 'the care of rivers is not a question of rivers, but of the human heart'; 'the care of rivers is the Way of Heaven'; or, in a favourite, oft-repeated phrase, 'to care for mountains, your heart must be as the mountains — to care for rivers, your heart must be as the rivers'.

This sense of identification with the natural world Shozo had learnt, not, like most Japanese, from a combination of literary sources and the subtle arts of Japanese gardening or flower-arrangement, but from his peasant upbringing, and in a more vital way from his Yanaka experience, of which living literally cheek by jowl with nature was one of several equally significant components:

I have no learning. Heaven and earth are my teachers. Disaster is good fortune indeed. Five times in prison have only made me stronger. My past life was all error. This I learnt since coming to Yanaka.

At a deeper level there is the mystical sense of unity with nature, which finds expression in his diary only in gnomic fragments, or in poetry:

> *If I make*
> *The sea and sky my home,*
> *My home is without possessions.*
> *And having nothing,*
> *All things are mine.*[1]

> *If all men would make*
> *The grassy plains their bed*
> *And the mountains their pillow*
> *They would wake to the glory*
> *Of the dawning sun.*

This two-fold conviction of the need for precise study 'in the field' of the characteristics of the rivers of Shimotsuke and for the propagation of what is in essence a philosophy of conservation, based on a moral attitude to nature, was the propelling force of Shozo's last years.

Soon after the floods of the summer of 1910 began to recede, he started on the long labour of fact-finding, tramping up and down both banks of the bigger rivers, the Tone and the Watarase, shod in straw sandals, or in high wooden clogs of his own design if the mud was deep, his haversack on his back, a stick in one hand to help him walk and another on his shoulder carrying his straw cape. These journeys, of which he was to undertake many, were mostly made on

---

1. A more forceful version of a poem he had written eleven years before. See above, p. 104

foot, for he had vowed never to use rickshaws again.[2] They lasted for from two to four weeks, and would average some eight miles a day. Sometimes he would go alone, sometimes take along a few of the younger men from Yanaka. Besides making detailed maps and measurements of unusual features in a river's course, he built up a record, by careful enquiry among farmers in every area, of the levels and duration of floods over the years. One or more of the notebooks containing all this information he always carried around with him in his haversack, so that whenever he could find a willing listener on the subject of the care of rivers (and often when the listener was less than willing) he could back up his arguments with facts and plans. In time, indeed, he became so familiar with the material that he could produce from memory instant and accurate drawings of any section of the hundreds of miles of river country he had visited.

After some months of this initial fact-finding he was in a better position to tackle his other and more difficult aim, that of teaching to an indifferent rural population a new attitude to 'mountains and rivers'. There were public meetings in various towns and villages, and many attempts to enlist the support of prominent individuals.

The climax came in November, 1911, when under Shozo's sponsorship an association called the 'Shimotsuke Conservation Group' was launched. For centuries the rulers and people of each of the several feudal enclaves into which Shimotsuke was divided had planned and built only to secure the best water supply and the maximum flood protection for themselves, with no thought for their neighbours; the new group was to bring together those, in Tokyo and in the five prefectures that had replaced the old feudal domains, who cared for both rivers and men, so that the traditional sectionalism could be superseded by a new breadth of vision and the region's most vital natural resource made less dependent on the expensive bungling of a centralised bureaucracy.

The formation of the group was Shozo's last striking achievement in the field of public affairs. It had some influence, but was not

---

1. He was not able to keep this vow very strictly. His incessant travelling had made him well-known to many rickshawmen who over the years came to revere him as a friend of the poor and a traveller who treated them with unfailing (and unusual) courtesy; and they would often offer him a free ride. Often, indeed, he would have nothing to pay them with: having borrowed a few sen specifically for a rickshaw, if he happened to meet some children in the street on his way to the rickshaw-stand, he would as likely as not give them the money he had just borrowed, or buy a few baked sweet potatoes from a roadside stall, which he would then share with them. For he had a soft spot for both children and rickshawmen. One of the friends at whose house he often spent the night in Tokyo was a prominent journalist. When he arrived from Yanaka late at night and found the door locked, he would go and stay with a rickshawman who had a shack nearby. The next night he might spend with a Dietman or with Marquis Okuma; or at a Salvation Army Hostel or a Buddhist temple. (He seems to have been in the habit of arriving at awkward hours. The abbot of one temple in Tochigi Prefecture where for thirty years Shozo had sought overnight lodging whenever he found himself in the vicinity recalled that in the last year of his life it would often be after midnight that they would hear Shozo banging on the gate with his stick: 'it became a habitual joke with us that anyone knocking like that, and so late, must either be a sick man, a robber, or Tanaka Shozo'.)

notably successful. Only a handful of enthusiasts, none of them with Shozo's single-minded energy, took up his ideas. The Assemblymen for whose support he had hoped were mostly indifferent.

One evening in October, 1911, during an emergency session of the Tochigi Assembly that had been summoned to discuss flood control, he called on the homes of the Assemblymen representing the worst affected areas, to be told that they were attending not the Assembly but the theatre. Their 'levity' provoked an outburst of anger in his diary at what he saw as their betrayal of his fight against pollution:

These are the men I trained. They betray my name, the fruits of my work. They break the laws of Heaven and of earth. The children eat the flesh of their fathers. . . .

But their indifference was not really surprising. Many thought his ideas out-of-date, a re-hash of ancient wisdom that in the modern Meiji state had been discredited; though from a less superficial point of view he was ahead of his time, not behind it. Also against him was the fact that in a society where initiatives were customarily launched from the top downwards he was a mere private individual with no 'position', and an unkempt old eccentric into the bargain. There were not a few even now who were very willing to dismiss his pleas for the proper care of mountains and rivers as the self-advertisement of a *seijiya*, a 'politician' in the most pejorative sense of the word, though what profit he might be extracting from such an undramatic cause these critics never troubled to explain.

Despite all the opposition and indifference Shozo worked on without wavering, and with all his usual intensity. So preoccupied was he with Yanaka and his fact-finding journeys that when his wife Katsu had to leave the relatives with whom she had been living for a number of years to spend some weeks in hospital in Tokyo, he did not once visit her; though he twice had business in the city while she was there, he went straight back to Yanaka the moment his business was done. This 'coldness' to the faithful, uncomplaining Katsu was the one fault which his disciple Shimada Sozo could never forgive.

Shozo himself was deeply troubled; his own record of the conflict between his feeling of guilt and the conviction that nothing should be allowed to interfere with his public work is evidence that for all his single-mindedness he was never a mere fanatic, contemptuous of ordinary human responsibilities:

My not going to see her wasn't deliberate; it just happened that way because I have been so busy. Yet I couldn't in any case put private affairs before public. From the standpoint of ordinary humanity I shall be thought unfeeling, I suppose. Certainly my wife can't believe I am truly sympathetic. . . . But what I do, I do not for myself. The Way to Heaven is steeper than any mountain; it leads above the clouds, and the climber must travel light, throwing off all desire, pride, and selfish wants and whims. . . . She was in Tokyo more than

30 days. Twice I stayed overnight in Tokyo, not far from the hospital. For the sake of the Way I transgressed the Way and broke the law of Heaven for the law's own sake. But does this accord with the mind of God? I may forgive myself, but how does the divine spirit look on what I have done? ... The mind's first resolve is God.[1]

The spring and early summer of 1912 brought more trials for both Shozo and the villagers. As the rivers rose with the melting of the winter snow, the prefecture ordered them to stop all work on the makeshift dykes within which each year they were still managing to grow a few crops — disobedience to be punished with imprisonment or with fines they clearly could not pay — and to *demolish* the dykes with their own hands (on the ground that they had been erected without permission) when the spring floods were over. In the event the spring floods, though brief, were particularly severe, and the dykes were destroyed before their eyes. If they were to survive there was no choice but to rebuild them as best they could.

While they were setting about this task, in early April, the five-year old lawsuit in which they had been claiming proper compensation from the prefecture entered a critical stage, with what promised to be the final hearing in Tochigi Court. Shozo had been telling the villagers that the bringing of the suit had been a mistake, foisted on them by the lawyers of the Aid Yanaka Association — in that it had led them and the newspapers that carried reports of the case to suppose that money was more important than principle. Nevertheless he had taken a prominent part in the proceedings. At a hearing the previous September he had harangued the court for an hour and a half on the unconstitutionality of the destruction of Yanaka, the day before departing on one of his fact-finding walks.

The court atmosphere drew from him all the eloquence with which he had so often addressed the Diet on pollution — and when the judge repeatedly tried to silence him, provoked him to an explosion of anger such as he had not displayed for many years.

Much the same thing happened at his final appearance in the court on 15 April, 1912. He had intended, as he said with a smile to a friend afterwards, to make a reasoned statement of the villagers' case, but got so carried away by the presiding judge's interruptions that he found himself giving instead a long lecture on conservation — which ended with a demand that the judge order the arrest of the 'robbers' in the prefectural and central governments who had permitted the

---

1. This final sentence illustrates the danger of interpreting Shozo's frequent references to 'God' only in traditional Christian terms. The thought here is probably derived from Yoshida Shoin (1830-1859), the short-lived but celebrated samurai patriot and teacher of so many of the leaders of the Meiji Restoration, who was later the subject of a biography of R. L. Stevenson: 'All-important is the mind's first resolve. It will follow a man everywhere.' (Yoshida Shoin, *Komo sakki*.) Shozo's first loyalty, he is probably implying, is to the vow of public service he had made thirty-three years before.

despoliation of Yanaka. Scandalised, the judge got up and walked out, while Shozo was pacified by the two lawyers then in charge of the villagers' case. Surprisingly, after this incident, the finding of the court (when it was finally announced five days later) was in favour of the villagers.

But only just. They were awarded additional compensation which was only marginally above the original offer from the authorities, and less than a sixth of the token sum they had pleaded for; this was not the clear victory of principle for which the case had been fought. With Shozo deliberately absenting himself, so that he could not influence them, the villagers met to discuss whether or not they should appeal, and decided unanimously that they should.

The Tokyo lawyers of the Aid Yanaka Association, understandably, felt they could give their services no longer; but Arai Osui came to the rescue by recommending a lawyer friend of his own, one Nakamura Akizaburo, who with colleagues he persuaded to join him took charge of the appeal throughout the seven years it took to bring it to a successful conclusion.[1] Working feverishly, he and Shozo just managed to prepare and submit the appeal documents by the statutory date.

A few days later Shozo was back in Yanaka, helping the villagers in a desperate attempt to salvage a small crop of wheat that with the arrival of the summer rains had lain for a day and a half under three feet of water.

Late in July, while away in the town of Sano for a few days to submit more protests against the official refusal to admit the villagers' right to any form of flood protection, Shozo heard the newsboys crying special extra editions of the Tokyo papers: the Emperor Meiji was dying. There is pathos — and irony, though Shozo intended none — in the following letter he at once wrote to the Yanaka villagers, suggesting that they send 'best wishes for his recovery' to the titular head of the state that had wiped their community off the face of the map, and the man to whom Shozo had tried to appeal on behalf of the Ashio pollution victims eleven years before:

Saw report of His Majesty's grave illness in extra editions today. Let us send the message below to the Governor, to be forwarded to His Majesty.

---

1. Nakamura, who is given only the briefest mention in Japanese accounts of the Yanaka saga, is nevertheless one of its heroes. At great physical and financial cost to himself and his family he undertook the brunt of the work, not only in the Yanaka compensation case, but in its sequel, the so-called 'reed-cutting incident' (see below, Epilogue). In the spring of 1924, only four months after winning the latter case on the villagers' behalf, he died of sheer exhaustion. His wife and daughter died soon afterwards; his only son had died while the case was still in progress.

> We humbly pray for your Majesty's recovery.
>
> With the utmost respect,
>
> from the people still resident
> in the former village of Yanaka
>
> To His Excellency the Governor of Tochigi Prefecture:
>
> Being unlettered folk, we have no knowledge of politeness and etiquette. Before sending our humble message, please alter it as may be necessary.

The Emperor died that week. Te state funeral was held six weeks later. Shozo, who was by then in the middle of one of his river-survey journeys, had stopped for some hours at the home of a farmer in a village not far from Yanaka. As the clock struck the precise hour at which the Emperor's funeral was due to begin, Shimada Sozo recalls, 'Tanaka turned to face south, in the direction of Tokyo. For over an hour he sat erect, silent and motionless as a stone', filling the neighbours who had gathered in the house with awe at the solemnity of the ragged, weather-beaten figure.

One wonders what passed through his mind during that hour of silence: the man who all his life had defended the weak against the arbitrary authority of fief, prefecture or state, meditating on the death of the man in whom above all that authority was incarnated. If in many ways, Shozo's ideas were far ahead of his time, in his profound instinctive reverence for the Emperor — balanced though it was by a clear perception that the Sovereign was used by the oligarchy to cloak its policies with spurious authority — he belonged to the old, not to the modern, Japan. And as if to underline the fact that he too was a man of Meiji, that era of extra-ordinary men, he himself was to survive the Emperor by little more than a year.

A shack built by a Yanaka family after their house had been destroyed

14

'Over withered fields'

The last few months of Shozo's life were among the busiest he had ever known. 'Drunk with work' he calls himself in February 1913. Some quiet moments there were. New Year's Day and the two following days he spent with the anarchist Ishikawa Sanshiro at the Yokohama house of Fukuda Hideko, the woman Socialist and writer, triumphantly producing a five-yen note when he arrived on her doorstep, for her to buy oranges and sweet New Year saké as his contribution to the festive occasion. For him, five yen was now a sizeable sum, as little likely to pass through his hands as five hundred — as he implied in the poem he gave his hostess along with the money:

> *A country bumpkin,*
> *But rich enough*
> *To buy a geisha —*
> *Look what he's brought:*
> *Five hundred yen!*

The little party was a singularly happy one, Mrs. Fukuda records, with Shozo more lively than she had seen him for years, breaking for a brief space his no-saké vow, talking freely of the past, and writing a whole series of New Year poems in his powerful but flowing calligraphic hand. Later that month he visited some friends in western Tokyo, finding shapely stones by the roadside, as his custom was, to present to any he thought might appreciate them.

Between these interludes he drove himself as hard as ever, conferring with Nakamura and his associates on the Yanaka appeal, canvassing in city and country for support for his Conservation Group, journeying the length and breadth of Shimotsuke to record the topographical facts without which his ideas would carry no conviction. On one of these journeys he wrote to his native village of Konaka to arrange for the disposal of the Tanaka property, of which he was still the nominal owner, though it was nearly forty years since he had lived in it, and the successive doctors he had found as tenants had occupied it rent-free in return for their service to the village. The house had been mortgaged to his nephew for the sum of ¥400 so that he could repay two debts of ¥200 each to his friend Shimada Saburo, the Tokyo editor and parliamentarian, and to a well-to-do sympathiser in Tochigi. Neither creditor, as it turned out, would accept repayment. But Shozo's conscience would not let the matter rest there.[1]

He now left the house and land to the Konaka Farmers Cooperative Club (which he himself had founded), on condition that *they* repaid the money. When this too failed, he still would not accept the money for himself, but gave it too to the Club. Shozo was now in an even more literal sense without possessions of any kind.

His first visit to Yanaka in the New Year was simply to arrange with the young men of the 'village' a children's party — not to celebrate the New Year, but to console the children for the loss of their 'school'. Yanaka Primary School proper had been destroyed along with the peasants' homes. Ever since, some of the remaining children had been attending school in Koga, the nearest town; a temple on the fringe of the original village territory was serving as a temporary schoolhouse for the others. Now this temple too was arbitrarily closed by the Prefecture and included within the 'lake' area, the pupils being transferred to a school in another small town nearly four miles away, which they were to reach by boat and on foot as best they could. Having done what little he could to offset the bewilderment and sense of deprivation of these youngest members of the tiny community, Shozo was soon back in Tokyo for the fourth court hearing of the Yanaka appeal.

While in the capital he witnessed angry mobs setting fire to public buildings and the offices of newspapers supporting the government, in protest against the authoritarian regime of Prime Minister Katsura. The violence did not surpuise him; it merely confirmed what he saw as the lesson of the long pollution struggle and of the destruction of Yanaka — that as a 'community' in any true sense of the word Japan was dead, and that a government which acted as the Japanese oligarchs did was not a government at all, and would inevitably provoke, in the absence of an opposition acknowledging a religious dimension to politics, violent reaction from the governed. Even his once-prized Constitution he now saw as a tool unscrupulously manipulated by politicians sheltering behind the prestige of the Imperial throne.

Yet so far there was no alternative to using the existing political process, and it was this realisation that kept Shozo from following the radical but unrealistic notions of the early Japanese socialists and anarchists:

> *Today is today, the future is the future. Never think so much of the future that you neglect today . . . Today is enough for itself. That was Christ's teaching, and it's my belief too.*

In this spirit Shozo called on Ozaki Yukio,[1] one of the government's most outspoken critics in the Diet, to encourage him in his independent stand. Unlike many lesser men, Ozaki recognised Shozo's moral stature — and showed it gracefully by writing this poem for him:

> For Tanaka Shozo
>
> *On receiving a visit from a great man*
> *It speaks for itself —*
> *The fragrance*
> *Of the plum blossom!*

There were many signs during the early months of 1913 that Shozo knew, however obscurely, that he had not long to live. One was his disposal of the family house already mentioned. Another was the series of letters he sent to the Yanaka villagers during his stay in Tokyo; long letters, written hastily and following one after another in rapid succession, as if he were afraid he might not have time to say all he wanted. They are not always consistent. One day he castigates them for the brusqueness they have shown on certain past occasions to visitors from the capital, and enjoins them at great length to be polite and welcoming, and not to parade their hardships unduly when any of the lawyers or other Tokyo sympathisers show up; the next day, in language that would have bewildered them indeed if they had not grown used over the years to his strange ways, he speaks of them as 'god':

In their work the young men of Yanaka must respect what their elders say and value the advice of the fine spirits that you have among you. If you worship the God of Heaven, he is there in your homes. But there are gods among men, too. For Yanaka folk, to revere the noble ones among you is the same as to revere the gods and Buddhas whose shrines you keep in your homes. The people of Yanaka are God. Though Japan is bent on destroying herself, the spirit of the people of Yanaka will not die ... The people of Yanaka have no learning, no money, no food, no houses; but they are God ... Japan must die, for there are wild beasts here in Tokyo among the men of wealth and rank. Ueno Police Station was burnt to the ground last night: a rioting crowd of twenty-thousand rampaged through the city centre till dawn ... God is in Yanaka. You yourselves are your Bible. Knowledge won through suffering is just as precious as the Bible. Books in themselves have no life! Read the 'book of Yanaka', then compare it with the Bible. Look back over what you have been through the last ten years, ponder it, learn it by heart — this is the way to discover new truth. This is the Way to Heaven.

---

1. 1858-1954. The most outstanding liberal in the parliamentary history of modern Japan. He was then at the height of his career.

Earlier notions of 'studying religion more seriously, after the Yanaka struggle was over' had given way to such an overwhelming conviction of the *identity* between religion and the Yanaka experience that he cannot keep off the subject for long. And always accompanying the profundities and the practical advice in these letters is an affectionate interest in the daily problems of individual members of the Yanaka community, of which he now felt himself so completely a member that as often as not he would sign himself simply 'Yanaka survivor'.

His refusal to rest throughout the bitterest weeks of winter took its toll, and one morning in the second week in March, at a little inn in the Shiba district of Tokyo where he had arrived a day or two before, he found himself unable to get out of his bed. The inn had long been one of his favourite stopping places. But the friendly proprietor who had always kept a bed for him at a nominal charge of ten sen a night had been replaced by someone less sympathetic, who put him in a servant's room, a tiny unlit box of six feet square, and demanded fifty sen, without meals. Sick and without the money to pay even for this rock-bottom lodging, Shozo records in his diary no complaint, only a judgement on himself and on the evils of extravagance:

I have been punished for staying in this inn. Heaven's punishment for accepting too much comfort. 50 sen they charge — three times what I need to live on.

Many, not even of the highest but of the middle classes, spend five yen on a single meal. Compare this with the three or four sen the peasants and others like them spend on a whole day's food. The well-off need five hundred times as much money for one meal as the poor. Like one man eating five hundred shares of bread — robbing five hundred others of their share: starving them. The Great Learning says: 'If but one man is covetous, the country cannot be at peace.' How true!

For his own survival, he wrote off at once to a friend in Tochigi, asking to borrow ten yen. His illness and need are mentioned briefly, almost as an afterthought, the bulk of the letter being taken up with a catalogue of the forces arrayed against Yanaka — the two prefectural governments of Gunma and Tochigi, the central government, the Ashio mine, most of the Diet — and a statement of his unshaken faith that resistance is still meaningful, for even though so tiny an entity, Yanaka can be made to carry a universal significance 'as the small orbs of the sun and moon transmit light through infinite distance'.

The recipient immediately brought the money to Tokyo in person, and would willingly have given him more, but Shozo would only accept the ten yen he had asked for. Fortunately, Mrs. Fukuda happened to call on him at the inn that day; and she arranged for him to be moved to the nearby house of an anarchist friend who, though wretchedly poor himself, was glad to offer Shozo shelter so that he could take the rest he needed.

In these more congenial surroundings he at once resumed his letter-writing to the villagers. This time he gave them detailed instructions as to how to receive the assessors from the Court of Appeal, whom he himself would have accompanied to Yanaka if he had not been ill; they must receive them as courteously as possible, but in their usual sedge-hats and straw coats, which they could spread on the ground for the assessors to sit on if they wished to rest. They should not talk overmuch, but let the facts speak for themselves. And in case, eventually, they were to win their appeal, they should be preparing themselves now to hand over whatever compensation might be awarded them to the Prefecture, as a contribution to the building of a new Yanaka.

A few days in bed were enough to restore Shozo to something like his usual vigour. At once he set off back to Shimotsuke, calling first at Yanaka and then going on to speak at a big public meeting on conservation, attended to his delight by several hundred enthusiasts, in a nearby village.

During the next six weeks three more fact-finding journeys followed, interspersed with quick visits to Yanaka and Tokyo, studying the tributaries of the Watarase. During the first of these journeys Shozo stopped at the town of Kiryu to pay an unusual call — on his wife Katsu, who was now living there with relatives. To her astonishment, he stayed for three days; longer than they had spent together for many years. Cheerful and kindly, he talked at length of their early days, and asking for fine quality calligraphy paper wrote out a number of poems and maxims for her to make into hanging scrolls. These mementoes, she recalled afterwards, and the very length of his stay, gave her the sense that this was a final leave-taking.

Back in Yanaka in June, he spent a day picking barley, and cooked it in the evening as a rice-substitute supper — and an object-lesson — for several villagers who had been complaining they could not grow enough rice to support themselves and that rice in the town shops was too expensive to buy. Then he moved to Koga, staying alternately in temples and inns to rest and write up for publication a report of his river-studies. The report was duly written, but the rest he needed more than ever was hard to come by.

The police, who had been renewing their pressure on the Yanaka villagers to leave, called at every inn where Shozo stayed, till the proprietors began to feel it was bad for business to take him in. Ironically, some admirers chose this moment to suggest the erection of a memorial stone to commemorate his life's work. Shozo was merely angry. Such an 'honour', in his view, would be a stupid waste, nothing more than an excuse for not acting on the principles he stood for. He himself was nothing: when he died — and he would be content to die in a lean-to or by the roadside — they could feed his body to the horses, or throw it in the river if they chose; but *no* memorial.

Death was even nearer than he guessed. When on 2 July, weary from days of moving from inn to inn, he suddenly vomited all his food, his disciple Shimada Sozo realised there was something wrong with him beyond mere exhaustion. But he would not see a doctor. Two short letters he wrote on the 4th and 6th show an awareness of approaching death together with a tranquillity of spirit to which physical decay is scarcely relevant. On hearing that he was unwell, his dearest friends in Tokyo, Kinoshita Naoe and Henmi Onokichi, had sent him a postcard on which was printed the following saying by Chu-ko Liang:[1]

> *Unless a man be without desire*
> *He cannot make clear his intent;*
> *If his spirit is not tranquil,*
> *He will accomplish nothing great.*

In the traditional Japanese fashion, Kinoshita and Henmi had expressed their sympathy for Shozo in his illness, not by any conventional formula of enquiry after his condition, but by poems of their own composition, which they wrote beneath the quotation from Chu-ko Liang:

> *On the blossoms —*
> *White, purple,*
> *Of every colour,*
> *Of the first chrysanthemums,*
> *Falls the steady rain.*
>
> Kinoshita Naoe

> *The quiet rain falls,*
> *And you, our friend,*
> *Lie ill.*
> *Deep indeed is the stillness*
> *As we 'sit in silence' here.*[1]
>
> Henmi Onokichi

Shozo's answers (I give them in full, though the allusions and the compressed expression make further annotation unavoidable):

July 4

Priest Saigyo wrote, after visiting the Grand Shrine at Ise,
> *Although I do not know*
> *Whether any being men should reverence*

---

1. A celebrated Chinese scholar and statesman of the 3rd century A.D.

1. Again in the traditional manner, both these poems take as their starting-point a seasonal phenomenon that was occurring at the time they were written — the long, steady, but not violent downpours that mark the Japanese rainy season in June and July. In the first, the many-coloured chrysanthemums suggest the varied facets of Shozo's long career; and the rain, his illness. In Henmi's poem, the stillness of a *seiza* ('sitting in silence') meeting, accentuated by the patter of the summer rain that softens all external sounds, is deepened still further as those present think of Shozo and his illness.

> Dwells there,
> Yet in extreme awe
> My tears well forth.[1]

The depth of Saigyo's feeling draws my own tears. I say, when the farmers are short of water in the paddy-fields at planting-out time,

> All men
> Purify your lips
> And pray to God
> That through every sluice into every field
> Water may flow.[2]

Random thoughts:

> Though it is summer,
> Over withered fields my dreams
> Are wandering still,
> As on a borrowed pillow,
> Travelling, I lay my head.[3]

Again,

> Sing today,
> Cuckoo-bird, sing today
> Of all days,
> For that voice of yours
> Shall have no tomorrow.[4]

I look forward to worshipping 'the myriad gods' who meet at Nippori before long.[5] Take care of yourselves in this steamy weather.

July 6

They say of Hideyoshi that he was 'open', and of Ieyasu that he was 'tranquil of spirit'; neither combined these two qualities. All the sages have had them both, and wisdom, insight, and warmth too. They seem like ordinary men, yet are more than human; they resemble gods

---

1. This famous poem of Priest Saigyo (1118-1190) records his experience of the numinous atmosphere of the great Shinto shrine at Ise, set as it is among deep forests.

2. Responsive as Shozo is to the religious awe that Saigyo speaks of in his poem, for him the 'divine' is always inseparable from man and his daily needs. Ise is of course a Shinto shrine; and before praying at a Shinto shrine the mouth must be cleansed or purified with sacred water.

3. Shozo incorporates in his own poem the death-verse with which the great poet Basho (1644-1694) took leave of his disciples and friends:
> On a journey, ill —
> And my dreams on withered fields
> Are wandering still. (tr. Henderson)

In Basho's verse, 'withered fields' are seasonal words, indicating that it was composed in the autumn of the year (as well as of the poet's life); the poet longed to be able to continue the country journeys that had so fed the springs of his poetry. Shozo too, lying 'on a borrowed pillow', is 'on a journey, ill'; but in his case it is summer, not autumn, and the withered fields are the polluted and flooded fields of the Shimotsuke plain.

4. In traditional Japanese culture the cuckoo was associated with early summer and with death: it was said to vomit blood and die after it had sung eight thousand and eight times. Hearing its cry was sometimes regarded as an evil omen. Shozo's cuckoo, needless to say, is himself.

5. Shozo's illness had not dulled his sense of humour. 'Nippori' refers to a temple in the Nippori district of Tokyo, where big 'sitting in silence' meetings were regularly held. The 'myriad gods' are both the nameless deities the sitters might individually worship, and the sitters themselves, among them Kinoshita and Henmi.

yet are not divine. Perfect single-mindedness is riches indeed, yet if a man lacks wisdom and insight, the Great Joy of the universe is beyond his reach. This wisdom lies locked in the earth, in the skies, in all the world about us. I have not yet learned its secrets. But I long for those 'that have a wealth of years before them'[1] to obtain the Great Joy. The lesser joy I do know. I pray that the Greater will be yours. Give me your guidance!

The following day, 7 July, being a festival day,[2] Shozo left the inn at Koga, telling his old friend the innkeeper (who tried hard to make him stay longer) that the presence of a 'shabby old man like himself' would spoil the festive atmosphere. Physically, he was a little better, though weak still — too weak to eat even rice; he lived now on little else but gruel and water. Sheer force of will kept him tramping eight or nine miles a day along the muddy roads for another three weeks, making detailed notes as usual.

At the end of each day his exhaustion was extreme. Yet on the 20th, while staying with a sympathiser in the town of Ashikaga, on the upper reaches of the Watarase, he could fill pages of his diary with leisurely meditations on a dozen different subjects: on the need to let truth speak for itself without adornment or special pleading (with an implicit warning to himself against the gut-reaction of anger that stupidity or narrowness still aroused in him all too easily); on the corruption of children by affluence and excessive freedom, because proper freedom is the product of constraint; on the analogy between physical and spiritual purity and the true care of rivers:

I often see people washing and rinsing their hands. Not their minds. They wash their faces, their bodies, their mouths, eyes, noses. But these are only the branches, not the root. So with rivers. If a man thinks clearing a river's passage and helping it flow is conservation, that's because he knows only the branches and not the root; the root of river-care lies at the source, in the mountains, lakes and forests ... Minding a river while neglecting the mountains is like a man who gorges himself on poison and dirt but protests he's healthy and hygienic because he religiously washes and rinses his mouth ...

Three days later, once again unable to walk and confined to bed, he was addressing a long circular letter to a number of influential acquaintances asking them to intervene in support of an enterprising friend (an old helper of Shozo's in his early Diet days). The person concerned had started a horse-drawn 'bus' service from Sano, near Shozo's birthplace, to Koga — principally to help the weavers of Sano, who had hitherto made the journey on foot, to expand their market. Tochigi Prefecture (Sano being in Tochigi) had granted the

1. A Chinese phrase for 'the young'. Kinoshita and Henmi were both much younger than Shozo.
2. The Festival of the Weaver, sometimes called the Festival of the Stars, is observed throughout Japan on this day. It celebrates the love of the celestial weaver princess and the herdsman, who so neglected their duties in their passion for each other that the Emperor of Heaven ordered them to live apart, except for one day in each year — the 7th day of the 7th month.

entrepreneur a licence to run the service; but the writ of Tochigi did not run in Koga, which was in Gunma Prefecture — the border being about a hundred yards outside the town limits — and the chief of police of Koga, supported by local interests, forbade the buses entry into the town.

Trivial in itself, for Shozo the issue was symbolic in that the attitudes it aroused typified the sectionalism and bureaucracy poisoning many areas of Japanese society. In page after page, as if there were nothing else in the world to claim his attention, he appeals to his readers for more modern attitudes, for greater openness to the needs of the wider community beyond one's own village or town, for — in sum — a deeper sense of the 'Way of humanity'.

A summons to give evidence at another hearing of the Yanaka Appeal case found him too ill to travel. On 25 July he wrote to Shimada Sozo that he thought he would not live beyond the end of the year, and was 'preparing himself' accordingly.

The rain that day was torrential. Worried that the Yanaka crops might be in danger, Shozo sent the villagers a small sum of money he had managed to borrow, about enough for a day's supply of rice for every household. Paradoxically, anxiety for Yanaka seemed to give him new energy. Another letter to Shimada, dated 30 July, tells of his hope of coming soon to Yanaka, where he would like to recuperate for a while in the Raiden Shrine[1] before going on to Tokyo to attend the Appeal Court; restricting himself to liquid foods had done him some good, he thought. But his handwriting told another story. So, indeed, did another letter — the last he was ever to write — of the same date, addressed to Kinoshita and Henmi, asking them to do all they could after his coming death for Shimada Sozo, his faithful disciple and secretary.[2]

Unknown to Shozo, a relative in Ashikaga, alarmed by his looks, sent for his wife (who was now living with her family in the neighbouring town of Kiryu), naively hoping she would be able to persuade him to regard himself as really ill and let her look after him. When he was told Katsu had arrived, Shozo's only reaction was a flash

---

1. A small Shinto shrine in the shade of a clump of trees, dedicated to the spirits of thunder and lightning. It was the only building in the village that had not been completely destroyed when the houses were razed in 1907. For a while the villagers used it for their meetings; but successive floods had washed away the walls and floor, and now only the corner pillars and roof remained. For Shozo it had these attractions: it would be cool even in the worst of the summer heat; if he had to be ill, he would be less of a burden to others in this public place than in the shack of some hard-pressed villager; and thirdly, it was in Yanaka, where he most wanted to die.

2 The devotion to Shozo's memory that Mr Shimada showed in collecting, checking and preserving all kinds of information on the last years of Shozo's life has been matched by the disciple's desire to minimise the importance of his own role during those years. When his completed account was published in 1972, Mr Shimada would not allow the text of this last letter to be included, 'because it praised him too highly'. But we do at least know — and may be moved by the knowledge, as he was — that not the least of Shozo's 'preparations for dying' was the endeavour to acknowledge in this way the debt he felt he owed to the Yanaka boy, fifty years younger than himself, who had in effect loved and served him like a son.

of the old anger. They didn't understand him, he retorted; he had work to do in Yanaka and Tokyo, work that wouldn't let him idle his time away here in Ashikaga. So he left, without even greeting the luckless Katsu.

Later that day, the 31st, at the house of an old Diet colleague not far from Yanaka to which he had made his way with some difficulty, he said he had come 'to take his leave, for he would not be passing that way again'. If man's allotted span was a hundred years, he said jokingly, he was lucky indeed; for having in his youth forfeited ten years to alcohol, ten years to tobacco, and ten years to syphilis, at seventy-two he had already lived two years longer than his due.

When his host suggested calling a doctor, he refused. His only worry, he said, was that by the manner of his dying he might give others trouble in looking after him. Best of all would be to die suddenly on the road from village to village; failing that, he would want the end to come at Yanaka, or at Unryuji, the Zen temple that had played such an important part in the fight against pollution.

On 1 August, at the local primary school, he addressed a meeting of village leaders on river conservation, education and the 'Way of Man'. The headmaster of the school, who had never seen him face to face before, recalled afterwards his amazement that anyone looking so desperately ill could speak for over an hour with such cogency and vigour. Next morning, however, he was so weak he could not even tie his kimono sash by himself.

After making the following entry in his diary (it was to be his last),

2 August: If a man lacks the strength to repulse the devil, it is because he has that of the devil in himself. Being of the devil, he cannot resist him. It is then that a man has need of repentance and baptism, for they can wash away all past evil.

Why have — me[1]

he set out by rickshaw from his friend's house, apparently for Yanaka. But he was never to reach it. After calling on friends in two villages, he made his way to Unryuji Temple; but the priest was away, and ironically the acolyte had never seen Shozo and did not know who he was.

A hundred yards from the temple were two farmhouses belonging to related families who had taken an active part in the pollution struggle. Dismissing the rickshawman, Shozo managed to walk over to the first of these cottages. It was empty; on this hot summer's day a week or so after the rains had ended, all the family were out in the fields.

Outside the second house two young children were playing. Shozo sat down on the veranda, intending perhaps to rest until the priest of

---

1. This last line is omitted in most printed versions of the diary, no doubt because most readers would not be able to make anything of such a fragment. Shimada Sozo, however (in whose possession the diary remains), is in doubt that the words stand for Jesus' saying on the cross, My God, why hast thou forsaken me? (Matthew XXVII, 46).

Unryuji should be back. The children, startled as he took off his peasant's hat of straw by the deathlike expression on his face, ran off to fetch their parents. When they came back Shozo had collapsed.

For three days he hung between life and death, in an improvised sickroom where the only sounds were the singing of summer insects and the munching of hay in the stable, from which the room was separated only by a thin partition.

Repeatedly, in the intervals when he was conscious, he would demand to be carried on a stretcher to Yanaka, 'where he still had work to do'. But the risk of moving him would have been too great. Then there was some improvement, and he was able to sit up and talk. As word of his illness spread, visitors began to arrive, first in twos and threes, then in larger groups, till in the third week of August, when the Tokyo papers carried a report of the seriousness of his condition, several hundreds came every day in the hope of catching a glimpse of the old rebel before he died.

Kinoshita Naoe left his home in Tokyo to organise the nursing and to help protect Shozo and the two peasant families from the crowds of visitors who were descending upon the remote cottage, and who according to Japanese custom had to be given some show of hospitality before they left. The task was not easy. When, as very soon became necessary, Kinoshita had to put up a notice outside the house announcing that Shozo was too ill to see anyone, several of the visitors objected vehemently and were only with difficulty kept from violence.

Kinoshita obtained the assistance of many helpers. Food and bedding were donated in ample quantities; young men who could be spared from Yanaka gave what help they could, and no less than thirty villagers from Konaka undertook a variety of duties under Kinoshita's direction, two of them cycling back every day to Konaka to report on Shozo's condition.

Shozo himself was unmoved by the crowds. He had fought too many battles on his own to be greatly impressed with this show of sympathy, offered as it was when there was little prospect of his troubling the comfortable, conformist world much longer. To some visitors the old unbending, uncompromising spirit showed itself openly.

One day when he was well enough to see a visitor or two a Buddhist priest, a friend of forty years, brought one Yamada Yujiro to see him. One of Shozo's most loyal supporters in the early years of the anti-pollution campaign, Yamada had later proposed a highly individual solution to the pollution crisis — that Furukawa should be induced to buy up all the polluted land on both banks of the Watarase, on the ground that once the land was his, such a successful entrepreneur would surely find some way of restoring it to full productivity with the same speed with which he had developed Ashio. The government showed interest in the idea; Yamada, a skilled negotiator, was summoned for consultations by two successive Ministers of Agriculture. Absurd though it may seem at first sight, the plan was a genuine attempt at a compromise put forward by a practical man who saw very clearly that the government was bound 'in the national interest' to support Furukawa, and that simple attacks on the mine-government combination, however sincere, would get nowhere.

Shozo would have none of it. Compromise to him was unthinkable — and for the peasants to sell their inherited land, a kind of sacrilege. In his eyes Yamada was a traitor, with whom no further cooperation was possible. They parted company, and Yamada gave up public work to return to his farm. They had not met for ten years. Now the priest, whose hope it was that by making possible a reconciliation he could do a last service to the dying man, brought the two men together once more. Yamada went into the sickroom first. When he bowed his head to the floor by way of apologising for his part in their past differences, Shozo merely stared at him, angry and contemptuous, then demanded to know 'Who brought you?' 'The priest of Sosoji Temple in Sano,' replied Yamada. Gradually Shozo's expression softened, till at last he offered a hand to Yamada, saying simply, 'The world goes neither my way nor yours!' As Japanese readily do on such occasions, Yamada wept copiously at this sudden breaking of the barrier between them.

But most often during these last days Shozo was calm and cheerful. Though it was certain now that his death could not be delayed for long,[1] he was anxious for nothing but that the visitors should be treated kindly and the nurses get their due share of rest. With the latter he indulged in his own special kind of banter, telling them he couldn't help distrusting their gentle, reassuring manner, 'they were so like government officials tricking the peasants'. But with his closest friends — Kinoshita, Shimada Sozo and others — he would speak still of his deepest concerns, briefly now but with a solemn prophetic note in the words:

Shozo shares the life of all natural things. If they die, so must he. When he fell, it was because the rivers and forests of Aso and Ashikaga are dying, and Japan herself too . . . If those who come to ask after him hope for his recovery, let them first restore the ravaged hills and rivers and forests, and then Shozo will be well again . . .[2]

Urging them to take a lead in the work he had started, he went on:

Can you do it, or can you not? If you cannot, Shozo will die with the forests, with the rivers — and even if when he is dead you deck his coffin with gold and silver and the fruits of the earth, he will not thank you for such folly.

1. At first he had stubbornly resisted all attempts to bring in a doctor to examine him; but he relented on the arrival of Dr Wada, who for two years had commuted from Tokyo to give free treatment to the pollution victims. According to Dr Wada, Shozo's illness was pyloric stenosis (caused by a cancerous swelling in the stomach), from which there was no hope of recovery.

2. Shimada Sozo took down these words, and those that follow, as they were spoken.

Whenever he felt strong enough, he would have himself carried to the verandah so that he could continue even in sickness the 'sitting in silence' that he found so restful, looking out through clumps of bamboo to the fields beyond.

Then on 22 August there was a sudden relapse. Shozo lost consciousness,[1] and it was thought that the critical moment had come; but with the help of artificial respiration he revived, and seemed much as before, though continually weakening. Heavy rain fell in the next few days, and as Shozo had early prophesied, the Watarase (which was less than a quarter of a mile away) began to rise in flood. A boat was procured and kept in the garden, in case the water should reach the house and Shozo have to be evacuated; but it proved not to be necessary. Days of intense heat followed the rain.

It was the season of *O-bon*, the Festival of All Souls, and of the gay open-air dances with which the spirits of the dead are welcomed back on their brief annual visit to their former homes; on more than one evening the sounds of drum and flute and singing drifted over the fields to Unryuji Temple and the two cottages by the river.

The end came peacefully on 4 September. Before dawn, when Kinoshita, on taking over the watch from Shimada, had asked Shozo how he was, Shozo had replied, 'It's not my being ill, it's the ruin Japan is heading for —' Then, slowly and as if in sorrow, he gave his own final judgement on his life:

In the pollution struggle I roused many men to action, drove them to do this and that. But I did not teach them. No, not that — I did not know what true teaching, true education, was. This Tanaka Shozo, he was so ignorant! He set himself alone, apart from other men. That was the mistake. Everything since has followed from that.

Later that morning he suddenly called for Iwasaki Saju, who was in charge of the arrangements for receiving visitors, and told him,

There seem to be a lot of them outside, but they're no comfort to me. They sympathize with Shozo, but not a single one of them believes in his work. Go outside and tell them so!

About noon he announced that he would sit up. Very slowly, Kinoshita raised his back. To one side sat Katsu, gently fanning his face. Erect, his hands clasped in front of him — rocklike, as it seemed to Shimada, who on someone shouting that Shozo was worse had woken from a nap in the garden and come running to the sickroom, Shozo began the long, deep breathing he had learnt from Okada Torajiro as the first and most fundamental lesson in 'sitting in silence'. Eight or nine times the slow breaths came and went; till suddenly, as his eyes were trying to take in once more the little circle gathered round his bed, all movement ceased.

---

1. Before doing so he cried out twice, '*Genzai o sukue! Arinomama o sukue!*' — cryptic phrases which could be literally translated 'Save the present! Save the present as it is!' a cri du coeur, it would seem, for men to rise above their petty divisions and help each other — and 'rivers and forests' — without insisting on first trying to convert each other to this ideology or that.

'It is finished,' said Katsu quietly, still fanning his face.

The possessions he left: a haversack, a list of persons interested in the care of rivers, a New Testament, a copy of the Japanese Constitution bound in one cover with an edition of Matthew's gospel, three notebooks and a few stones.

* * *

A 'provisional' funeral was held two days later at Unryuji Temple, in the presence of those who had attended him during his illness. Sixty young men then carried the coffin six miles on poles lashed together to a length of thirty feet, to enable all who wanted the honour of shouldering the burden to take their share — to the crematorium in Sano, near his birthplace of Konaka.

The real funeral service took place in the grounds of a Sano temple on 12 October. As if in final ironic comment on Shozo's insistence that he did not want sympathy for himself but only for his work, no fewer than 30,000 men and women,[1] of whom perhaps not more than one in a thousand had understood and supported his lonely campaigns, came to pay their last respects.

His 'sincerity', indeed, had become almost legendary, and during the months following his death many of Japan's most distinguished men, not least among them Count Okuma, who had been the first and only Minister to respond positively to Shozo's pleading, bore witness to the rare combination in his character of pugnacity, gentleness, and total devotion to the causes for which he fought. The right-wing nationalist thinker Miyake Setsurei spoke of him as one of a trio who had made the greatest spiritual impact on Meiji Japan, the others being Saigo Takamori[2] and General Nogi.[3] Shozo's friend and teacher of his last years, the recluse Arai Osui, wrote in a letter to Shimada Sozo of the 'childlike' simplicity and integrity that shone through all his words and actions.[4]

1. Including 140 priests, and a strong contingent of police, whose presence may have been occasioned by a false rumour that before his death Shozo had asked that his ashes be taken to the Appeal Court that was hearing the Yanaka compensation case.

2 One of the key figures in the Meiji Restoration, Saigo later (1877) led a rebellion against the new government, and committed suicide when it failed. The strength and 'sincerity' of his character have been the object of veneration ever since.

3 Nogi committed suicide on the day of the Emperor Meiji's funeral — the most dramatic example of the 'following one's lord in death' that was the supreme test of samurai loyalty.

4 Arai gives a moving account of his last 'encounter' with Shozo. Two nights before Shozo died, Arai dreamed he saw Shozo walking slowly towards him along a river bank. 'His footsteps were light and made no sound. I asked him, How is your illness? He smiled, and answered in his old voice, I am well....' Arai awoke, then fell asleep a second time, and saw the same dream again. It was still widely believed in Japan that the spirits of the dying visited their closest relatives or friends in their dreams to say farewell; and Arai felt sure, particularly since as a rule he never dreamed, that this must be the explanation on this occasion. He was surprised, therefore, to see no report of Shozo's death in the paper next day, either in the morning or the evening editions. The dream seemed after all to have been a meaningless coincidence, and he began to hope that his friend might still have long to live. On the following morning, however, the paper did carry the report he had been expecting.

But perhaps the best tribute, and the one most in keeping with Shozo's own lifelong distaste for mere sympathy, came from the Christian leader Uchimura Kanzo. After speaking of Shozo's love of nature, and of his intimate, encyclopedic knowledge of all its manifestations, from rivers and mountains to trees, flowers, fishes and insects, Uchimura went on:

'Shozo was the protector of the farmers. There could be no greater mistake than to think he was important only to those who live along the banks of the Watarase. Eighty per cent of the Japanese people are farmers ... He was their spokesman, their defender: his voice, the voice of forty millions who live from the land. Yet the people of our country did not heed that voice.

As sincere and quick to feel for others as a child, of all men that I have met, Tanaka Shozo was the most lovable.'

Despite the immense respect accorded in public to Shozo's memory for some months after his death, it was quickly apparent that neither the people of Shimotsuke nor their appointed rulers had heeded his repeated appeals for the sinking of sectional interests and viewpoints in a larger vision of the good of society as a whole. No sooner was the cremation over than a squabble broke out — a perfect symbol of continuing sectionalism — as to which community should have the privilege of retaining Shozo's ashes. The protracted quarrel was only settled when it was finally agreed to divide the ashes into five portions, each to be laid to rest in a different village.

An equally symbolic action on the part of the authorities showed how little they too had changed. In December 1913, three months after Shozo's death, two Yanaka villagers erected in front of the shack where one of them was living a small makeshift shrine to his memory. The following March a charge was brought against them of having erected an 'unauthorised structure' on land covered by the Rivers Law, and soon after they were convicted and fined.

For a generation and more after his death Shozo was almost totally forgotten by the world at large, though Kinoshita Naoe and Shimada Sozo laboured with quiet patience to collect and preserve the records of his work. In 1953 the prophet received a measure of permanent recognition in his own country when a small band of admirers built a shrine, with a rock nearby on which is engraved a summary of his career, on a stretch of high ground overlooking the 8,000 acres of wasteland where once the village of Yanaka stood.

It was not until the late 1960s, with the rapidly rising awareness among ordinary Japanese of the huge scale of the pollution their economic miracle had brought in its train, that his name came once again to be widely spoken of. Today radio, press and television make frequent reference to him as the 'hero' of *kogai dai-ichigo,* the first of the great pollution scandals.

The will to fight pollution is stronger than ever before; citizens are increasingly conscious of the need to combine in defence of their environment, and much excellent anti-pollution legislation has been enacted by the Diet. Yet because of the lethargy of the bureaucracy and its historical — and until recently no doubt inevitable — tendency to side with industry against attacks from the citizenry, the curbs so far achieved have been relatively modest, and the vastness of the problem makes measures to tackle it more urgent than ever. This account of Tanaka Shozo's life may properly close with a poem of his that remains as relevant today as when it was written, not only for Japan but for every other industrial country:

> Myonichi wa
> Kiyokarubeshi to
> Iu nakare
>
> *Say not that all*
> *Shall be made clean*
> Tomorrow!

15

Jottings

Shozo was a tireless correspondent and diarist, expressing himself with equal naturalness whether he was writing to his friends or for his own eye alone. In narrating his life-story I have quoted with some frequency from both sources. The following further selection of a few of the more translatable passages from his later letters and diary-entries (they cover the years 1909-1913) may help to round out the picture of this man whose hectic outward life was balanced by an unshakable inner serenity. The passages need no explanation, for Shozo's vision in his maturity was not intellectual but childlike. Inevitably his style loses much of its delightful flavour in translation, but the reader in whom the story of Shozo's career has struck a chord of sympathy may perhaps be able to sense, nevertheless, something of the limpid directness of these extracts.

PUBLISHER'S NOTE: *Whereas through the book we have italicized all Shozo's own words for ease of identification, we are leaving the section that follows in roman type to make for easier reading.*

*

If a man picks some egg-plants from his field and sends them to a friend, his friend will be grateful, and enjoy them at his table... But if the egg-plants are not fresh, as heaven made them, they will give no pleasure to him who receives the gift. Yet if a man offers his inmost feelings unadorned, he is accused of rudeness. No one sends flowers as a gift unless they are fresh and pure; but the gift of one's heart must be decked in fine words. What senseless foolishness!

*

I sought to observe other men truly, and could not. I did not know that to see a man truly, you must become one with him. Not to observe, but to become one with him: this is the Way.

*

Some days I'm proud of . . . the 25th and 26th, drenched to the skin, no clothes to keep the rain off. 27th: by boat to Yanaka. Fell asleep in the boat. Felt bad later, my old illness coming back . . . stopped at an inn at Koga that night — they wouldn't lend me dry clothes, so slept in sodden kimono. To Akiyama's on the 28th. Travelling on the 29th, soaked again. Akiyama lent me a warm kimono. Back to Koga today, wearing three kimonos to keep out the rain . . . The first time in 66 years I ever slept in wet clothes. (The sun's dried them out today.) In this at least I'm as hardy as the Yanaka folk now.

*

Ill and sleeping in a wet kimono the other night — the most unpleasant experience I've ever had. All of a sudden, though, my troubles were dissolved. So with the Yanaka folk, as they go through the worst that life can bring them. This moment of extremity is all-important . . .

>*The moment*
>*An insect, even,*
>*Is trodden to death*
>*May be the moment*
>*Of its ascent to heaven.*

*

Last year the villagers built temporary dykes to protect their crops. Officials came and broke them down again.

>*Though its branches*
>*Are wrenched and broken*
>*By the storm,*
>*The blossoms are fragrant still*
>*On this wild cherry.*

*

Men argue about which is better, Western or Japanese music. I prefer the music of the winds.

*

They make idols for those who wish to see but have no eyes. Since idols were invented God has become more invisible than ever. Since music was invented, none listen to the wind.

*

Goodness is like air in an air-pillow: if it is not hidden, it is lost. What is seen is not goodness.

*

Your spirit is the gift of God. If a man collects paintings or pots, people think him foolish in the extreme if he does not know the maker of each piece and what its special qualities are. What are we to say if a man is ignorant of something much greater, the spirit within him? His spirit is a part of God's spirit . . . if he would see God, he must look within himself. Look in yourself, if you truly wish to see God; looking upward will not find him. Look within, with all your strength. If your words and deeds are clear, and you look for him sincerely within yourself, you will find him. God is not an idol. 'God is invisible,' they say — what pitiful folly!

*

If a man keeps treasures of art hidden in his storehouse and does not show them to the people, it is as if they were buried in the ground; they are treasures no longer. The sun and moon hang in the sky for all creatures on earth to see, the greatest of treasures; would they be treasures if they were always clouded? Rain, frost and snow are precious in due measure, harmful in excess. River breezes, the moon over the mountains, are treasures of art, a heavenly garden for all men; heaven gives them to us that we may learn the spirit of sharing. The world's treasures are not treasures unless they are shared like the wind and the moon. It is thus with learning . . .

*

Stayed at Akiyama's for a meal. Apart from the mushrooms we had to eat, there were crimson maple trees, white clouds, and the cries of deer; the sights and sounds so beautiful one could hardly think of the meal . . . Spring, summer, autumn, winter, the gifts of heaven are everywhere — there is no limit to the banquet God provides . . . the judgement on a man is whether or not he partakes of this feast, that is all.

*

A man must question his fellow-men. But all things are my teachers; those nearest to me are the animals, the birds, the fishes, the insects, and I must listen to what they say — and much more to the sage among men . . . God's family is large and peaceful and loving. God never tires of teaching men, especially the foolish and the maimed. Enter God's school, and know the joy of growing without stress or strain!

*

This is the 6th year I have been in Yanaka. Five wasted years, it might seem. But it is not so. These men and women of Yanaka — they are like the ancients; like children. If they have enough to eat and to drink, they are content. For drink, they draw water from their wells; they eat the produce of their own fields. Their pleasure is in nature. Why their freedom was invaded, their prosperity and their homes destroyed, they do not know . . . Recently I have discovered that some of these families are not so ordinary as they look, and one especially, the Somemiyas . . . [there follow many examples of the public spirit of the husband, the support given him by his wife, and the thoughtfulness of their children] . . . Somemiya is illiterate; but the attention he gives to so many little things marks his family out from the others in a way that cannot be hidden.

When his eldest daughter was ill three weeks ago, the devil came to tempt the family twice, offering Somemiya (through his wife's younger brother) 200 yen of public money if he would abandon Yanaka. When his wife heard this, she asked why the man was afraid to speak to her in person? The devil did not come a second time. A few days later, a well-off relative who had long since fled from Yanaka met Mrs. Somemiya on the road. Have you seen our new house, said the relative; we know how hard things are with you — come and live with us, we have trees, bamboo, fields, — don't you envy us? I saw your house a while ago, said Mrs. Somemiya. We envy no one, and we live in poverty of our own free will, harming no one . . . The devil fled.

A beautiful family, with none to see such beauty and goodness. That's understandable, when Yanaka is so remote from the world — but that I should be so late in seeing Somemiya and his family as they really are, after more than five years in Yanaka! My foolish eyes . . . Mencius says, with a smile, 'I have eyes that can see the tip of a fine hair but not a cartload of firewood' . . . I see now that Somemiya and his family are citizens of the celestial city. Men say the Kingdom is nowhere to be seen on earth. A great mistake! It is not that it is not to be seen, only that they do not see it: they have ears but are deaf, their eyes are blinded, they have not the will to see or hear beauty and goodness. My eyes have for so long been unseeing. Who more foolish than I?

*

There are gentle, peaceable men and men of violence. The peaceable join with one another to tame the poisoned heart of the violent; their task it is to teach them patiently, that they may return to the ways of peace. Some say it is useless to struggle with the violent, for they are strong and the peaceable are weak. But the peaceable are strong in truth, which is the power of God and fills the universe. The strength of the violent is no more than the strength of claws and tusks . . . it is the naughtiness of children, while the strength of the gentle is the strength of the grown man . . . the grown man is like God, the child like the tiger or the wolf, strong, but only with the strength of the wild beast, that may be tamed as the tiger and the lion are tamed. Yet the lusts of the violent, which are for money and flesh, do not subside if they are given that which they lust after; in this man differs from the animals. His greed satisfied, the beast is submissive: pander to man's lusts, and he only rages the more. So men and beasts need different training. For the beasts, food: for men, the Way of God and the Way of Man.

*

In spring man may go to the hills to view the blossoms, in summer to the open moors, in autumn he gathers the fruits of the earth. When we see the autumn hills rejoicing in their dress of red maple leaves and white clouds, what need have we to dress ourselves in brilliant colours? The snow in winter is even more beautiful than the flowers in spring. An inexhaustible treasurehouse for God's and our delight. The moon, the snow, the blossoms, our bodies, all are sources of this boundless joy we share with God, a joy that defies description by brush or tongue, for it is without end. What need have we to strive to accumulate other treasure than this?

Nature accumulates — the snow, the flowers when they fall, warmth as the sun shines, the moon's brightness as it grows; that which accumulates melts away, flowers give way to fruit, the sun's warmth cools, the moon grows yet remains unchanged — and every sight and sound is a gift of infinite joy. So with the love of men. Love does not grow less with use, but increases, rather; a man's heart is a treasure-house he can never exhaust . . . Not his body, which is mortal, but the labour of his spirit, which cannot die. Yet most men see no point in this labour, in the labour of loving. How great is their loss! True, if love lessened with the using, there would be little point in loving, but since it suffers no loss but only grows, to be miserly with love is like refusing to draw water from the well, or regretting each mouthful of air we breathe. If love is not put to use, it will decay and lose its worth. Love is as necessary to man as the air, the water, the wind.

*

What joy! I see at last that I am nothing. I am emptiness, nothingness.

I possess nothing, I *am* nothing, my mind is nothing, my body is nothing . . . Nothing divides me from other men. I am poor indeed, yet this word 'poor' is nothing. For the first time I know that all heaven is mine. What delight . . .

*

Christ said, My God, why hast thou forsaken me. Only the deepest faith comes to this stage. He whose faith was not absolute would not speak these words.

*

Sakyamuni moved among men to find the truth of Man. When he had found it, he explained it in his preaching. Look around you — the sources of truth are everywhere and limitless: the lives of men, the laws of karma — all as plain to see as one's own hand. And now men 'believe' in Sakyamuni, and try to put truth into words: like climbing a tree to catch fish . . . It is sad that the people have been left so long with no guide to truth. I say, the cross of Christ is the Middle Way of Middle Ways, the heart of the universe and of the Way of Man; shining the brighter because it is without form and invisible to the eye. No man, however hard he may strive and study, can know this Middle Way with the eye of common flesh. They study and study, and are further than ever from the Way. How sad!

*

Left Eguchi for Kawamata on the morning of the 17th. On the way a squall blew up from the west, which made it almost impossible to walk. The mud surface of the road had only just been renewed, and my clogs couldn't get a grip on it. The wind blew so strong, I could hardly hold on to my stick, let alone keep my hat on, so I gave them both to the friend who'd come to see me on my way. It blew harder at once; nearly knocked me over. I kicked off my clogs — and what a change when I could stand firm! Every blast of the wind a pleasure, transformed into strength. I could go forward singing, rejoicing to see what good the mud which the floods had brought would do the fields . . . I am sad and happy by turns, as I think of the disaster the floods have brought to the poor farmers, and the hope of recovery. All depends, all life depends, on the mind's resolve.

*

Came back late at night from Sayama's to Shimada Eizo's. Stopped to urinate, when I was walking along the embankment, and heard the drops falling on the rotting leaves below. A bird asleep in the thicket, startled by the noise, flew up with a whirring of wings, and startled me in turn. Walked on again, but worried that it might have grazed an eye on a twig in its sudden flight upward, or hurt itself in some other way. Could think of nothing else as I groped my way through the darkness. All was cheerful at Shimada's, with lights burning. But I couldn't forget the bird. When I told them, they laughed.

Strong faith — no worry.

Confucius devoted himself with sincerity to worldly affairs. Buddha went beyond worldly affairs and achieved Nirvana. Christ lived truth. I follow Christ.

Two great fools:

Tanaka Shozo — for spending 7 years in Yanaka.

Tochigi Prefecture — for destroying Yanaka.

*

For many years I have not read the newspapers. So people mock me, saying my talk is of out-of-date matters. But they do not do the things of which I speak, they can only smile and say 'Old-fashioned talk! Old-fashioned talk!' When I speak of 'old' things, I speak of what I practise. What I do not practise, I do not speak of. Nowadays men only know, they see no need to act. They make me smile . . .

*

Lack of learning can be a blessing, precisely because men with learning look down on those without it. People meet each other with prepared attitudes, with caution in their minds, like the armour a fencer wears to protect himself. Before they speak or are spoken to, they stiffen their minds and bodies. It says in the Analects, 'When away from your home, behave as if interviewing an honoured friend.' Many follow this advice. And again, 'To tell, as we go along, what we have heard on the way, is to cast away our virtue.'

Men are ready to abase themselves before others if it will help them to avoid any hurt to their own vanity. I am without learning. In particular, I am ignorant of the polite forms. Having been brought up in a peasant household, I am rough and raw as when I was born, unrefined by learning. So it is natural that men should make little of me. How fortunate! The only time men do not wear their protective armour is when they speak with children; and to them I am a child, so they speak to me also without their armour. Meeting me without a mask, they do not deceive me, but speak truth, and often give me good advice, for their contempt for my lack of learning turns to pity. A paradox: lack of learning is close to truth.

Looked at from high enough above, there are no evil men.
>   *Seen*
>   *From the lofty sky*
>   *All are white —*
>   *Snowmen, Mount Fuji,*
>   *Beauties in their finery.*

Things I hate: laziness, dissipation, dried noodles, people who chatter without sincerity.

*

We were going to go on from Ogawa to Nanai, but the rain was torrential. Oshima, my policeman shadow, went to get rickshaws, but the rickshawmen said they had stomachache and couldn't come. Oshima said it was because they knew policemen weren't allowed to tip above the fare. So we spent the night in an empty hut opposite Takano's. It's supposed to be a police sub-station, but the police are below strength, so there was no one there . . .
>   *Sleeping*
>   *Under a leaky roof —*
>   *Rain all night.*
>   *What an honour, to stay*
>   *In an official residence!*
>
>   *I wash my hands*
>   *In the leaking rainwater —*
>   *Police sub-station!*

*

The kindness of the folk (the Aizawas, in Mizuho Village) at whose cottage I stopped last night.

The wife: Surely you've never stayed at a place as mean and dirty as ours?

Shozo (humbled by their sincerity): My home is a hut on the water, I'm a duck.

The husband (puzzled): Then what do you do at night — sleep in a tree?

Shozo: The birds have branches for their pillow. I've had no bed of my own for many years. Last night I slept so peacefully!

The husband (still more puzzled): Nothing worse than not being able to sleep, is there?

Good folk, they do not understand what I say, but in spirit we are one. Unspoilt by learning, their minds are as clear as the full moon. They do not know God's name, nor even that he exists, but they see him without hindrance.

For men there is the Great Way, for plants the four seasons. If men do not walk the Way, they are like plants not responding to the seasons. Should scholars of agriculture be humbled by the plants they study, foresters by their trees, horsemen by their horses? . . . Man falls short of the animals. If plants and beasts could speak, how superior to Man they would be! This is why I love the plants and beasts. To love men is hard. First a man must learn to love himself, then to reproach himself — if he cannot be severe with himself, neither can he love himself; if he does not love himself, he cannot love others; if he does not love others, he has no right to criticize them. Tseng Tzu said: 'I daily examine myself on three points — in planning for others, have I failed in conscientiousness? In intercourse with friends, have I been sincere? And have I failed to practise what I have been taught?' Good! Self-examination is the Way. I have not mastered it yet.

*

It is in the nature of the Japanese that change is from the top downwards, not the other way round. Even 'popular rights', and the Constitution too, are handed down by officials; not demanded by the people. It's strange. Japan is a constitutional monarchy, and a robber state, all at the same time. I have nothing to do with 'politics', nothing. For me Japan is a family. To care for rivers is to make sure that the garden is properly watered; to get rid of pollution is simple hygiene. This people do not understand. They call me a 'politician', because they do not know the natural order of life in the family.

*

It's cold! I gave my lined coat away to someone. I'm glad, though. This cold isn't cold. It's the reward for loving. Heaven's gift.

*

If I had been made to study, I would have been taken on in some employment. If I had been employed, my present good fortune would never have been mine. My good fortune is to have been cast aside. Only by being abandoned by others could I learn the truth of human affairs.

*

I have loved stones a score of years or more, but did not know the true way to love them till now, for I loved them for their shape alone, not for their nature, their quality. The other day I gave two stones to Mr. Inokuma, one rather large, one middle-size. They were beautifully shaped, but of poor quality. I saw the folly of looking to the form of things alone. With people, I learnt this lesson long ago; with things, I have been so slow to learn!

*

10 March.

> *Crimson*
> *The crane's head*
> *As it perches on the pine-branch;*
> *White is my hair:*
> *The glory of spring!*[1]

*

I have done with all factions, all joys and sorrows. When I am in Yanaka, Yanaka is my centre; the same with Tochigi or Koga or Ashikaga or Tokyo. Everywhere is my centre. If a man seeks, he will not find. Let him find his centre in himself; then his spirit will reach to every corner of the universe.

*

Kawabe told me this morning of two bullocks that met on a mountain track, both loaded; each gave way to the other . . . Nowadays men knock each other down that they themselves can pass.

*

No men love mountains and rivers now. When trees are planted on the hillsides, it is not done from love, but from greed, for what the timber will fetch. Who plants a tree in his garden and thinks of nothing but the fuel it will give him? The gardener loves his trees. Planting in the mountains and in a garden may look the same, but the spirit is different. Forestry is based on greed, not love; even when trees are planted where they should be, where rivers rise, if it is not done with love, it is not the Way of forestry.[2]

---

1. White and red being the colours of felicitation. The hair on Shozo's head was still black, but his beard was white.

2 It is pleasant to be able to record that even as Shozo was writing, an unknown French peasant was following the Way of forestry precisely as Shozo so eloquently defines it here. Elzeard Bouffier had been a lowland farmer in Provence. At the age of 52, having lost both his wife and his only son, he moved up into the barren mountains, with their scattering of ancient villages long since abandoned by an impoverished peasantry, to live alone with his sheep and his dog. The year was 1910. Feeling that the countryside around him was dying 'for lack of trees', he began to devote all his spare hours to the planting of acorns. By 1913 he had planted one hundred thousand, of which ten thousand had survived. The years went by; he continued planting acorns and beech-nuts by the thousand, always unaided and alone. Twenty years later he had created many square miles of forest. Given the trees, other vegetation began to take root; streams appeared; cool breezes replaced the hot mountain wind; and with these changes farmers began at last to repopulate the whole region, not by government fiat but in response to the favourable conditions created by one man's patient work. Bouffier did not stop his planting till shortly before his death in 1947. It is estimated that over 10,000 people owe the stability and happiness of their lives to this thirty-odd years of solitary, dedicated labour.

This remarkable story is told by the French writer Jean Giono, who first met Bouffier by chance in 1913 — the year of Shozo's death — and visited him annually thereafter. (See the journal *Resurgence*, Vol. 7 No. 6, January-February 1977.)

Epilogue

The fate of Yanaka

Even after Shozo's death the sixteen remaining families still refused to leave. The final denouement did not come in fact till November 1916, when the Prefecture (all attempts at persuasion having failed) told the villagers that if they did not move out of the 'lake' area their shacks would be as ruthlessly destroyed as their original homes had been nine years before. After mediation by a nephew of Shozo's who was a member of the Tochigi Assembly, the villagers agreed to go; most of them settled eventually in the neighbouring community of Fujioka.

The Yanaka compensation case — on which Shozo's widow Katsu worked in close cooperation with the villagers and the group of lawyers who were conducting it — ended at last in August 1919, with victory for the villagers after twelve years of litigation.[1] If the victory was incomplete (the compensation awarded, though more than double what had originally been proposed, was still far less than that recommended by the independent assessors, and amounted to no more than a fraction of the costs that had been incurred, the villagers accepted it with relief, recognizing that to some extent at least their stand had been vindicated. But even now they were not to be left in peace. Some had been helping to make ends meet by cutting reeds for thatching from the old Yanaka land; and now the authorities, implacable still, charged them with illegal activity on land that was no longer theirs.

The lawyer Nakamura gave himself as tirelessly to their defence now as he had to the conduct through the courts of their claim for compensation. Three years later the court decided once again in favour of the villagers. But within a few months of this second victory Nakamura, worn out by the privations which the conduct, without payment, of the two marathon cases had imposed, was dead.

---

1. A tiny incident at the end of the last hearing before the final judgement was delivered reveals something of the effect Shozo could have even on his bitterest opponents. As Shimada Sozo was going round the courtroom asking some of the lawyers to write down in his notebook some maxim or reflection that would commemorate the occasion, a man came up to him and asked that he too might be allowed to contribute. Shimada having agreed, he wrote *Aa kaiketsu Tanaka Shozo-o*, roughly translatable as 'In memory of Tanaka Shozo, a great and beloved man'; and signed himself 'former police officer', with the cryptic nom-de-plume 'Sword cutting water', implying that his own profession had been ineffective and meaningless. After writing these words, he hurried away without speaking, but Shimada recognised him: it was Uematsu, the Tochigi police chief who had directed with such ruthlessness the destruction of Yanaka in 1907. See above, p. 172 ff.

For nearly fifty years nothing more was heard of Yanaka. All trace of the homes and shrines and school of this once prosperous community have long since vanished. When I visited the site in February, 1970, it was like a vast stretch of moorland, marshy in patches, and with the monotonous brown of the winter grasses broken only occasionally by a clump of evergreen trees. Here and there, it is true, if one kicked among the grasses, one could find low tombstones, marking the ancestral graves that sixty-five years ago the villagers were so loath to abandon.

Otherwise, nothing.

There was talk of turning the area into a boating-lake, or even into a huge golf-course — with the implicit admission that if plans like this could be seriously considered, the destruction of Yanaka had after all contributed nothing (as Shozo had correctly insisted) to its ostensible object, the permanent prevention of flooding elsewhere.

But attachment to Yanaka still survives in those who were born there, though two generations have passed since they were forced to leave. In 1971, as public knowledge of Yanaka and its history was spreading, a Mr. Kanda Kichizo, a retired farmer of 76 whose family had left the village in 1905, completed after several years work a register of the present whereabouts of 371 descendants of the original 400-odd families. This in turn led to the formation in 1972 of an Association for the Preservation of the Remains of Yanaka.

Tall wooden markers with inscriptions now locate the site of each of the tombstones that until recently were hidden by the grasses. It is hard to say what the future may hold. Perhaps one can even envisage the realisation of the dream that seemed so absurdly unrealistic when Shozo fought for it nearly 70 years ago — of a new Yanaka rising on the site of the old, as a symbol of the regeneration of the spirit of community that he feared might have perished along with its destruction. But whether or not the village achieves a physical resurrection, its place in the history of the developing world movement for the reconciliation of man and his environment is now assured, thanks to Tanaka Shozo and the handful of families who refused to allow its name to die.

The Ashio mine and the pollution situation after Shozo's death

The recovery of the poisoned land that began in 1902 continued, with some setbacks, throughout the following years. It was probably aided by the huge government works to strengthen and straighten the banks of the Watarase that were carried out between 1910 and 1917. (Shozo would have no truck with these grandiose operations, which he regarded as wholly unnecessary. Some parts at least of his own much simpler solution were incorporated into the government plan, without acknowledgement, after his death.)

These preventative measures, despite their enormous cost, have never been altogether effective. In 1929, 1958, and 1964 the Watarase broke its artificially reinforced banks, and as its waters still contained traces of poisonous substances, significant pollution of certain districts of agricultural land resulted on each occasion, though there was no recurrence of the widespread and sensational damage of the 1890s.

A newly-formed Farmers' Alliance against Pollution petitioned in 1964 for the cleansing of the waters of the Watarase to the level of purity that had been normal before large-scale mining had been started at Ashio in 1878. The attitude of the authorities to the Alliance and to the industry differed little from that of officialdom in Shozo's day. When the farmers of the Alliance were asked to nominate a representative to a committee on purification, they nominated their president and founder, only to be told that if he was to be the 'representative', he must first resign from the Alliance; while a director of the mine was accepted without question for the same committee.

Much as Count Mutsu had complacently spoken of foreign machines in 1891, the Mayor of one town on the Watarase sought to persuade the Alliance not to sue the mine on the ground that 'he had been to Ashio and had seen for himself how much money the mine had spent on anti-pollution measures.' Statements of similar import were made by the prefectural authorities and by the responsible organ of the central government, the Ministry of International Trade and Industry.

More recently, however, there have been two developments which suggest that the long saga of Ashio pollution and the human distress it has caused may at last have come to an end. In 1972 it was announced that copper reserves in the area were all but exhausted, and that mining would cease.

Whether the farmers of Shimotsuke have in fact seen the last of the deadly 'blue water' remains problematical, since the possibility was left open that copper mined elsewhere might still be refined at Ashio. And even if all refining does permanently cease, there remain in the still denuded mountain ravines around the sources of the Watarase the vast mounds of potentially dangerous copper waste, deposited during a century of headlong mining activity. There is as yet no known way of restoring these hills and ravines to their natural (and beneficent) state; for the foreseeable future, the black mounds will stay, a 'surrealist's nightmare',[1] and a constant threat to the Shimotsuke plain if the rains should break them up and wash the

---

1. I borrow this phrase from a recent book, *Kogai retto* (The polluted archipelago), by the leading contemporary Japanese campaigner against pollution, Ui Jun.

poisonous lumps down into the Watarase. Nevertheless, the end of mining at Ashio was a major event for all those who live on the plain below.

Perhaps even more significant in the long term was the decision of another group of farmers in 1971 to invoke the arbitration machinery newly established within the government's Environment Agency, to claim compensation for pollution damage to their crops during the previous twenty years. Initially about 100 farmers were involved in this new campaign; later the number rose to 971, all from the small area along the banks of the Watarase in Gunma Prefecture where pollution was now concentrated.

When their leaders called at the Environment Agency in Tokyo to ask for financial assistance in drawing up the necessary documents, the Agency's Director reacted with surprise and some scepticism; he is reported as saying that he thought Ashio pollution had ceased to be a problem in Tanaka Shozo's day.[1]

But the farmers, conscious of the growing public concern about pollution all over the country, were not deterred. In March 1972 they filed with the Agency a claim against Furukawa Mining Industries for ¥3,877,000,000.[2] Furukawa Mining Industries' first reaction, as in the 1890s, was to deny — against all the evidence — that Ashio could have had anything to do with the poor performance of the farmers' land.

After a year of arbitration meetings, it reversed its stand, and for the first time in the 85 years since the pollution of the Shimotsuke plain had begun, openly admitted its responsibility and the right of the farmers to demand compensation.[3]

Finally, in May 1974, the government's Pollution Disputes Mediation Committee announced an award to the claimants of ¥1,550,000,000.

This sum was less than half their claim; and the farmers were uneasy at other aspects of the proceedings — the Committee remained officially 'neutral', and the precise basis of its award, unlike that of the farmers' claim, was not made public. Yet the settlement[4] could fairly be described as epoch-making. This was the first major case to be brought to a successful conclusion by the Pollution Disputes Mediation Committee, and the result gave some promise that the Committee was on the way to fulfilling the public expectation that it would serve as a 'pollution court', from which even uninfluential and impecunious citizens might hope to obtain redress.

1. The *Asahi Shinbun* (evening edition), May 10, 1974.
2. The claim was based on a detailed assessment of crop damage on 468 hectares of prime agricultural land over 20 years.
3. In all previous settlements, any money the company paid to pollution victims had been described as 'contributions' (*kifukin*), or 'gifts in token of sympathy' (*mimaikin*), the term 'compensation' being scrupulously avoided.
4 It was formally accepted by both parties on 11 May, 1974.

Epilogue

The Committee's work was clearly made easier by the recent and moderately successful (from the plaintiffs' point of view) outcome of each of the much-publicised 'four great court cases on pollution',[1] in which pollution victims had sought compensation by traditional legal means. Litigation in these latter cases, besides being inordinately expensive, had dragged on through an average of nearly five years. The Committee had come to its decision on Ashio in a little over two years, and at far less expense.

Taken together, the 'four great court cases' and the Pollution Disputes Mediation Committee's award, with the many measures enacted in the 'Pollution Diet' of 1970, offer grounds for real hope that Japan may now be beginning to master her enormous pollution problems. In this field as in others, it may yet turn out that the pragmatic Japanese, now that the hectic century of modernisation is behind them, will show themselves better suited to construct 'industrialism with a human face' than any other advanced industrial community.[2]

Certainly those who campaign against pollution and for the preservation of the environment in Japan today have a great weight of public opinion behind them. They have too a magnificent example of the courage and persistence they still need, in the person of Tanaka Shozo, who pioneered the first Japanese anti-pollution struggle before the word 'pollution' in its sinister modern sense entered the language.

In the Japan of 1977 his name is a household word. For those more visionary spirits in Japan and elsewhere — and they are growing in number — who look beyond contemporary industrial society to a new culture in which care of the land and a more harmonious relationship with all the natural world will be accepted as man's first duty, there is precious encouragement in the prophetic wisdom of his last years, grounded in ancient values yet pointing to a new age.

---

1. These cases concerned the most spectacular pollution scandals of the sixties and early seventies — the Minamata disease (centred on the town of Minamata in Kyushu), the Niigata Minamata disease (of a similar type but occurring at Niigata, on the Sea of Japan), the Toyama *itai-itai* disease (at Toyama on the Sea of Japan), and the Yokkaichi disease (at Yokkaichi, on the Pacific coast of the main island of Honshu).

2 As Professor Fosco Maraini suggests in his challenging *Japan: Patterns of Continuity* (Kodansha International, 1971).

Selected Bibliography

IN JAPANESE

AMEMIYA GIJIN, 'Tanaka Shōzō ni okeru shūkyōsha no keisei', *Rekishi kenkyū*, Vol. 3, No. 2, Nihon Shoin, 1955.
Tanaka Shōzō no hito to shōgai, Meikeidō, 1971.
ARAHATA KANSON, 'Tanaka Shōzō ō', *Shinshakai*, Aug. 1917.
Yanaka-mura metsubō shi, Meiji Bunken 1963 (reprint of edition of 1907).
ASHIO DOZAN KŌDOKU HIGAI KYŪSAIKAI (ed.), *Ashio kōdoku higai kyūsaikai hōkoku sho*, privately printed, 1902.
ASHIO DŌZAN RŌDŌ KUMIAI, *Ashio dōzan rōdō undō shi*, privately printed, 1958.
HAMAMOTO HIROSHI, 'Jōnetsu no hitobito (2), Tanaka Shōzō', *Shincho*, Sept. 1953.
HAYASHI HIROKICHI (ed.), *Tanaka Shōzō bannen no nikki*, Nihon Hyoron Sha, 1948.
HAYASHI SHIGERU, AMAMIYA GIJIN, et al. (ed., on behalf of the Tanaka Shōzō Zenshū Hensankai, *Tanaka Shōzō zenshū*. To be published by Iwanami Shoten in 17 vols., commencing June 1977.
HAYASHI TAKEJI, 'Seiji to kenshin', *Shisō no kagaku*, Oct. 1962.
Tanaka Shōzō no shōgai, Kōdansha, 1976.
'Tanaka Shōzō to Arai Osui', *Chūō kōron*, Oct. 1961.
'Teikō no ne', *Shisō no kagaku*, Sept. 1962.
'Watarase-gawa kōdoku jiken to Tanaka Shōzō', *Shisō no kagaku*, April & May 1971.
HIDA BUNJIRŌ, *Furukawa Junkichi den*, 1926.
HINATA YASUSHI, 'Yanaka-mura', *Shisō no kagaku*, Sept. 1962.
ISHIKAWA SANSHIRŌ, *Jijoden*, Riron Sha, 1956.
Nami, Sōru Sha, 1957.
ITSUKAKAI, *Furukawa Ichibē den*, Itsukakai, 1926.
IWASAKI KATSUSABURŌ, *Tanaka Shōzō kikō dan*, Daigakkan, 1902.
KINOSHITA NAOE, *Ashio kōdoku mondai*, Mainichi Shinbun Sha, 1900. Reprinted in Vol. 1 of *Kinoshita Naoe chosaku shū* (referred to below as KNC), Meiji Bunken, 1969-72.
Kikatsu (Shobundō, 1907), KNC, Vol. VI.
'Kōdoku mondai to Tanaka Shōzō', *Meiji bungaku kenkyū*, Aug. 1934.
'Rinjū no Tanaka Shōzō', *Chūō kōron*, Sept. 1933.
Rōdō (Shōbundō, 1909), KNC, Vol. IX.
'Seiji no hasansha Tanaka Shōzō oboegaki', *Chūō kōron*, April 1933.
Tanaka Shōzō ō (Shincho Sha, 1921), KNC, Vol. XIII.
Yajingo (Kanao Bunendō, 1911), KNC, Vol. XII.
Tanaka Shōzō no shōgai, Bunka Shiryō Chōsa Kai, 1966 (reprint of 1928 edition).
KOKKA IGAKKAI ZASSHI, *Kōdoku ron shū*, Kokka igakkai jimusho, 1902.
KURIHARA HIKOSABURŌ et al. (eds.), *Gijin zenshū*, 5 vols., Chūgai Shinron Sha, 1925-27.
KUROSAWA TORIZŌ, *Tanaka Shōzō o kataru*, Ozaki Yukio Kinen Zaidan, 1968.
MASAOKA GEIYŌ, *Jindō no senshi Tanaka Shōzō*, Meikō Shoin, 1902.
MATSUMOTO EIKO, *Kōdoku jiken no sanjō*, Kyobunkan, 1902.
MITSUE IWAO, *Tanaka Shōzō*, Ebetsu-shi Rakunō Gakuen Shuppan Bu, 1961.
MORI SENZŌ, *Meiji jinbutsu itsuwa jiten*, Tōkyōdō, 1965.
MORINAGA EIZABURŌ, 'Tanaka Shōzō to kōdoku jiken no saiban', *Tokubetsu kenkyū sōsho*, privately printed by Nichibenren, 1967.
NAGASHIMA TADASHIGE, *Arai Osui sensei*, 1933.
NAGASHIMA YOHACHI, *Kōdoku jiken no shinsō to Tanaka Shōzō*, privately printed, 1938.
NAIKAKU KŌDOKU CHŌSA IINKAI, *Kōdoku chōsa hōkoku sho*, government publication, 1902.
NAKAGOME MICHIO, *Tanaka Shōzō to kindai shisō*, Gendai Hyōron Sha, 1972.

OSHIKA TAKASHI, *Watarase-gawa*, Chūō Kōron Sha, 1948.
Yanaka-mura jiken, Kōdansha, 1957.
SATŌ GISUKE, *Bōkoku no shukuzu*, Shinsei Sha, 1902.
SATORI HIKOJIRŌ, *Kōdoku to jinmei*, privately printed, 1903.
SHIBATA SABURŌ, *Gijin Tanaka Shozō ō*, Keibunkan, 1913.
SHIMADA SŌZŌ, *Tanaka Shōzō no uta to nenpu*, Tanaka Shōzō ō jiseki kenkyūjo, 1934.
Tanaka Shōzō ō yoroku (ed. Hayashi Takeji), 2 vols., Sanichi Shobō, 1972.
SHIROYAMA SABURŌ, *Shinsan*, Chūō Kōron Sha, 1962.
TAGAWA DAIKICHIRŌ, *Aa, kōdoku ron*, Gendai Sha, 1903.
Kodoku mondai kaiketsu ron, Mumei Sha, 1902.
TAKAHASHI HIDEOMI, *Kōdoku jiken to genkō hōrei ron*, privately printed, 1902.
TAKAHASHI KIKUTARŌ, *Kōdoku mondai hibunroku*, Bunkaidō Shoten, 1904.
TAKAHASHI TETSUTARŌ, *Gijin Tanaka Shōzō*, 1913.
TAMURA NORIO, *Kōdoku: Watarase-gawa nōmin no kutō*, Shinjinbutsu Orai Sha, 1973.
Kōdoku nōmin monogatari, Asahi Shinbun, 1975.
Watarase no shisō-shi, Fūbai Sha, 1977.
(ed.) *Kikan Tanaka Shōzō kenkyū*. Published quarterly by Dentō to Gendai Sha. 1976-
TANAKA SŌGORO, 'Tanaka Shōzō', *Nihon hangyakka retsuden*, 1929.
'Tanaka Shōzō', *Nihon jinbutsu rekishi taikei*, 1960.
TORIYABE SHUNTEI, *Meiji jinbutsu gettan zenshū*, Hakubunkan, 1909.
UCHIMIZU MAMORU (ed.), *Shiryō Ashio kōdoku jiken*, Aki Shobō, 1971.
UI JUN, *Kōgai gen ron*, Aki Shobō, 1971.
Kōgai rettō 70 nendai, Aki Shobō, 1972.
USUDA SADANORI, *Hida Bunjirō-kun no shōgai*, Kōhikai, 1929.
WATANABE IKUJIRŌ, *Meiji-shi kenkyū*, 1934.
YAMASUGA YOICHIRŌ, *Gijin Tanaka Shōzō ō no hanmen*, Suigō Gakkai, 1921.

IN ENGLISH

MINISTRY OF FOREIGN AFFAIRS, TOKYO: Development of Environmental Protection in Japan. (Undated: 1974?)

PYLE, NOTEHELFER, & STONE: Symposium, 'The Ashio Copper Mine Pollution Case', *Journal of Japanese Studies*, Vol. I, No. 2, Spring 1975.

UI JUN: 'The Singularities of Japanese Pollution', *Japan Quarterly*, Vol. XIX, No. 3, July-Sept. 1972.

Shozo's own calligraphy for 'Disaster, gateway to joy'

For Product Safety Concerns and Information please contact our EU
representative GPSR@taylorandfrancis.com
Taylor & Francis Verlag GmbH, Kaufingerstraße 24, 80331 München, Germany

www.ingramcontent.com/pod-product-compliance
Lightning Source LLC
Chambersburg PA
CBHW050440240426
43661CB00055B/2460